D1097088

BMIT SUBMIT S

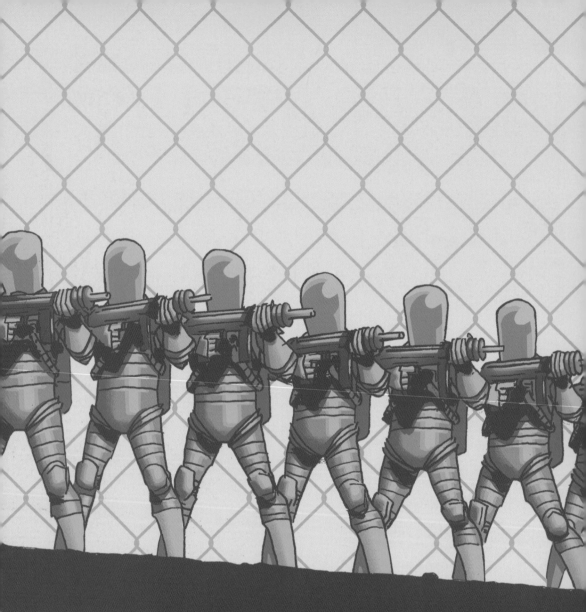

Facebook: **facebook.com/idwpublishing**
Twitter: **@idwpublishing**
YouTube: **youtube.com/idwpublishing**
Tumblr: **tumblr.idwpublishing.com**
Instagram: **instagram.com/idwpublishing**

COVER ART BY
JOHN McCREA

COVER COLORS BY
MIKE SPICER

COLLECTION EDITS BY
JUSTIN EISINGER
AND ALONZO SIMON

COLLECTION DESIGN BY
JEFF POWELL

PUBLISHER
TED ADAMS

ISBN: 978-1-63140-737-6   19 18 17 16   1 2 3 4

Ted Adams, CEO & Publisher
Greg Goldstein, President & COO
Robbie Robbins, EVP/Sr. Graphic Artist
Chris Ryall, Chief Creative Officer/Editor-in-Chief
Laurie Windrow, Senior VP of Sales & Marketing
Matthew Ruzicka, CPA, Chief Financial Officer
Dirk Wood, VP of Marketing
Lorelei Bunjes, VP of Digital Services
Jeff Webber, VP of Digital and Subsidiary Rights
Jerry Bennington, VP of New Product Development

MARS ATTACKS
OCCUPATION

WRITER/LETTERER
JOHN LAYMAN

ARTIST
ANDY KUHN

COLORIST
JASON LEWIS

SERIES EDITOR
DENTON J. TIPTON

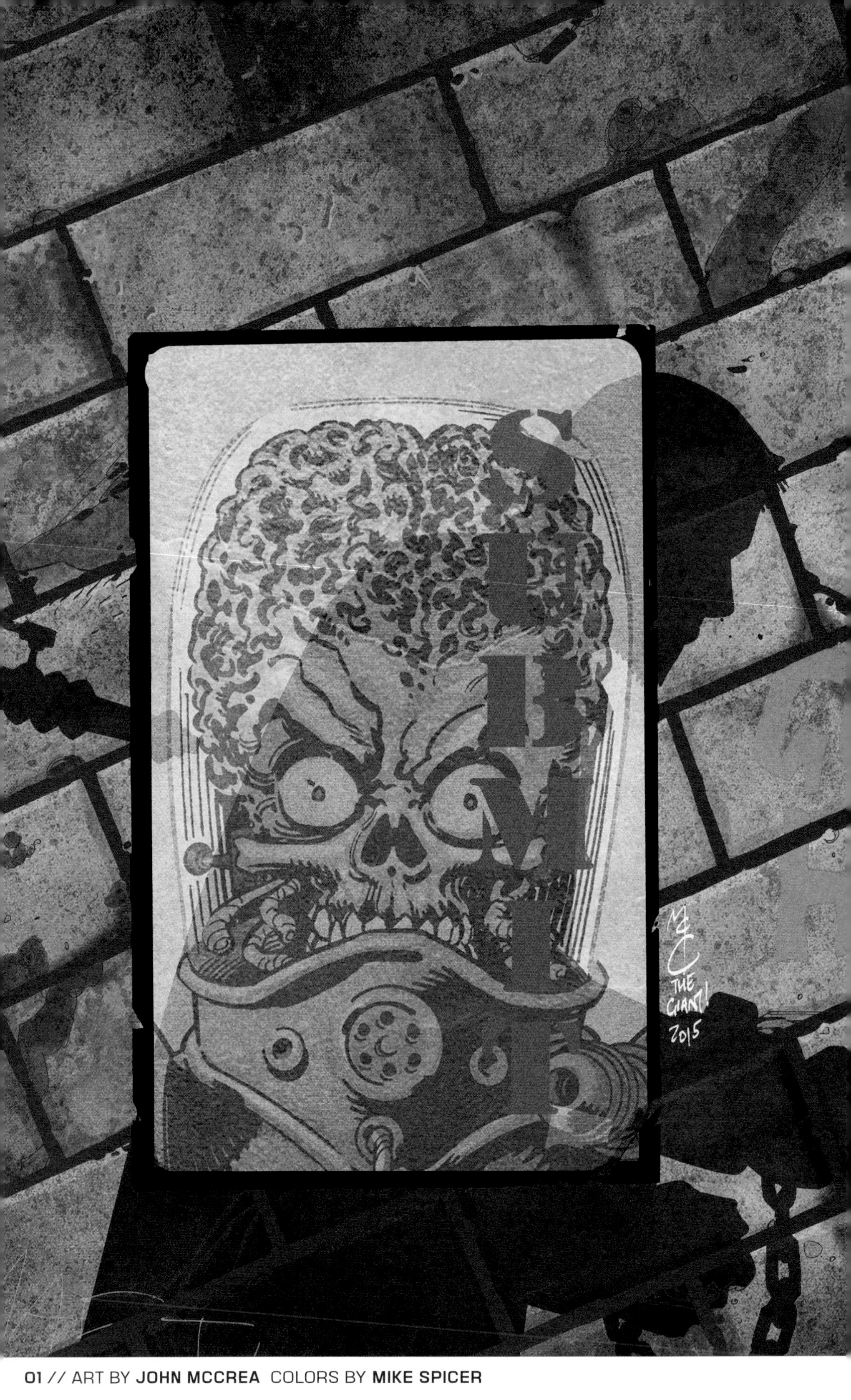
THE GIANT! 2015

01 // ART BY **JOHN MCCREA** COLORS BY **MIKE SPICER**

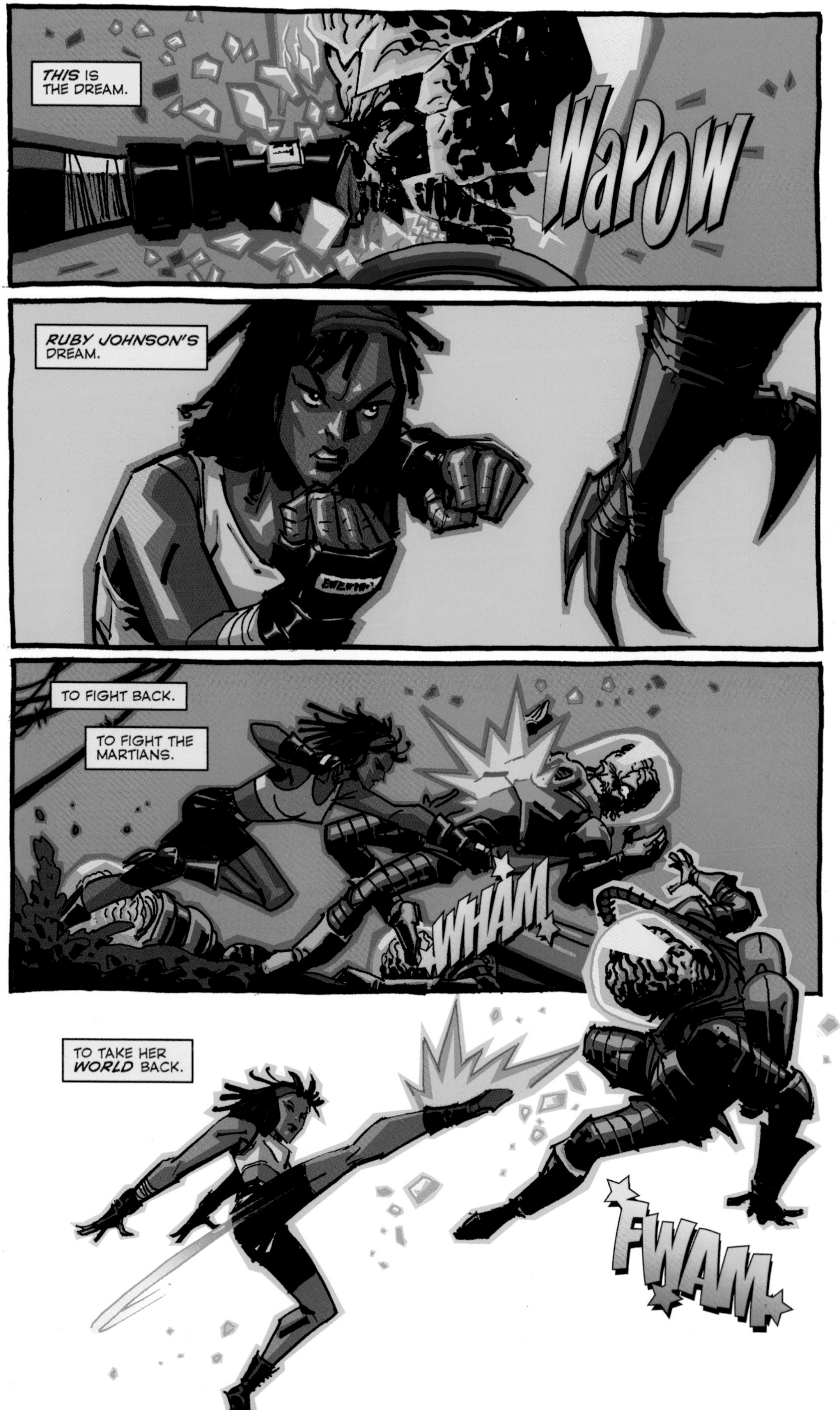
THIS IS THE DREAM.
WAPOW
RUBY JOHNSON'S DREAM.
TO FIGHT BACK.
TO FIGHT THE MARTIANS.
WHAM
TO TAKE HER *WORLD* BACK.
FWAM

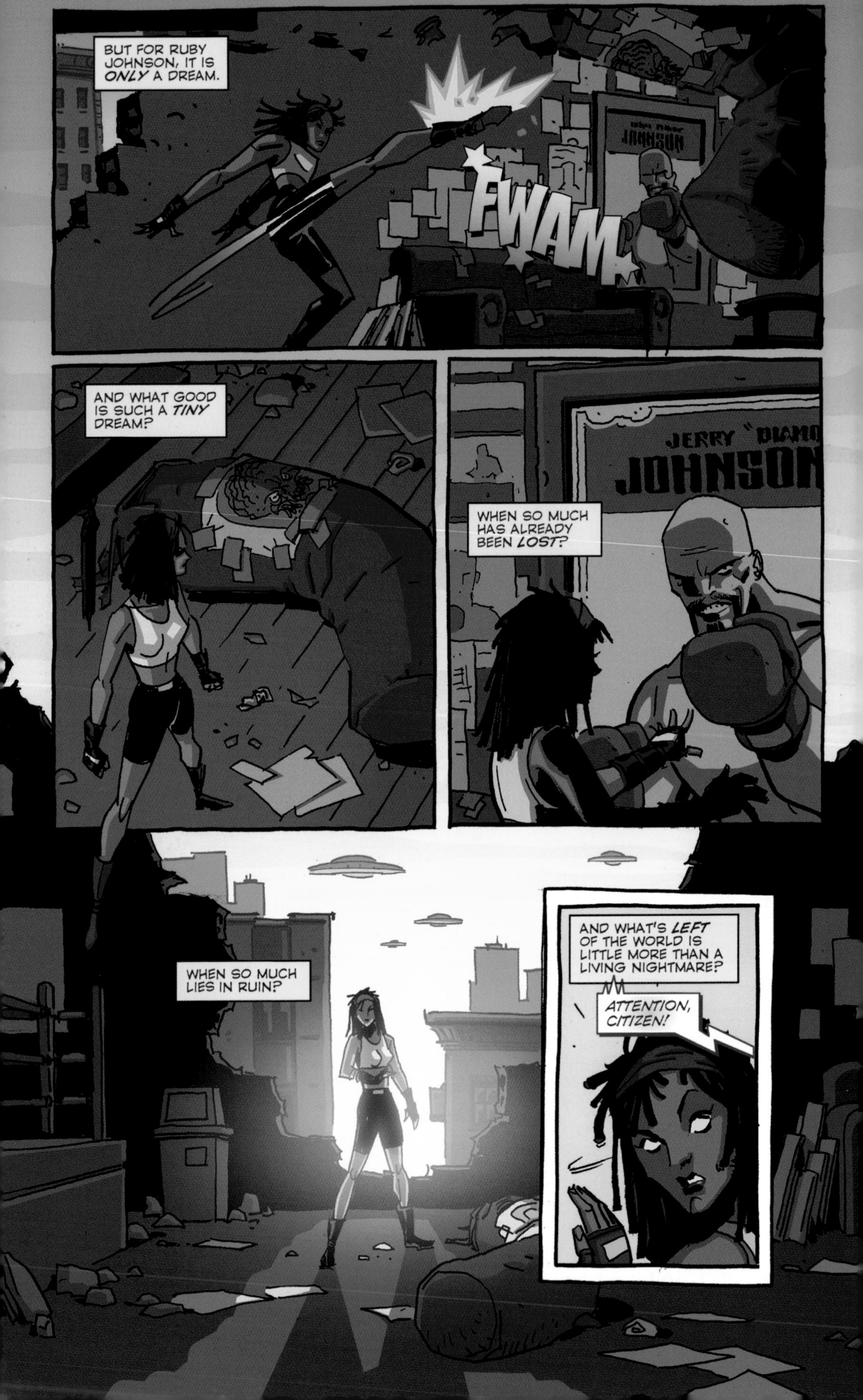
BUT FOR RUBY JOHNSON, IT IS *ONLY* A DREAM.
FWAM
JOHNSON
AND WHAT GOOD IS SUCH A *TINY* DREAM?
JERRY "DIAMO
JOHNSON
WHEN SO MUCH HAS ALREADY BEEN *LOST*?
WHEN SO MUCH LIES IN RUIN?
AND WHAT'S *LEFT* OF THE WORLD IS LITTLE MORE THAN A LIVING NIGHTMARE?
ATTENTION, CITIZEN!

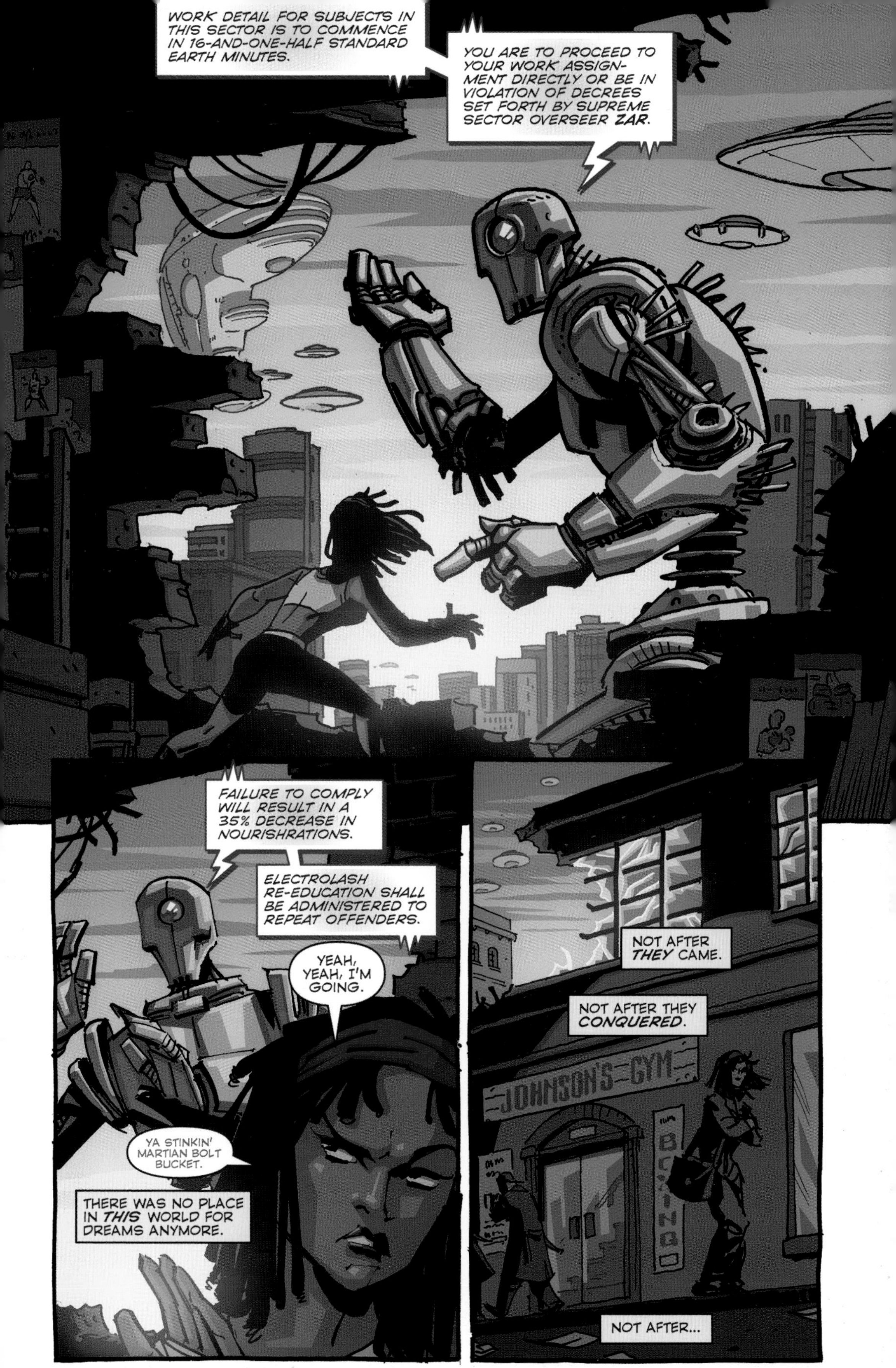
WORK DETAIL FOR SUBJECTS IN THIS SECTOR IS TO COMMENCE IN 16-AND-ONE-HALF STANDARD EARTH MINUTES.
YOU ARE TO PROCEED TO YOUR WORK ASSIGN-MENT DIRECTLY OR BE IN VIOLATION OF DECREES SET FORTH BY SUPREME SECTOR OVERSEER ZAR.
FAILURE TO COMPLY WILL RESULT IN A 35% DECREASE IN NOURISHRATIONS.
ELECTROLASH RE-EDUCATION SHALL BE ADMINISTERED TO REPEAT OFFENDERS.
YEAH, YEAH, I'M GOING.
YA STINKIN' MARTIAN BOLT BUCKET.
THERE WAS NO PLACE IN THIS WORLD FOR DREAMS ANYMORE.
NOT AFTER THEY CAME.
NOT AFTER THEY CONQUERED.
JOHNSON'S GYM
BOXING
NOT AFTER...

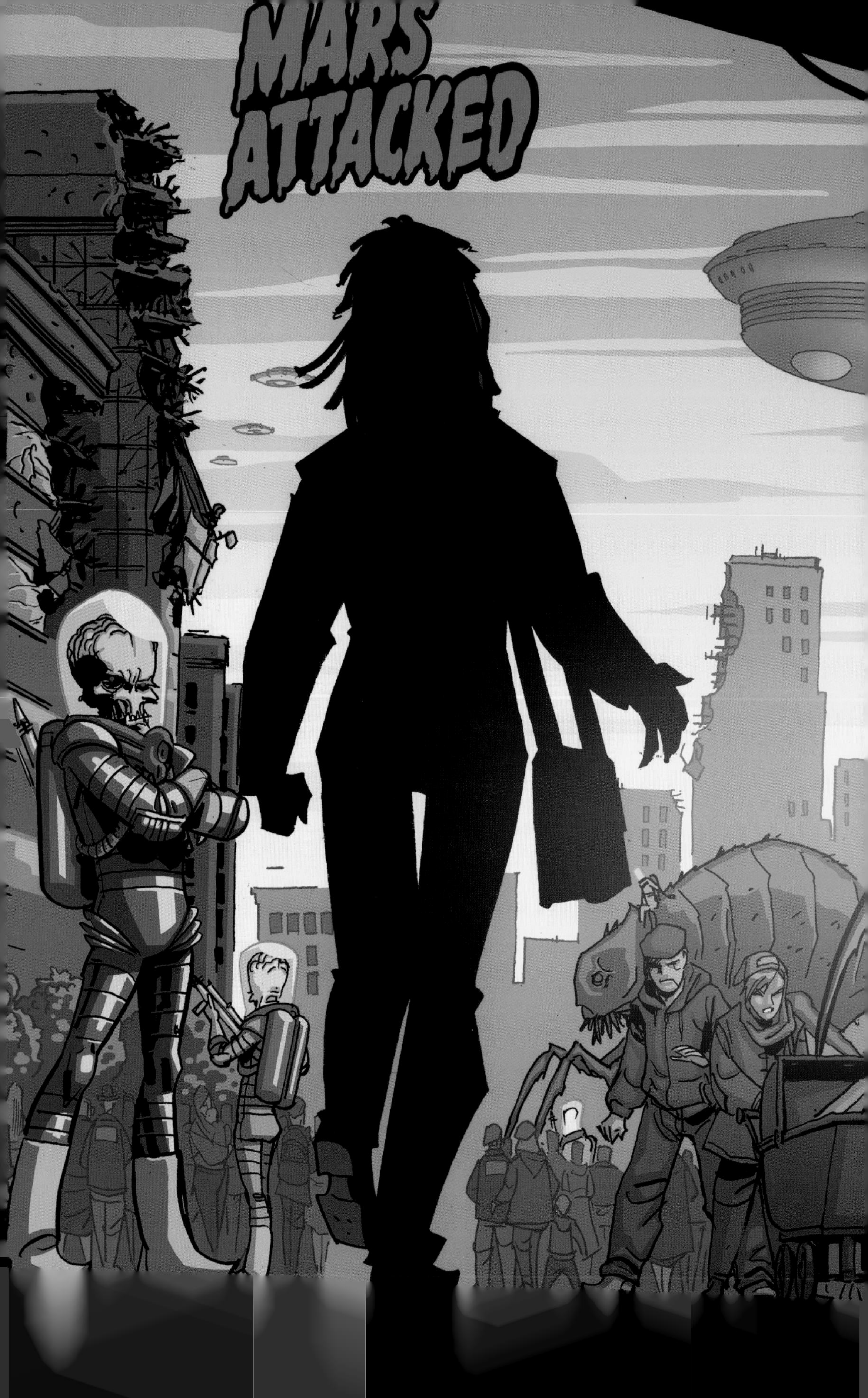
MARS ATTACKED

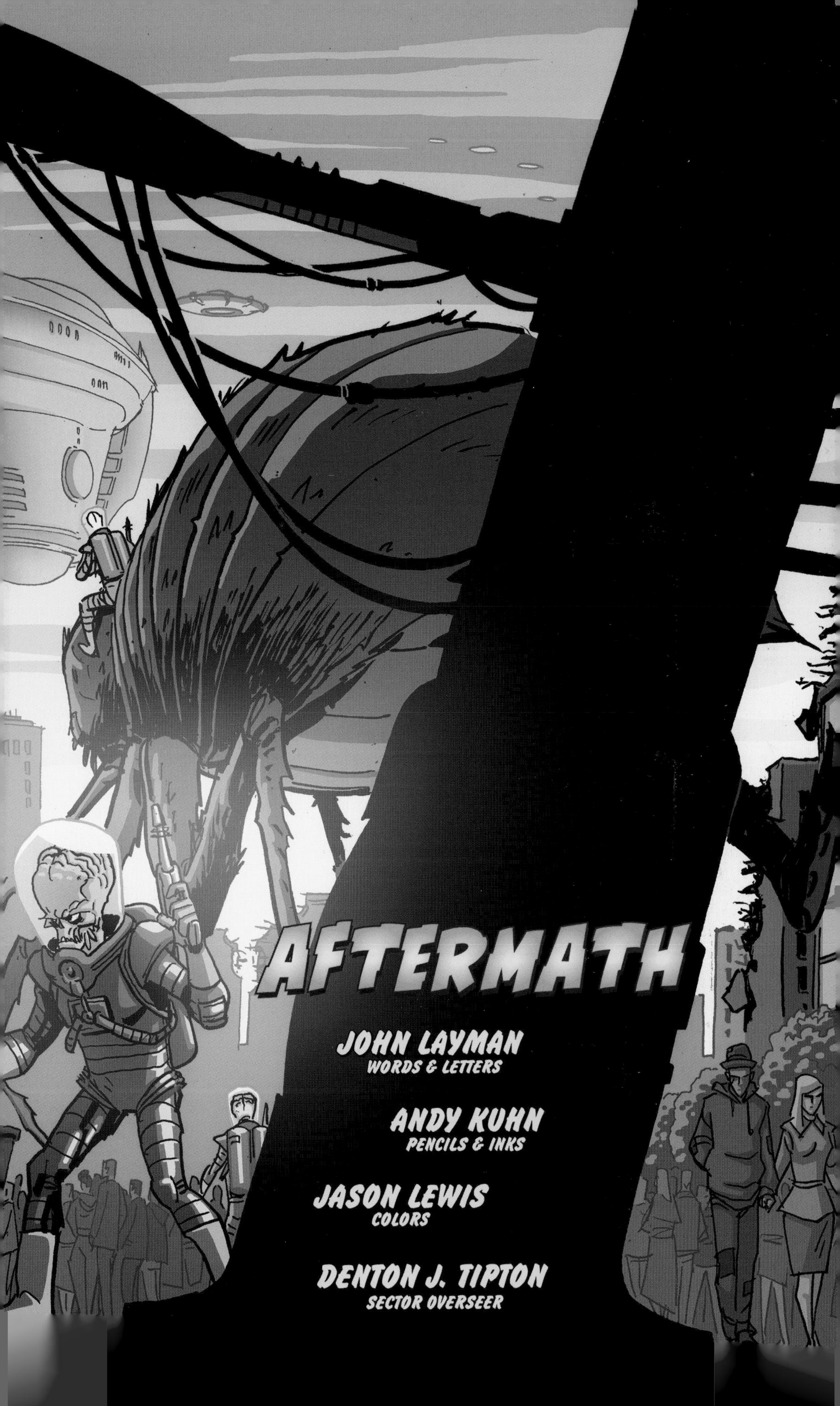
AFTERMATH
JOHN LAYMAN
WORDS & LETTERS
ANDY KUHN
PENCILS & INKS
JASON LEWIS
COLORS
DENTON J. TIPTON
SECTOR OVERSEER

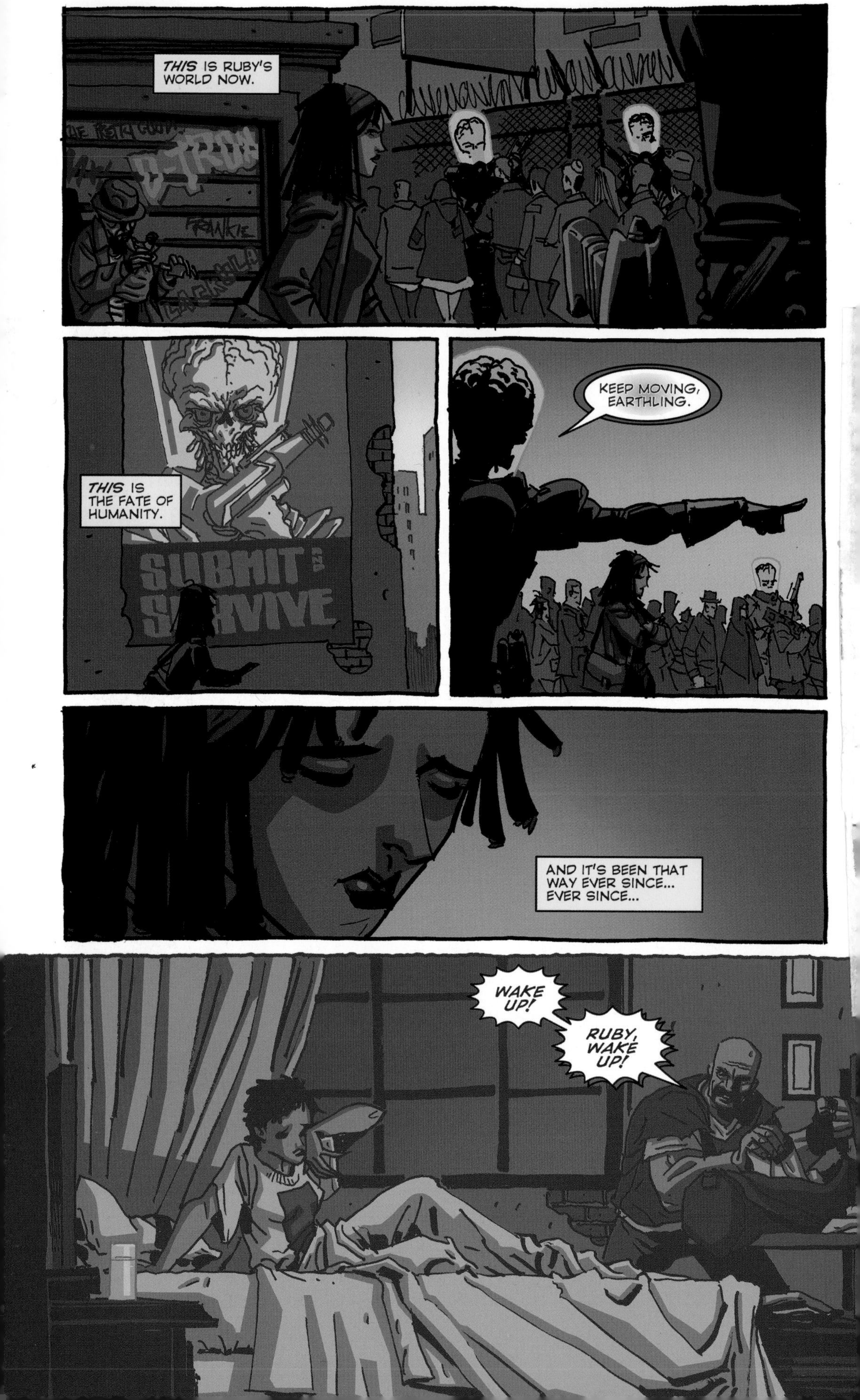

THIS IS RUBY'S WORLD NOW.
THIS IS THE FATE OF HUMANITY.
SUBMIT SURVIVE
KEEP MOVING, EARTHLING.
AND IT'S BEEN THAT WAY EVER SINCE... EVER SINCE...
WAKE UP!
RUBY, WAKE UP!

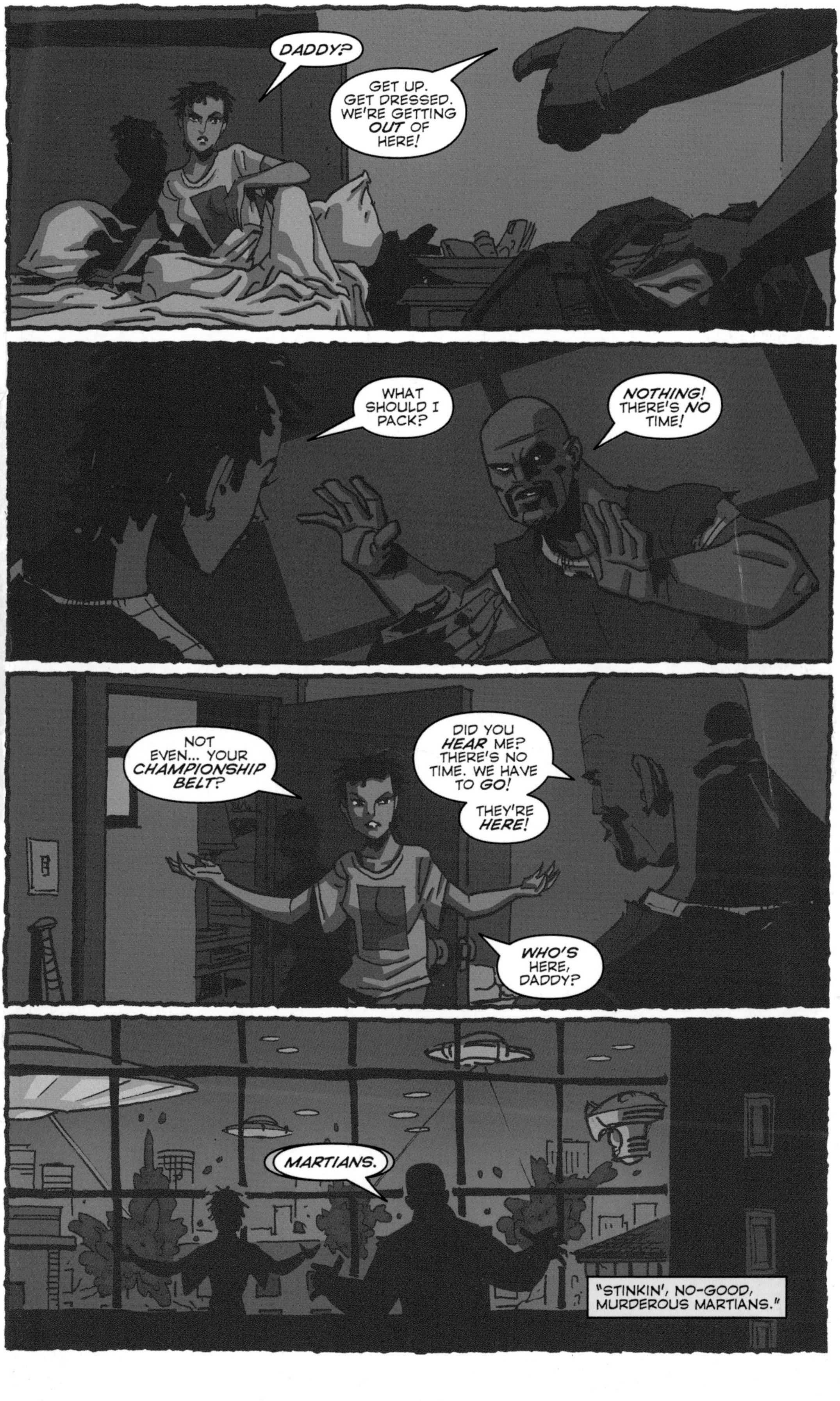
DADDY?
GET UP. GET DRESSED. WE'RE GETTING OUT OF HERE!
WHAT SHOULD I PACK?
NOTHING! THERE'S NO TIME!
NOT EVEN... YOUR CHAMPIONSHIP BELT?
DID YOU HEAR ME? THERE'S NO TIME. WE HAVE TO GO!
THEY'RE HERE!
WHO'S HERE, DADDY?
MARTIANS.
"STINKIN', NO-GOOD, MURDEROUS MARTIANS."

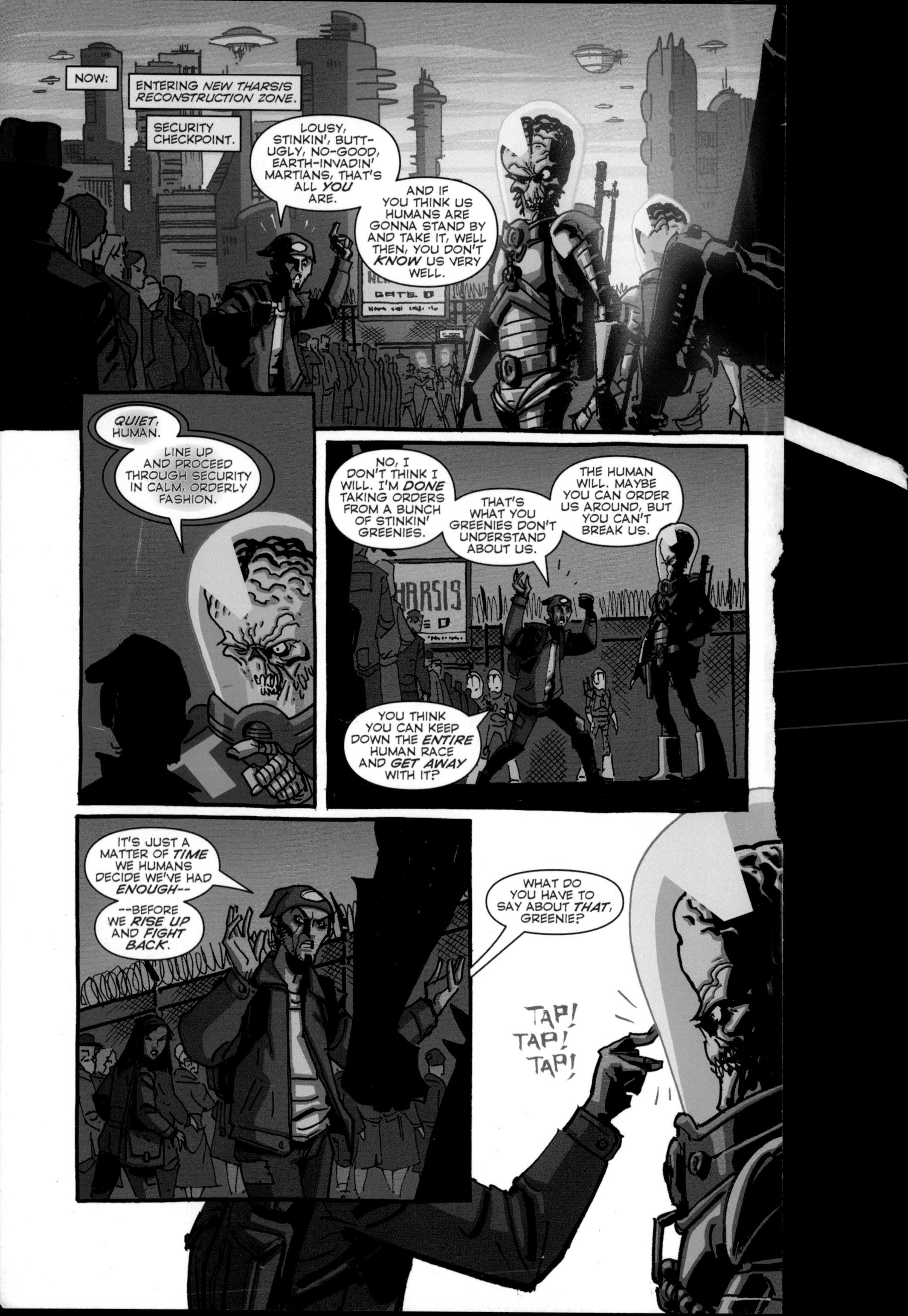
NOW:
ENTERING NEW THARSIS RECONSTRUCTION ZONE.
SECURITY CHECKPOINT.
LOUSY, STINKIN', BUTT-UGLY, NO-GOOD, EARTH-INVADIN' MARTIANS, THAT'S ALL YOU ARE.
AND IF YOU THINK US HUMANS ARE GONNA STAND BY AND TAKE IT, WELL THEN, YOU DON'T KNOW US VERY WELL.
GATE D
QUIET, HUMAN.
LINE UP AND PROCEED THROUGH SECURITY IN CALM, ORDERLY FASHION.
NO, I DON'T THINK I WILL. I'M DONE TAKING ORDERS FROM A BUNCH OF STINKIN' GREENIES.
THE HUMAN WILL. MAYBE YOU CAN ORDER US AROUND, BUT YOU CAN'T BREAK US.
THAT'S WHAT YOU GREENIES DON'T UNDERSTAND ABOUT US.
THARSIS
YOU THINK YOU CAN KEEP DOWN THE ENTIRE HUMAN RACE AND GET AWAY WITH IT?
IT'S JUST A MATTER OF TIME WE HUMANS DECIDE WE'VE HAD ENOUGH--
--BEFORE WE RISE UP AND FIGHT BACK.
WHAT DO YOU HAVE TO SAY ABOUT THAT, GREENIE?
TAP! TAP! TAP!

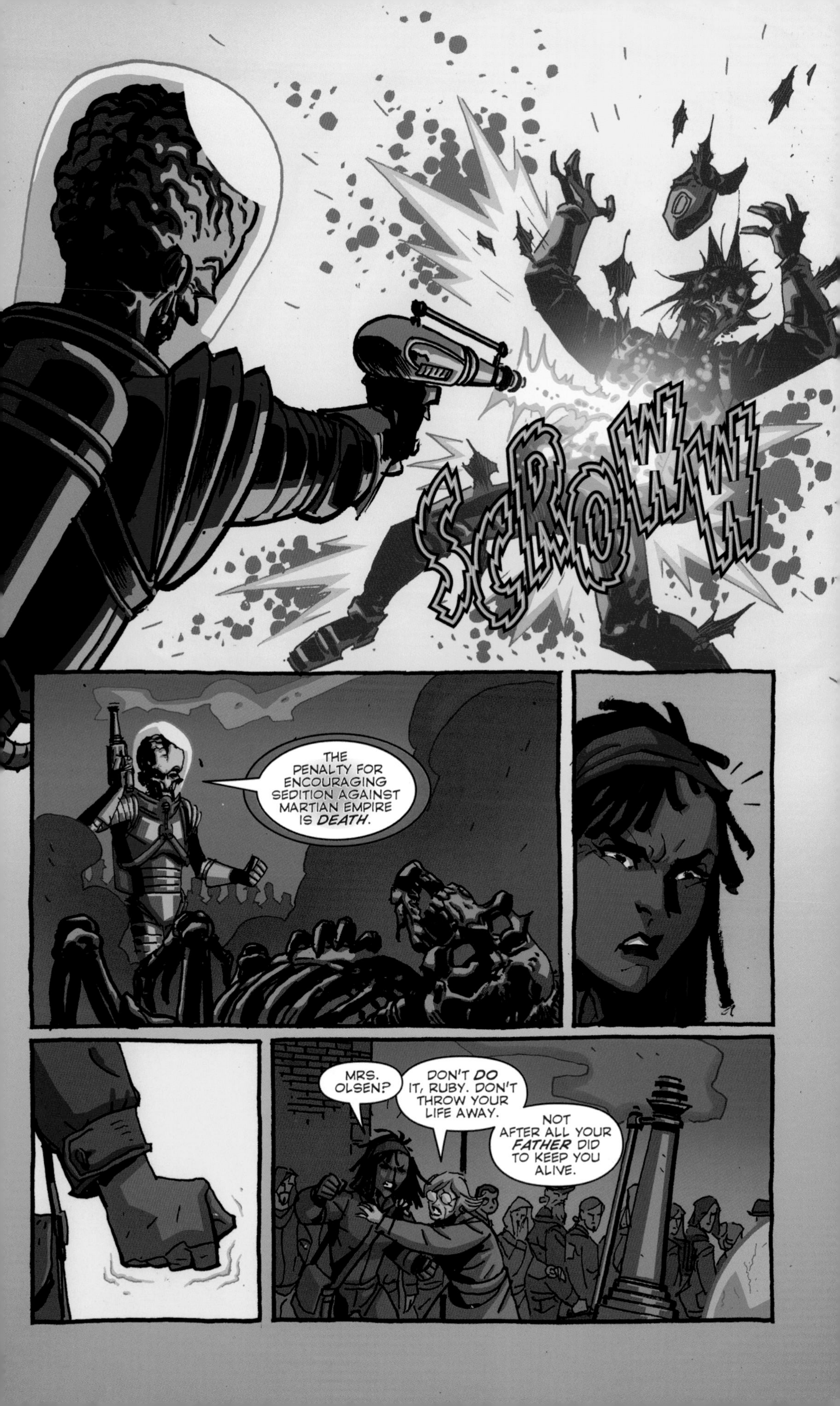
SCROWW
THE PENALTY FOR ENCOURAGING SEDITION AGAINST MARTIAN EMPIRE IS *DEATH*.
MRS. OLSEN?
DON'T *DO* IT, RUBY. DON'T THROW YOUR LIFE AWAY.
NOT AFTER ALL YOUR *FATHER* DID TO KEEP YOU ALIVE.

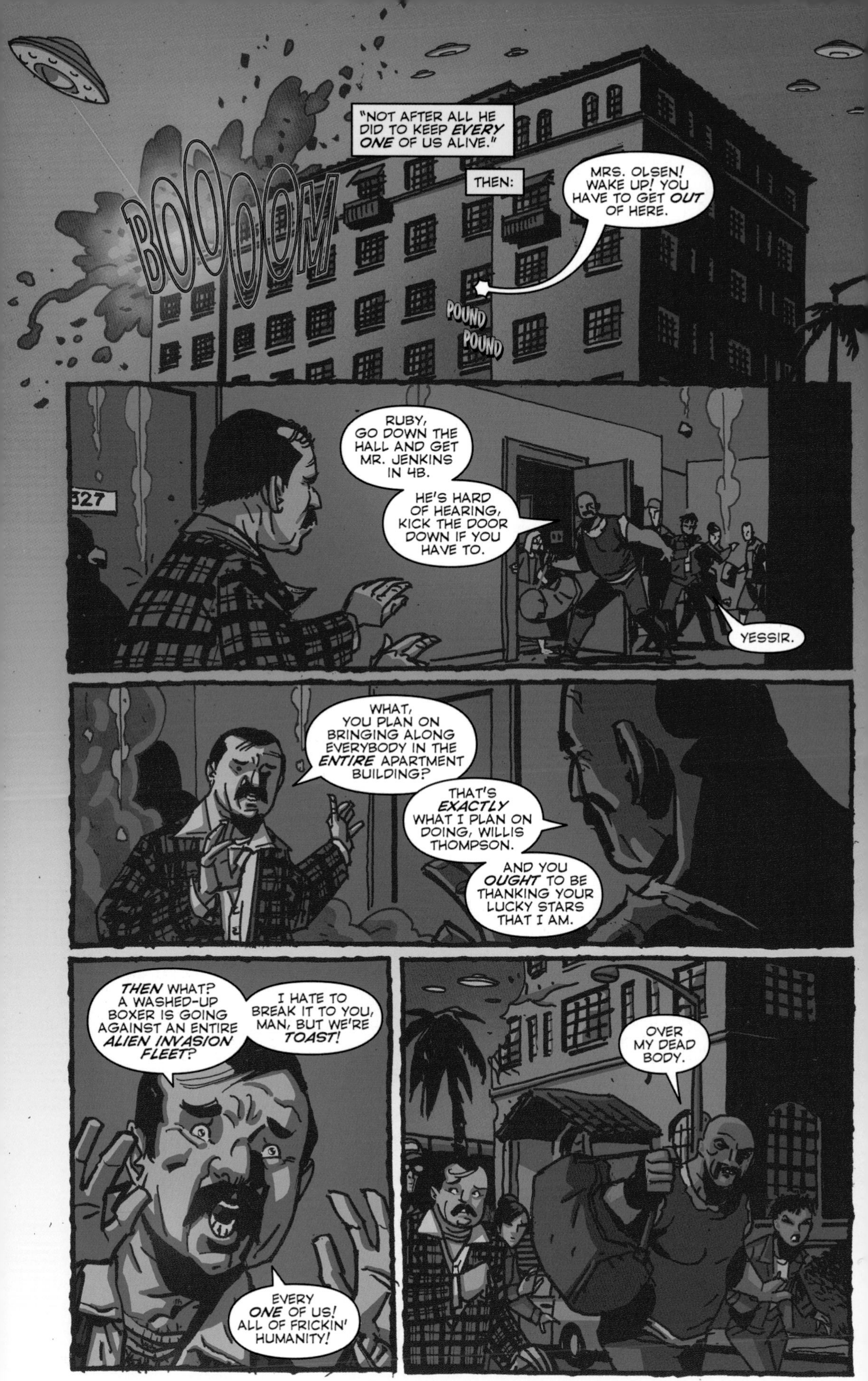
BOOOOOM
"NOT AFTER ALL HE DID TO KEEP EVERY ONE OF US ALIVE."
THEN:
MRS. OLSEN! WAKE UP! YOU HAVE TO GET OUT OF HERE.
POUND
POUND
327
RUBY, GO DOWN THE HALL AND GET MR. JENKINS IN 4B.
HE'S HARD OF HEARING, KICK THE DOOR DOWN IF YOU HAVE TO.
YESSIR.
WHAT, YOU PLAN ON BRINGING ALONG EVERYBODY IN THE ENTIRE APARTMENT BUILDING?
THAT'S EXACTLY WHAT I PLAN ON DOING, WILLIS THOMPSON.
AND YOU OUGHT TO BE THANKING YOUR LUCKY STARS THAT I AM.
THEN WHAT? A WASHED-UP BOXER IS GOING AGAINST AN ENTIRE ALIEN INVASION FLEET?
I HATE TO BREAK IT TO YOU, MAN, BUT WE'RE TOAST!
EVERY ONE OF US! ALL OF FRICKIN' HUMANITY!
OVER MY DEAD BODY.

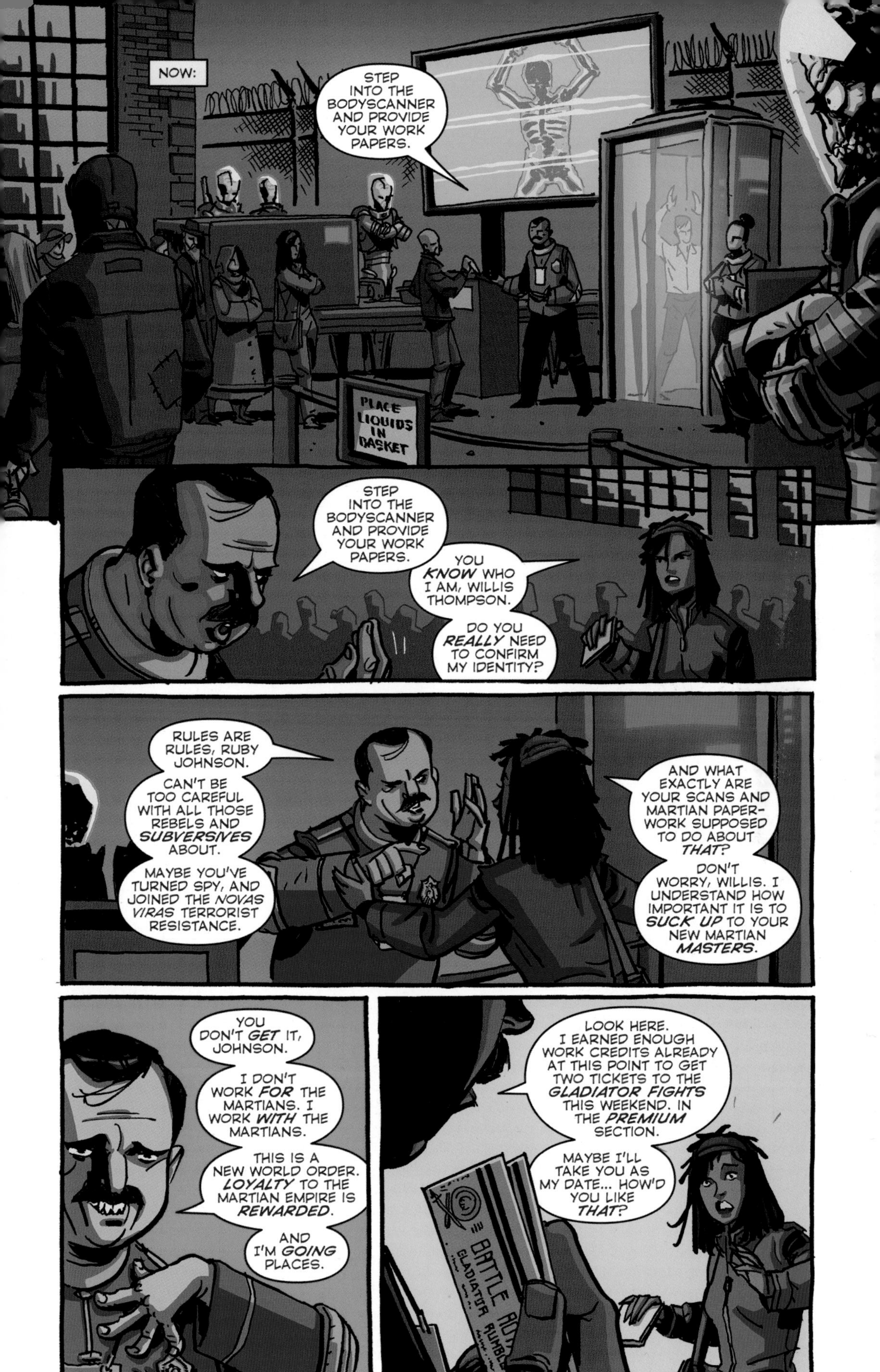
NOW:
STEP INTO THE BODYSCANNER AND PROVIDE YOUR WORK PAPERS.
PLACE LIQUIDS IN BASKET
STEP INTO THE BODYSCANNER AND PROVIDE YOUR WORK PAPERS.
YOU KNOW WHO I AM, WILLIS THOMPSON.
DO YOU REALLY NEED TO CONFIRM MY IDENTITY?
RULES ARE RULES, RUBY JOHNSON.
CAN'T BE TOO CAREFUL WITH ALL THOSE REBELS AND SUBVERSIVES ABOUT.
MAYBE YOU'VE TURNED SPY, AND JOINED THE NOVAS VIRAS TERRORIST RESISTANCE.
AND WHAT EXACTLY ARE YOUR SCANS AND MARTIAN PAPER-WORK SUPPOSED TO DO ABOUT THAT?
DON'T WORRY, WILLIS. I UNDERSTAND HOW IMPORTANT IT IS TO SUCK UP TO YOUR NEW MARTIAN MASTERS.
YOU DON'T GET IT, JOHNSON.
I DON'T WORK FOR THE MARTIANS. I WORK WITH THE MARTIANS.
THIS IS A NEW WORLD ORDER. LOYALTY TO THE MARTIAN EMPIRE IS REWARDED.
AND I'M GOING PLACES.
LOOK HERE. I EARNED ENOUGH WORK CREDITS ALREADY AT THIS POINT TO GET TWO TICKETS TO THE GLADIATOR FIGHTS THIS WEEKEND. IN THE PREMIUM SECTION.
MAYBE I'LL TAKE YOU AS MY DATE... HOW'D YOU LIKE THAT?
BATTLE
GLADIATOR RUMBLE

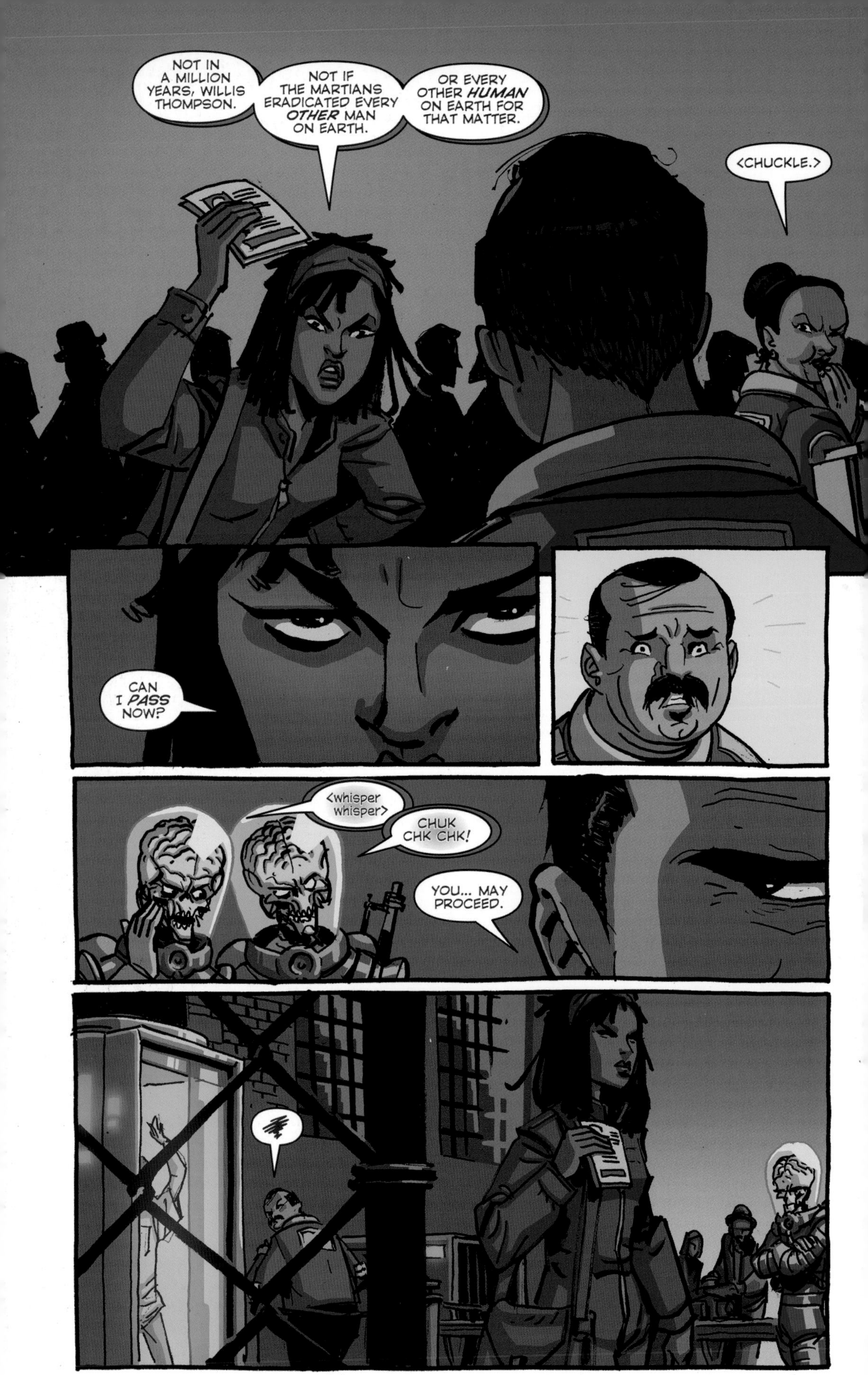
NOT IN A MILLION YEARS, WILLIS THOMPSON.
NOT IF THE MARTIANS ERADICATED EVERY OTHER MAN ON EARTH.
OR EVERY OTHER HUMAN ON EARTH FOR THAT MATTER.
<CHUCKLE.>
CAN I PASS NOW?
<whisper whisper>
CHUK CHK CHK!
YOU... MAY PROCEED.

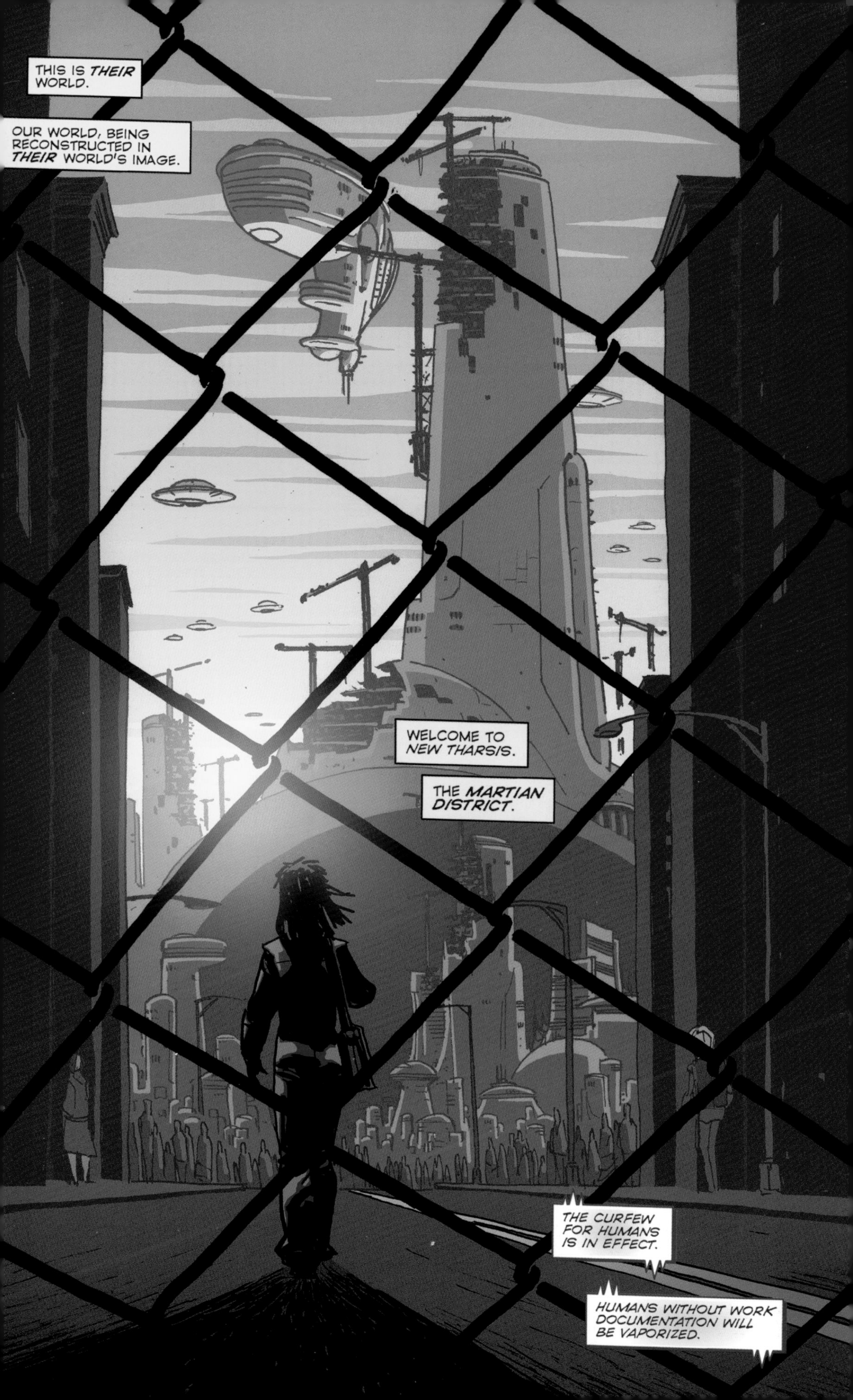
THIS IS *THEIR* WORLD.
OUR WORLD, BEING RECONSTRUCTED IN *THEIR* WORLD'S IMAGE.
WELCOME TO *NEW THARSIS*.
THE *MARTIAN DISTRICT*.
THE CURFEW FOR HUMANS IS IN EFFECT.
HUMANS WITHOUT WORK DOCUMENTATION WILL BE VAPORIZED.

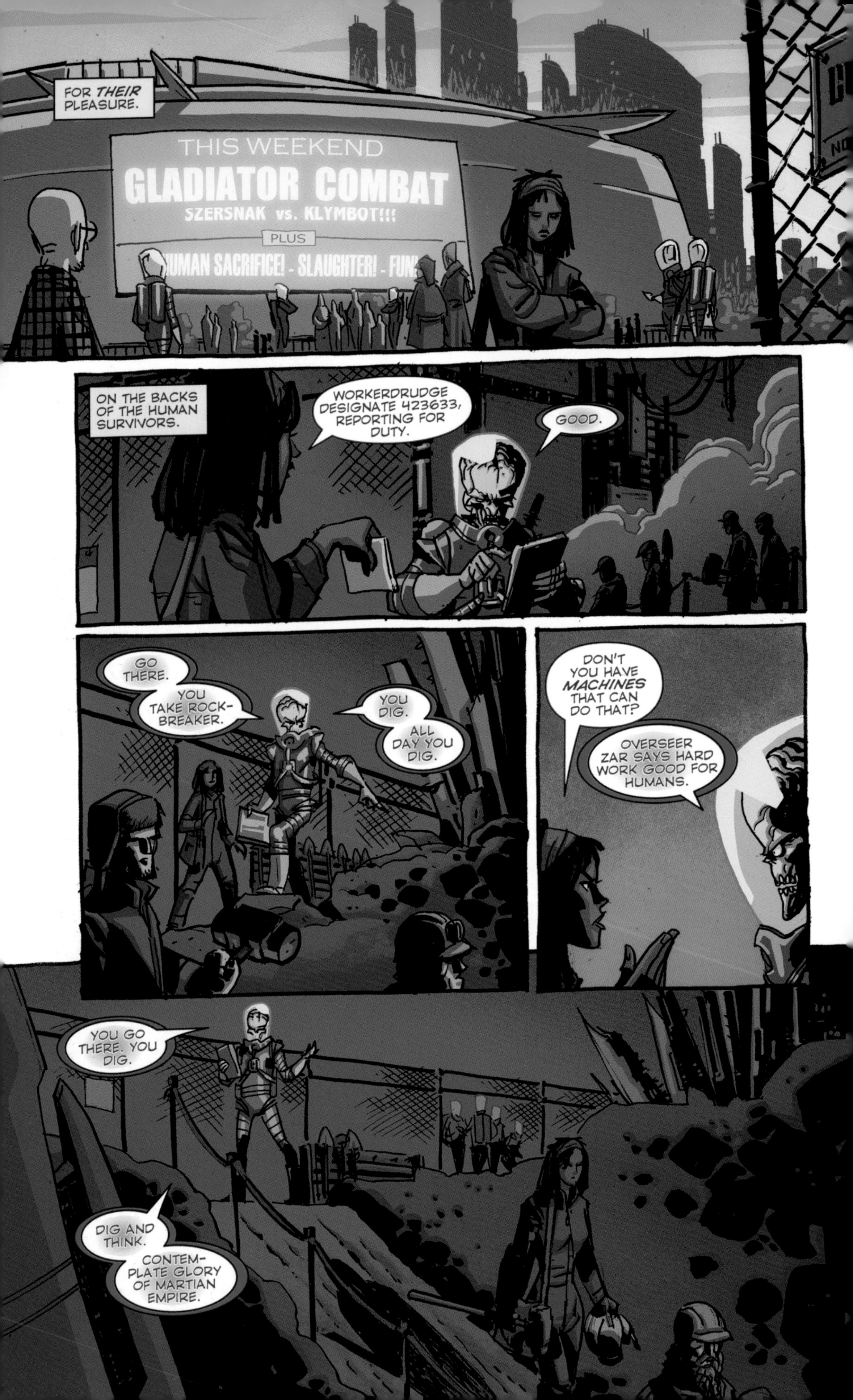
FOR *THEIR* PLEASURE.
THIS WEEKEND
GLADIATOR COMBAT
SZERSNAK vs. KLYMBOT!!!
PLUS
UMAN SACRIFICE! - SLAUGHTER! - FUN
ON THE BACKS OF THE HUMAN SURVIVORS.
WORKERDRUDGE DESIGNATE 423633, REPORTING FOR DUTY.
GOOD.
GO THERE.
YOU TAKE ROCK-BREAKER.
YOU DIG.
ALL DAY YOU DIG.
DON'T YOU HAVE *MACHINES* THAT CAN DO THAT?
OVERSEER ZAR SAYS HARD WORK GOOD FOR HUMANS.
YOU GO THERE. YOU DIG.
DIG AND THINK.
CONTEM-PLATE GLORY OF MARTIAN EMPIRE.

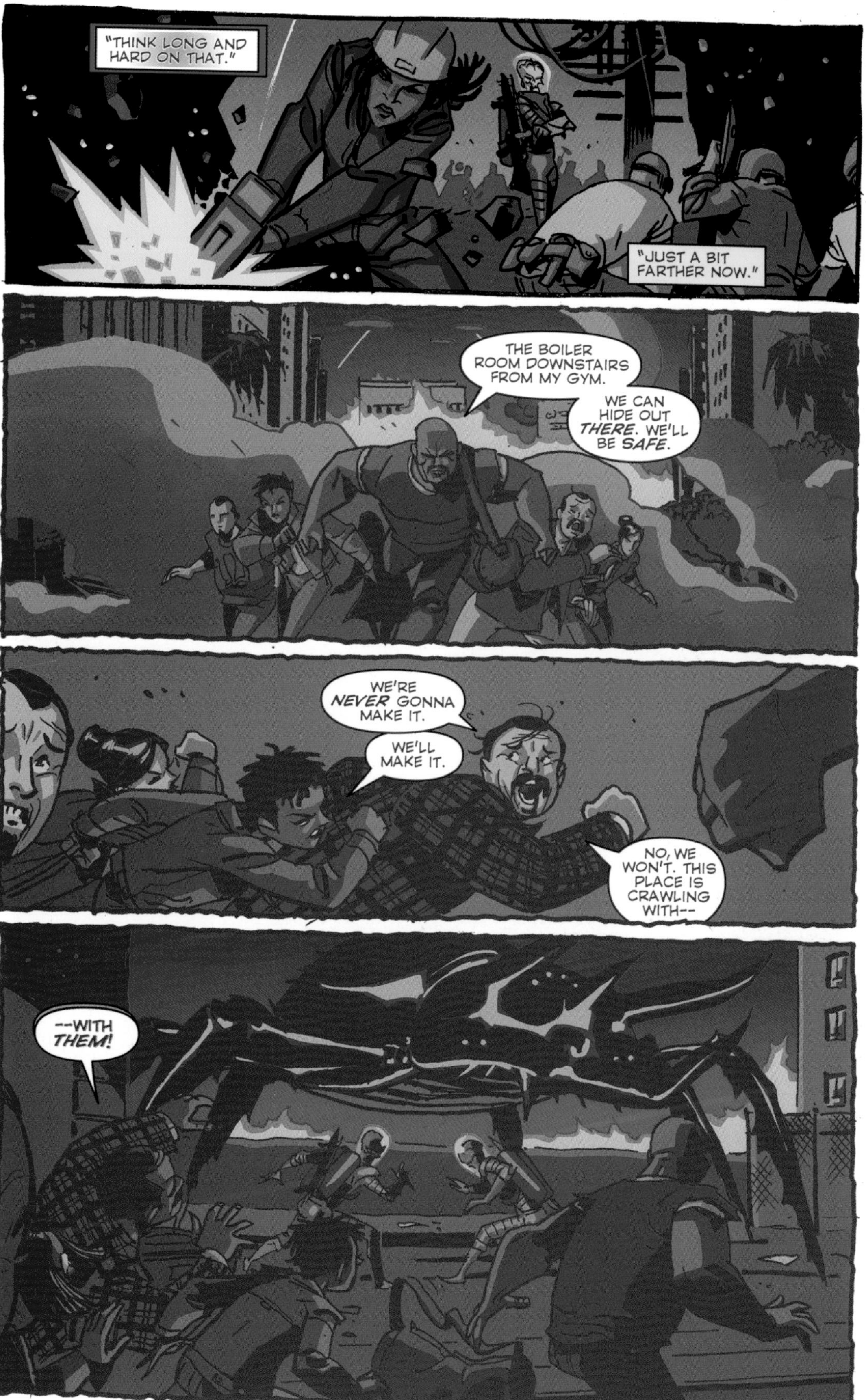
"THINK LONG AND HARD ON THAT."
"JUST A BIT FARTHER NOW."
THE BOILER ROOM DOWNSTAIRS FROM MY GYM.
WE CAN HIDE OUT *THERE*. WE'LL BE *SAFE*.
WE'RE *NEVER* GONNA MAKE IT.
WE'LL MAKE IT.
NO, WE WON'T. THIS PLACE IS CRAWLING WITH--
--WITH *THEM*!

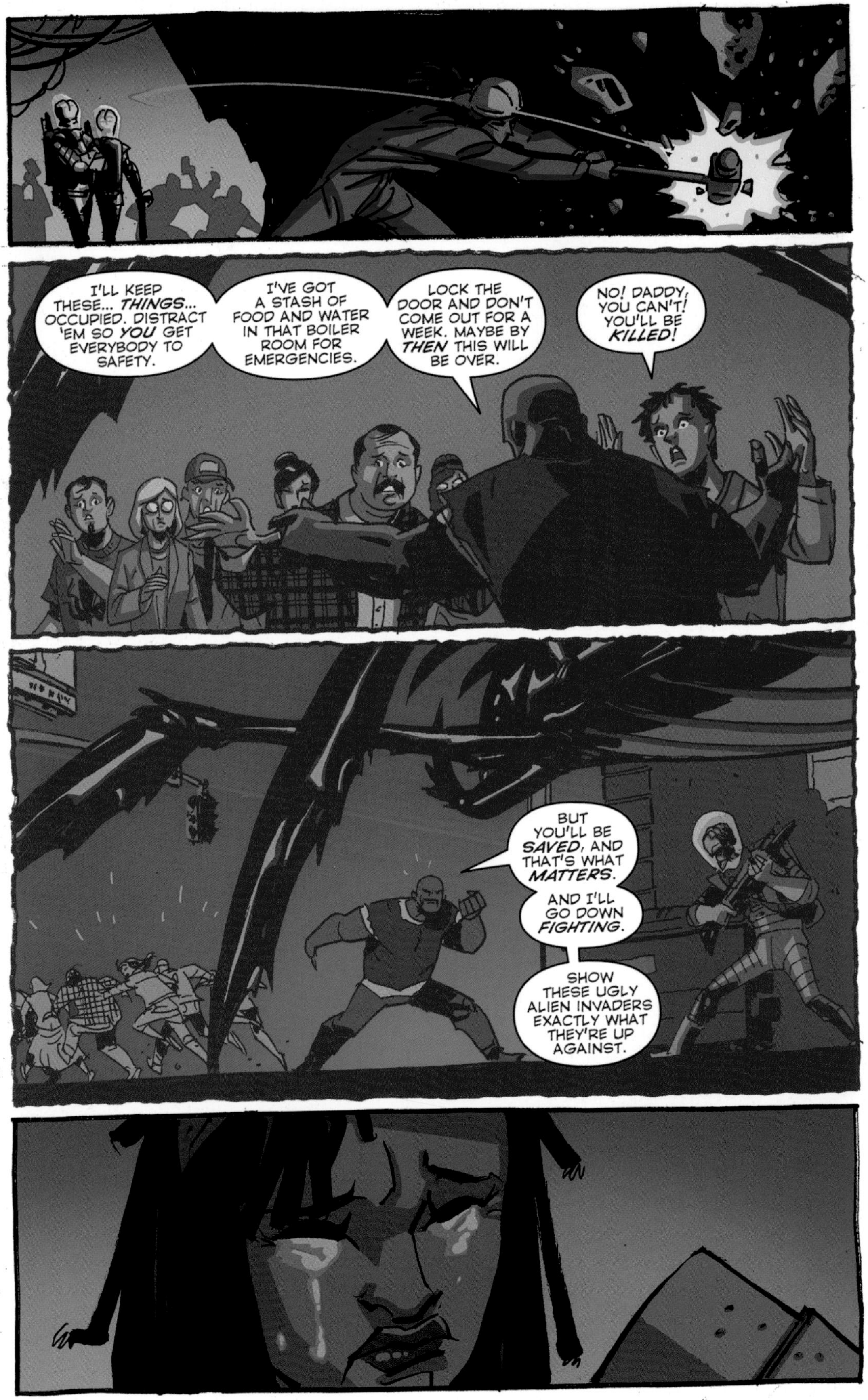
I'LL KEEP THESE... THINGS... OCCUPIED. DISTRACT 'EM SO YOU GET EVERYBODY TO SAFETY.
I'VE GOT A STASH OF FOOD AND WATER IN THAT BOILER ROOM FOR EMERGENCIES.
LOCK THE DOOR AND DON'T COME OUT FOR A WEEK. MAYBE BY THEN THIS WILL BE OVER.
NO! DADDY, YOU CAN'T! YOU'LL BE KILLED!
BUT YOU'LL BE SAVED, AND THAT'S WHAT MATTERS.
AND I'LL GO DOWN FIGHTING.
SHOW THESE UGLY ALIEN INVADERS EXACTLY WHAT THEY'RE UP AGAINST.

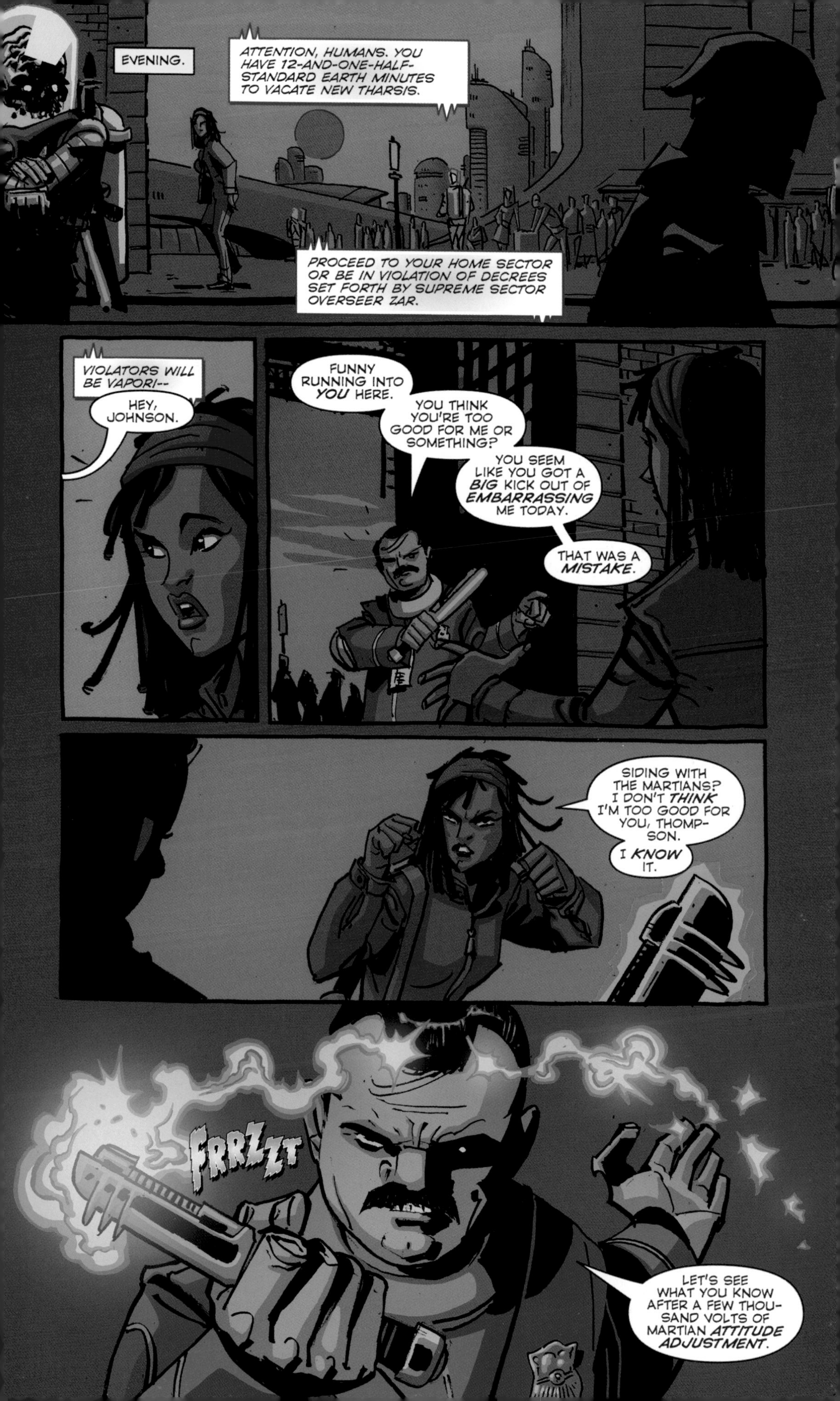

EVENING.
ATTENTION, HUMANS. YOU HAVE 12-AND-ONE-HALF-STANDARD EARTH MINUTES TO VACATE NEW THARSIS.
PROCEED TO YOUR HOME SECTOR OR BE IN VIOLATION OF DECREES SET FORTH BY SUPREME SECTOR OVERSEER ZAR.
VIOLATORS WILL BE VAPORI--
HEY, JOHNSON.
FUNNY RUNNING INTO YOU HERE.
YOU THINK YOU'RE TOO GOOD FOR ME OR SOMETHING?
YOU SEEM LIKE YOU GOT A BIG KICK OUT OF EMBARRASSING ME TODAY.
THAT WAS A MISTAKE.
SIDING WITH THE MARTIANS? I DON'T THINK I'M TOO GOOD FOR YOU, THOMP-SON.
I KNOW IT.
FRRZZT
LET'S SEE WHAT YOU KNOW AFTER A FEW THOU-SAND VOLTS OF MARTIAN ATTITUDE ADJUSTMENT.

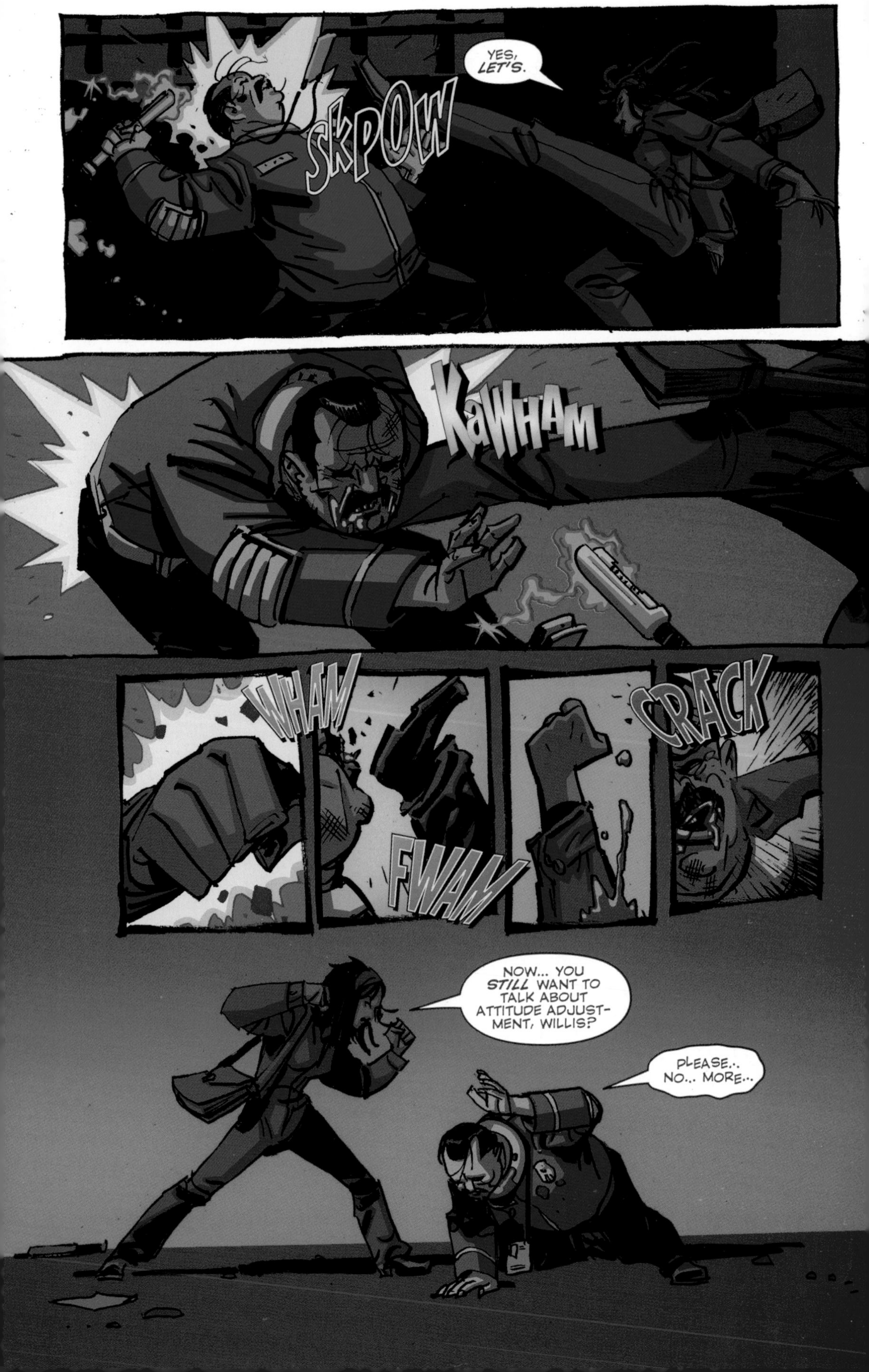
YES, LET'S.
SKPOW
KAWHAM
WHAM
FWAM
CRACK
NOW... YOU STILL WANT TO TALK ABOUT ATTITUDE ADJUSTMENT, WILLIS?
PLEASE... NO... MORE...

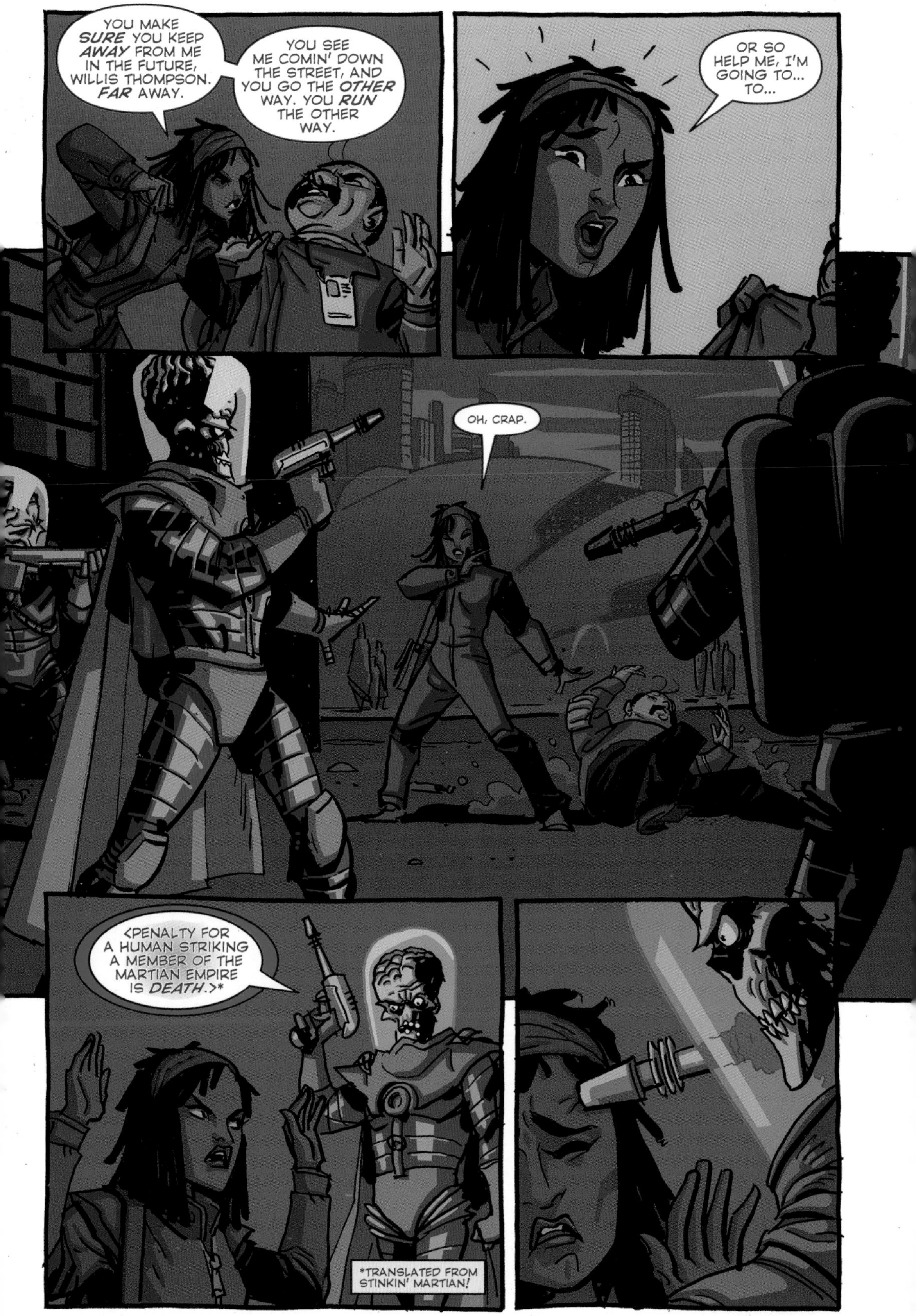
YOU MAKE SURE YOU KEEP AWAY FROM ME IN THE FUTURE, WILLIS THOMPSON. FAR AWAY.
YOU SEE ME COMIN' DOWN THE STREET, AND YOU GO THE OTHER WAY. YOU RUN THE OTHER WAY.
OR SO HELP ME, I'M GOING TO... TO...
OH, CRAP.
<PENALTY FOR A HUMAN STRIKING A MEMBER OF THE MARTIAN EMPIRE IS DEATH.>*
*TRANSLATED FROM STINKIN' MARTIAN!

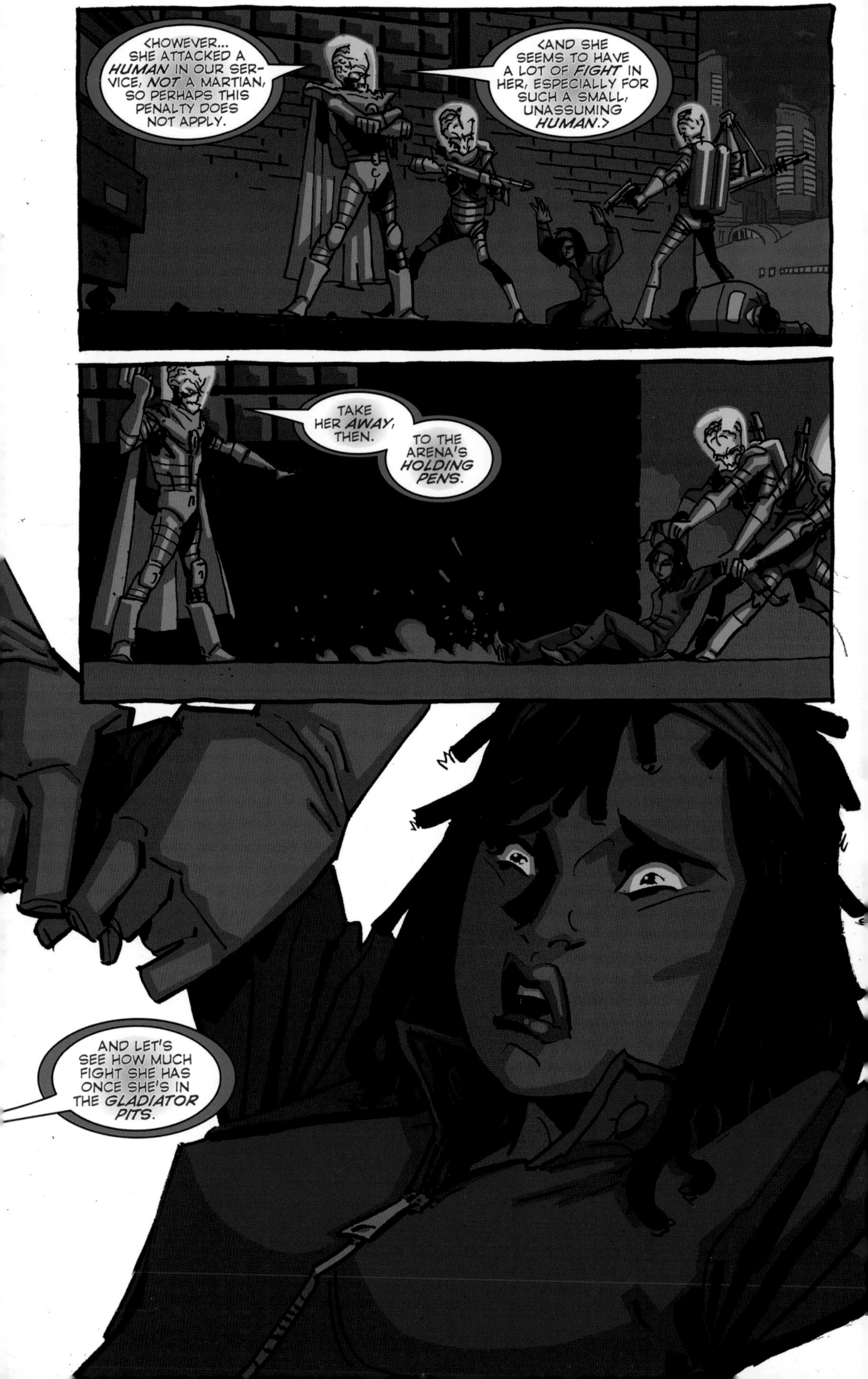

<HOWEVER... SHE ATTACKED A HUMAN IN OUR SERVICE, NOT A MARTIAN, SO PERHAPS THIS PENALTY DOES NOT APPLY.
<AND SHE SEEMS TO HAVE A LOT OF FIGHT IN HER, ESPECIALLY FOR SUCH A SMALL, UNASSUMING HUMAN.>
TAKE HER AWAY, THEN.
TO THE ARENA'S HOLDING PENS.
AND LET'S SEE HOW MUCH FIGHT SHE HAS ONCE SHE'S IN THE GLADIATOR PITS.

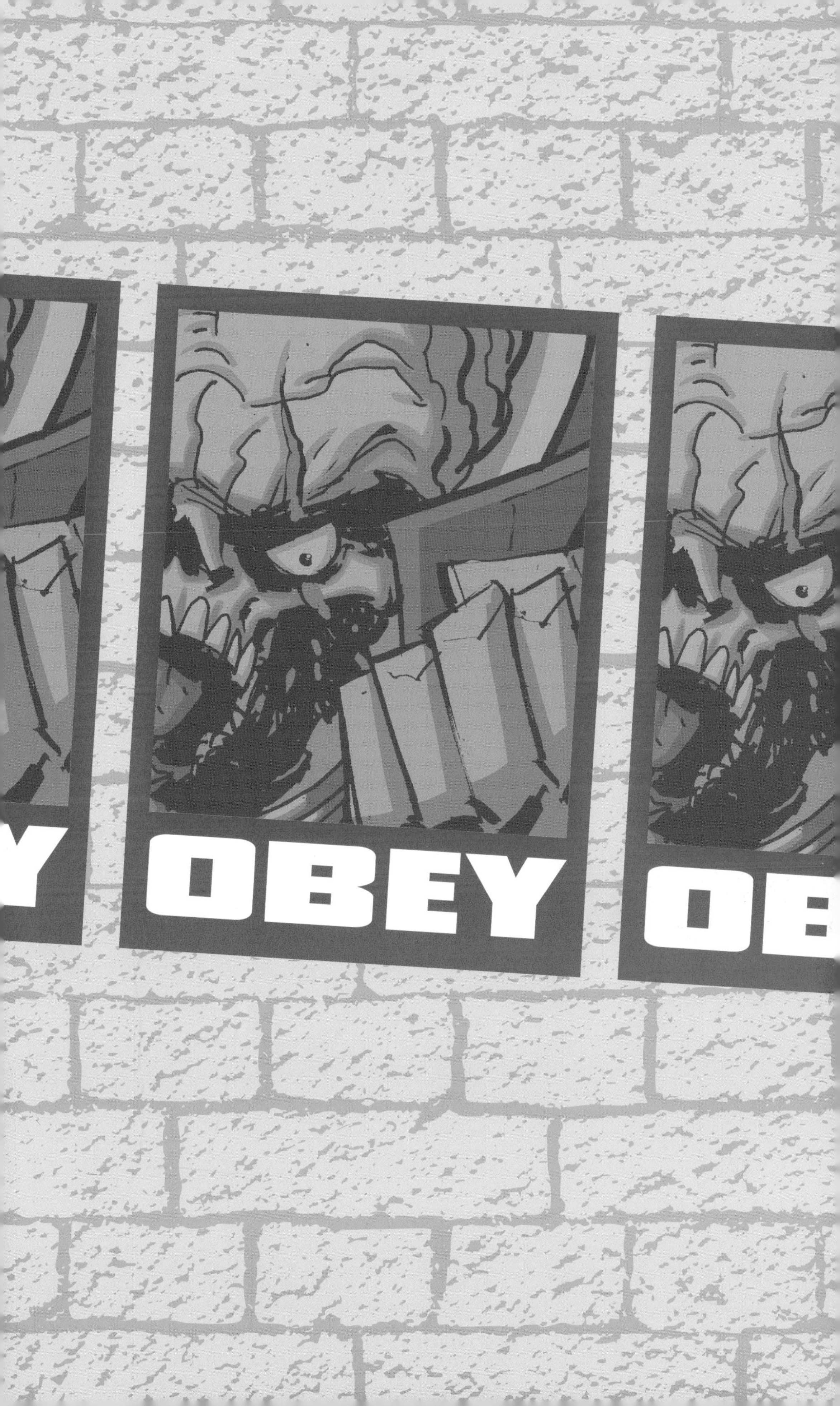
OBEY

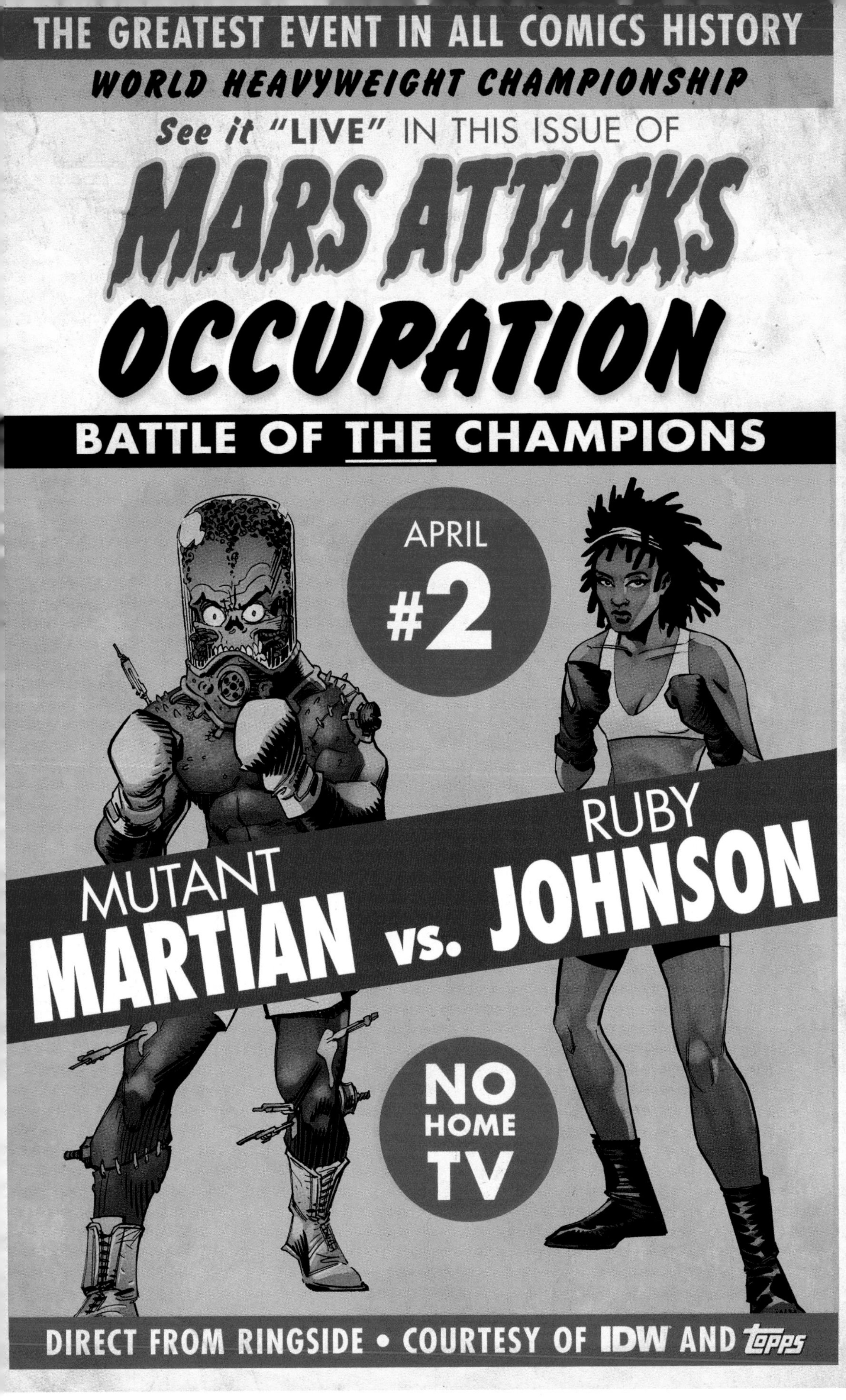
THE GREATEST EVENT IN ALL COMICS HISTORY
WORLD HEAVYWEIGHT CHAMPIONSHIP
See it "LIVE" IN THIS ISSUE OF
MARS ATTACKS®
OCCUPATION
BATTLE OF THE CHAMPIONS
APRIL
#2
MUTANT MARTIAN vs. RUBY JOHNSON
NO HOME TV
DIRECT FROM RINGSIDE • COURTESY OF IDW AND Topps

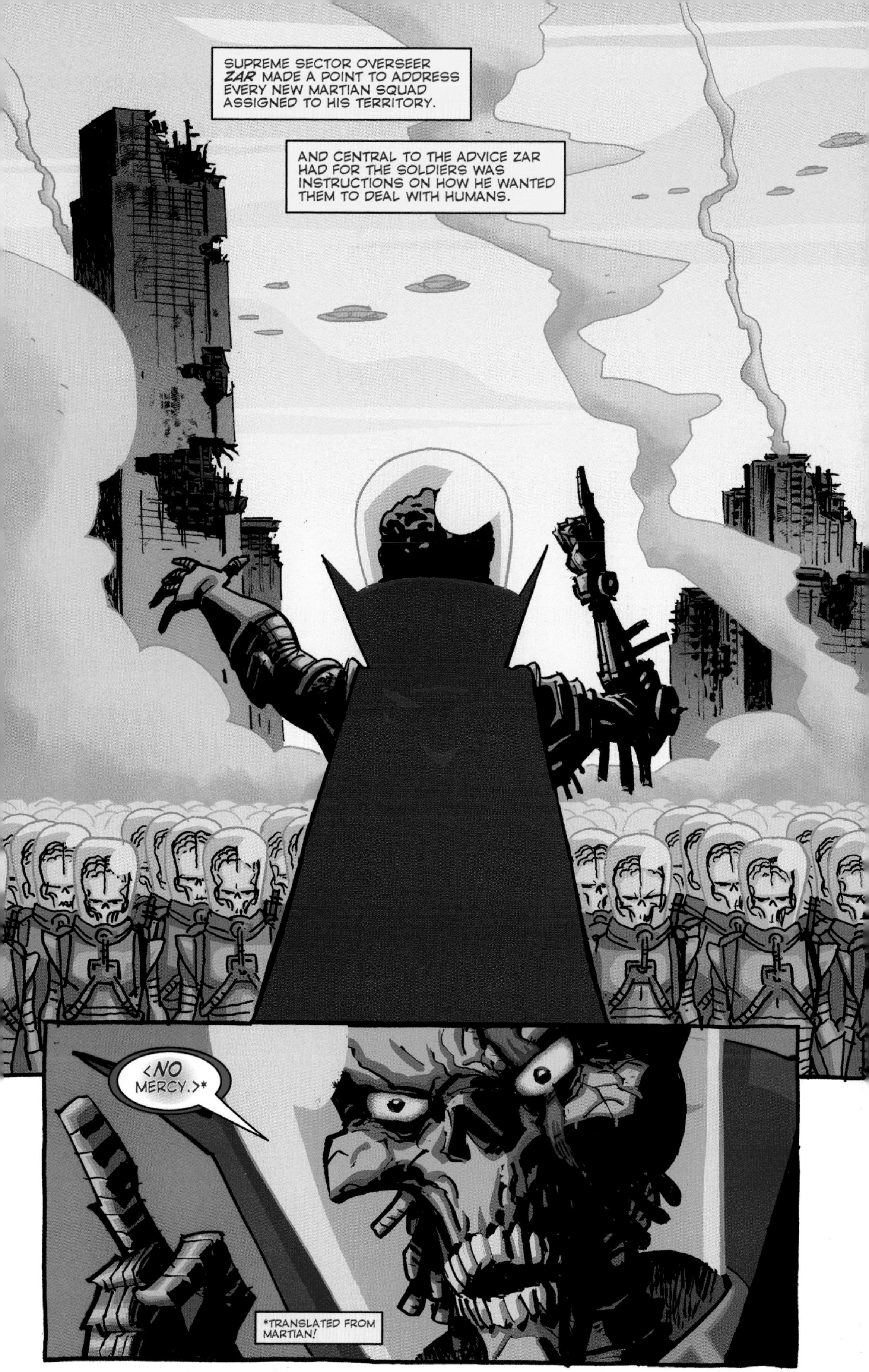
SUPREME SECTOR OVERSEER ZAR MADE A POINT TO ADDRESS EVERY NEW MARTIAN SQUAD ASSIGNED TO HIS TERRITORY.
AND CENTRAL TO THE ADVICE ZAR HAD FOR THE SOLDIERS WAS INSTRUCTIONS ON HOW HE WANTED THEM TO DEAL WITH HUMANS.
<NO MERCY.>*
*TRANSLATED FROM MARTIAN!

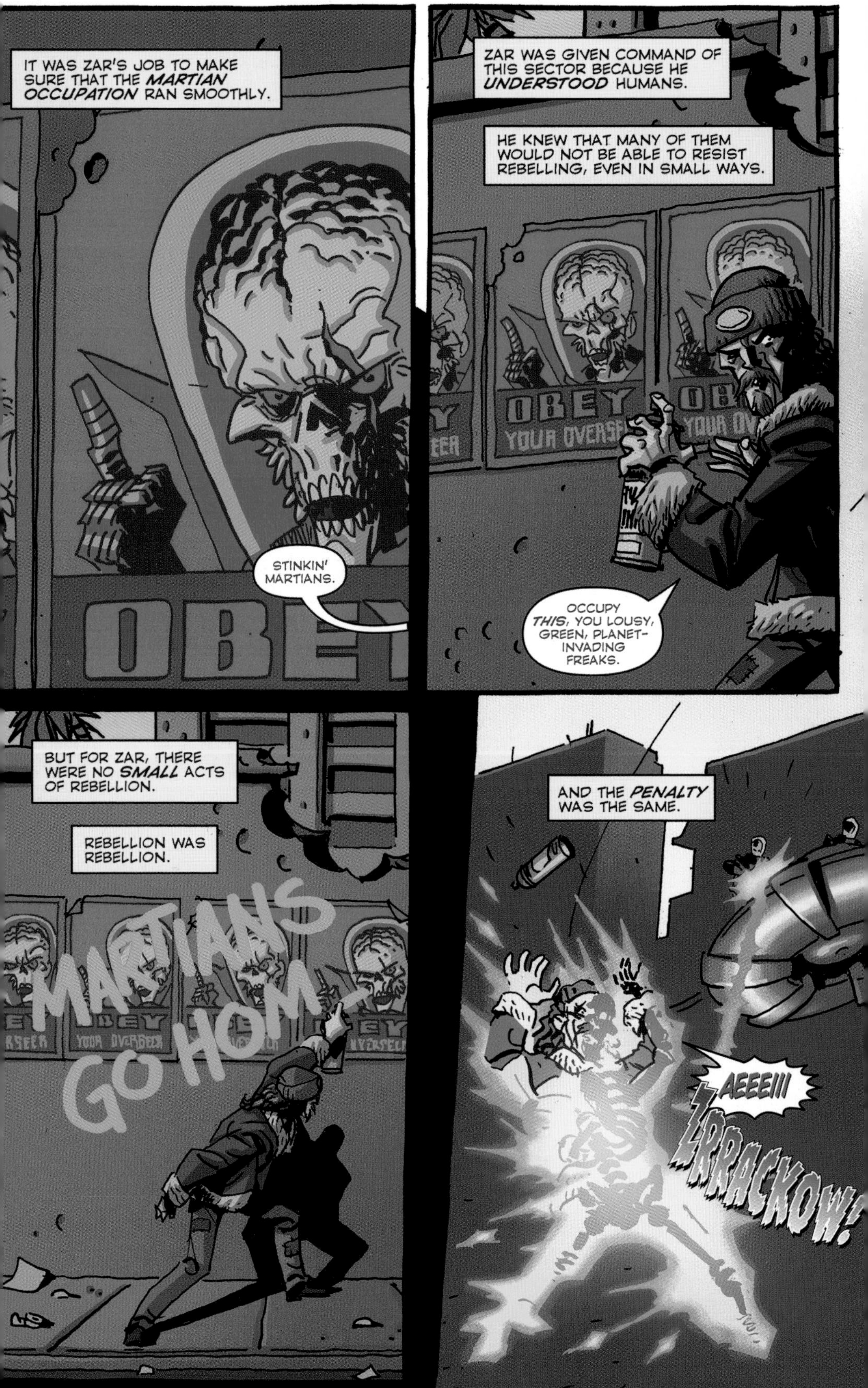
IT WAS ZAR'S JOB TO MAKE SURE THAT THE *MARTIAN OCCUPATION* RAN SMOOTHLY.
OBEY
STINKIN' MARTIANS.
ZAR WAS GIVEN COMMAND OF THIS SECTOR BECAUSE HE *UNDERSTOOD* HUMANS.
HE KNEW THAT MANY OF THEM WOULD NOT BE ABLE TO RESIST REBELLING, EVEN IN SMALL WAYS.
OBEY YOUR OVERSEER
OCCUPY *THIS*, YOU LOUSY, GREEN, PLANET-INVADING FREAKS.
BUT FOR ZAR, THERE WERE NO *SMALL* ACTS OF REBELLION.
REBELLION WAS REBELLION.
MARTIANS GO HOM—
AND THE *PENALTY* WAS THE SAME.
AEEEIII
ZRRACKOW!

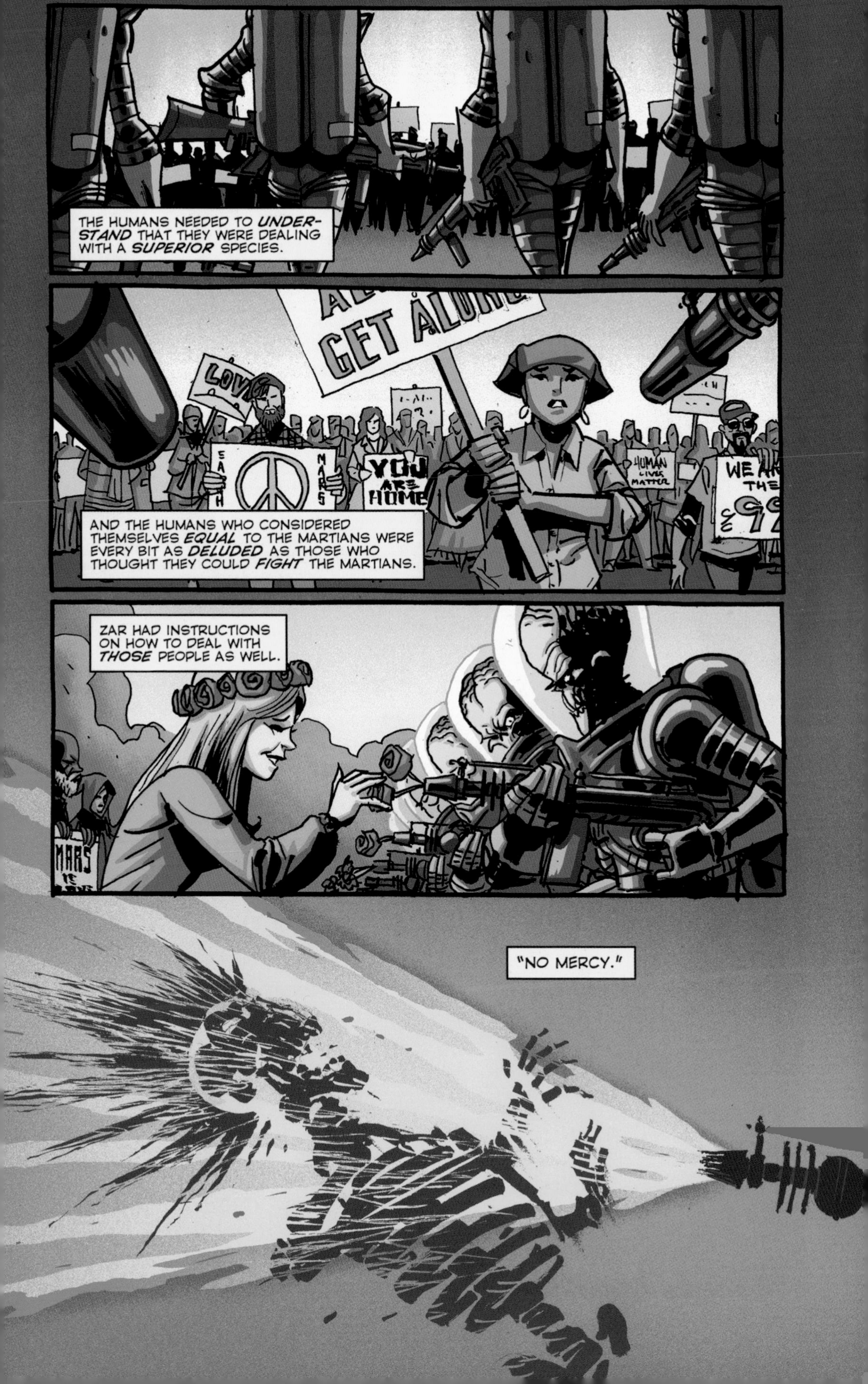

THE HUMANS NEEDED TO *UNDERSTAND* THAT THEY WERE DEALING WITH A *SUPERIOR* SPECIES.
GET ALONG
LOVE
EARTH
MARS
YOU ARE HOME
HUMAN LIVES MATTER
AND THE HUMANS WHO CONSIDERED THEMSELVES *EQUAL* TO THE MARTIANS WERE EVERY BIT AS *DELUDED* AS THOSE WHO THOUGHT THEY COULD *FIGHT* THE MARTIANS.
ZAR HAD INSTRUCTIONS ON HOW TO DEAL WITH *THOSE* PEOPLE AS WELL.
MARS
"NO MERCY."

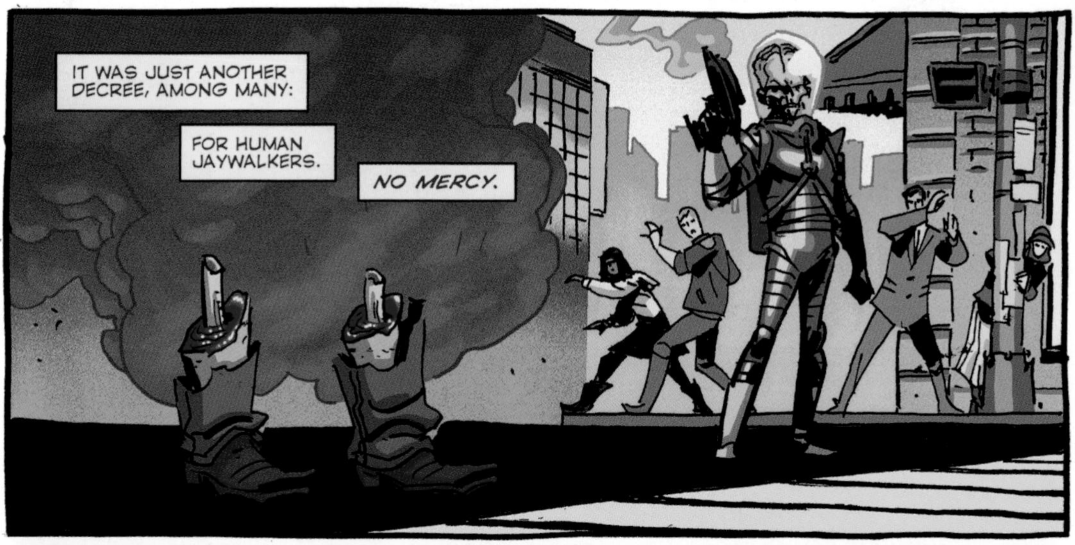
IT WAS JUST ANOTHER DECREE, AMONG MANY:
FOR HUMAN JAYWALKERS.
NO MERCY.

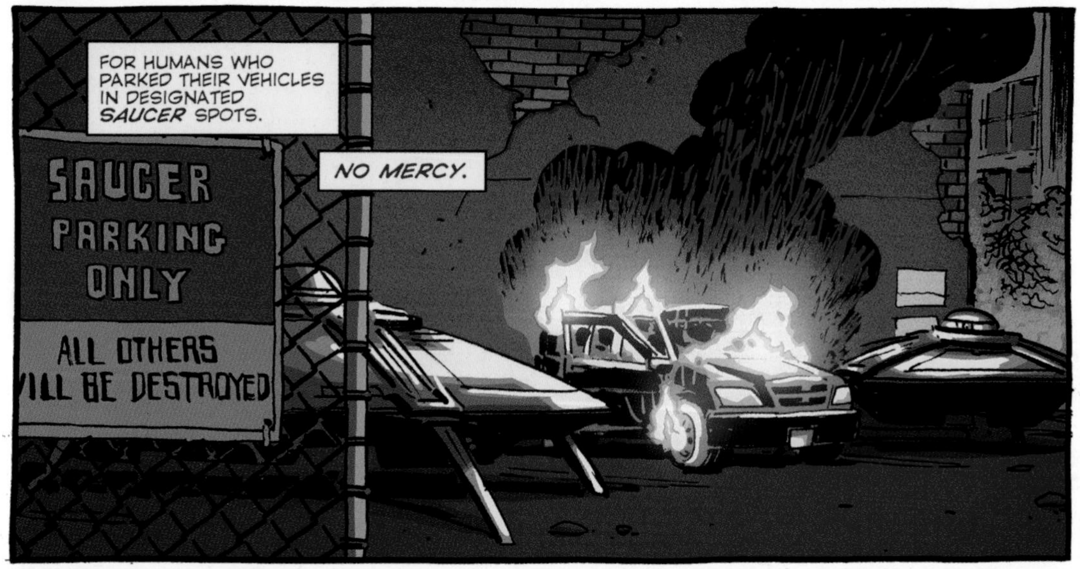
FOR HUMANS WHO PARKED THEIR VEHICLES IN DESIGNATED *SAUCER* SPOTS.
SAUCER PARKING ONLY
ALL OTHERS WILL BE DESTROYED
NO MERCY.

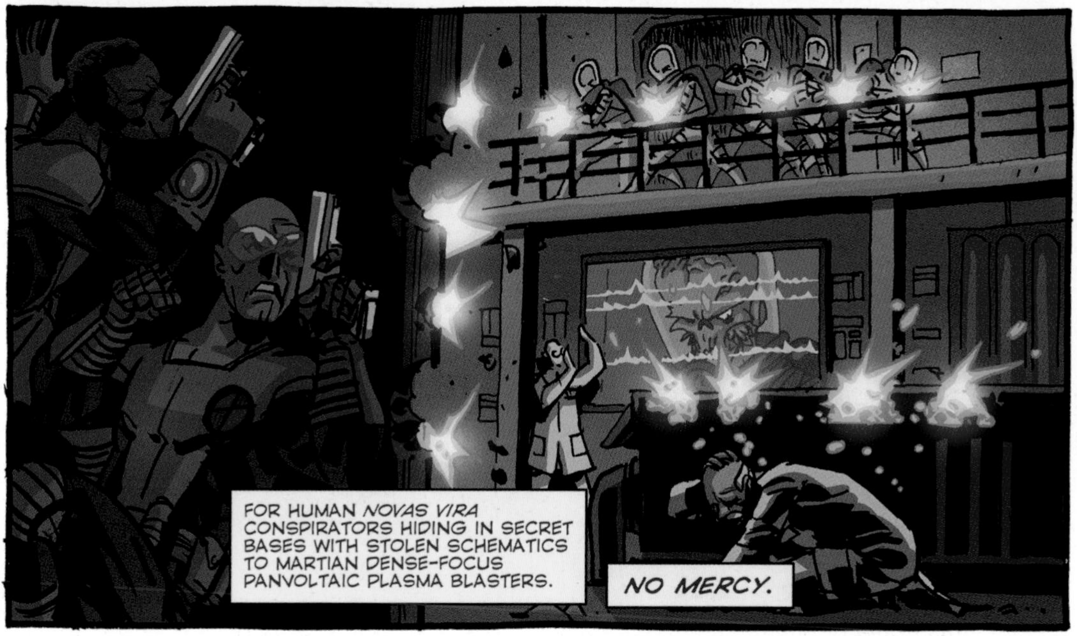
FOR HUMAN *NOVAS VIRA* CONSPIRATORS HIDING IN SECRET BASES WITH STOLEN SCHEMATICS TO MARTIAN DENSE-FOCUS PANVOLTAIC PLASMA BLASTERS.
NO MERCY.

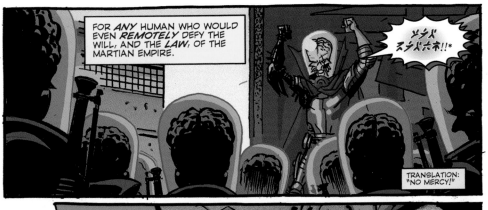

FOR *ANY* HUMAN WHO WOULD EVEN *REMOTELY* DEFY THE WILL, AND THE *LAW,* OF THE MARTIAN EMPIRE.

ソラバ スラバ六ネ!!*

TRANSLATION: "NO MERCY!"

THIS IS HOW SUPREME SECTOR OVERSEER ZAR KEPT THE HUMANS OF HIS SECTOR IN LINE.

HE DID, HOWEVER, ADVISE SOLDIERS TO KEEP AN EYE OUT FOR *CERTAIN* HUMANS.

KaWHAM

ONES WHO HAD JUST THE *RIGHT* AMOUNT OF *FIGHT* IN THEM.

FWAM

THE PRECISE MIX OF SPIRIT, DEFIANCE, AND WILL TO SURVIVE.

LISTEN, I CAN *EXPLAIN.*

THAT GUY *STARTED* IT. HE *THREATENED* ME. *JUMPED* ME.

I WAS JUST *DEFENDING* MYSELF.

IRRELEVANT, HUMAN.

YOU'RE COMING WITH US.

TAKE THEM ALIVE, KEEP THEM (MOSTLY) UNHARMED, AND BRING THEM INTO CUSTODY.

THIS IS *NOT* MERCY.

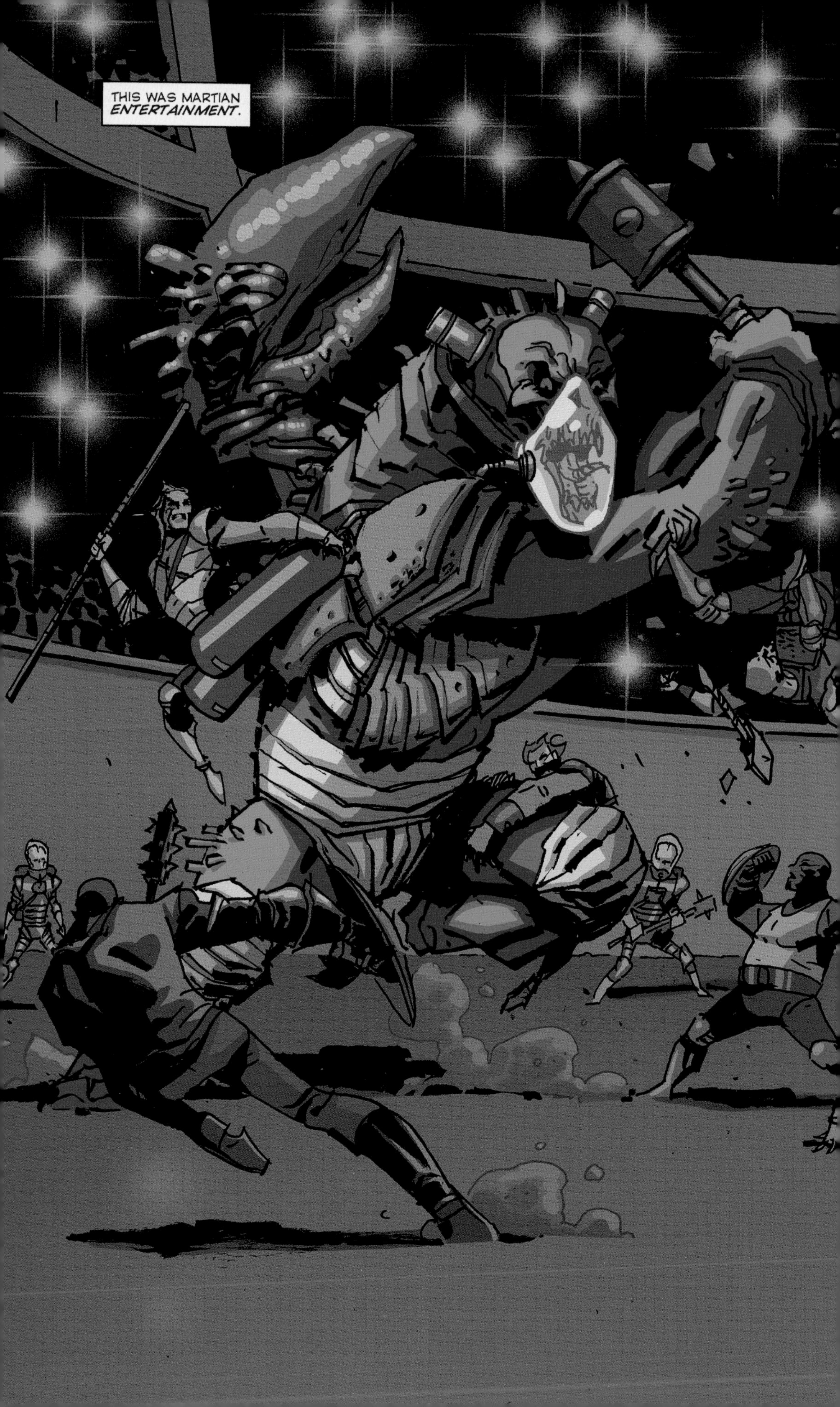
THIS WAS MARTIAN *ENTERTAINMENT*.

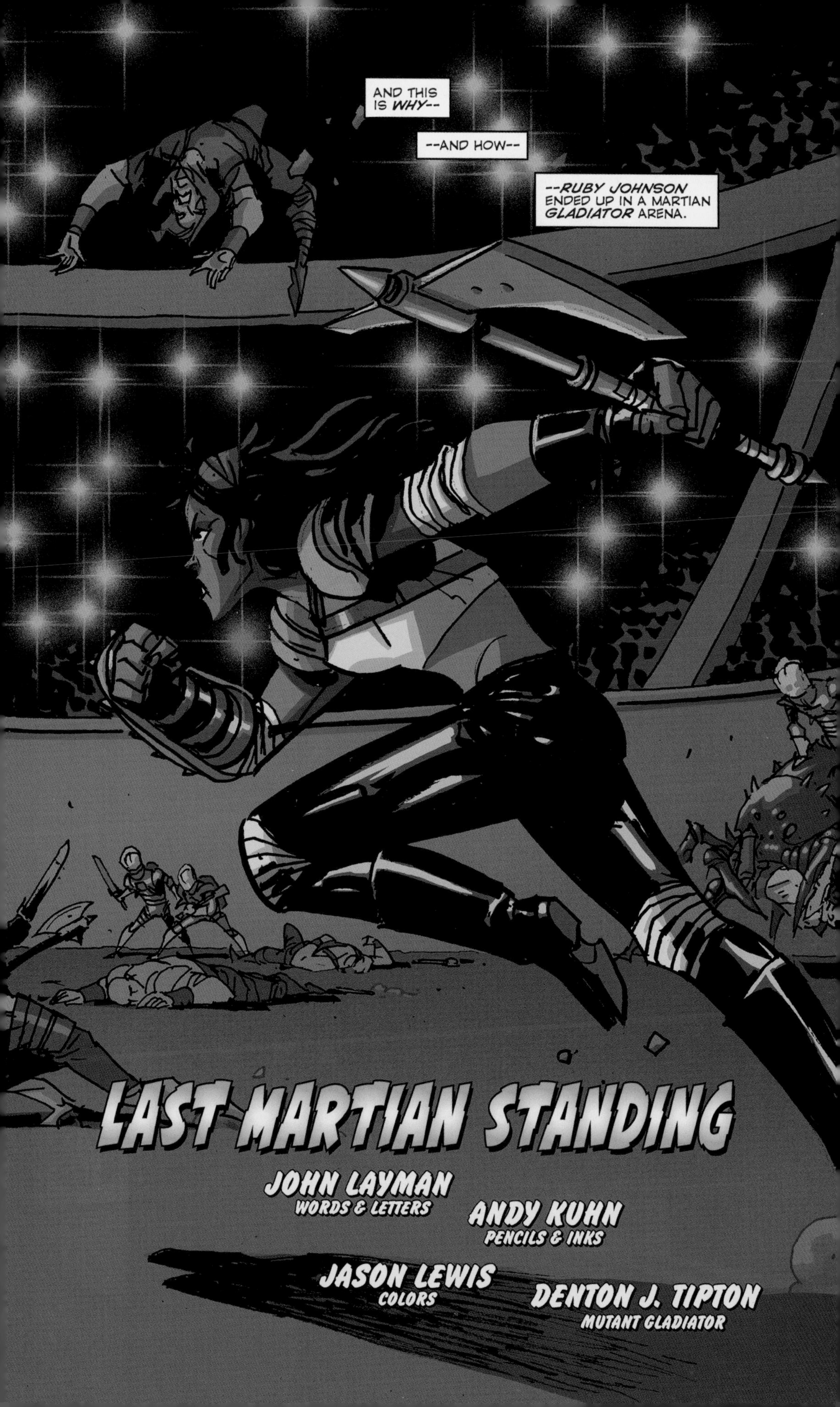

AND THIS IS WHY--
--AND HOW--
--RUBY JOHNSON ENDED UP IN A MARTIAN GLADIATOR ARENA.
LAST MARTIAN STANDING
JOHN LAYMAN
WORDS & LETTERS
ANDY KUHN
PENCILS & INKS
JASON LEWIS
COLORS
DENTON J. TIPTON
MUTANT GLADIATOR

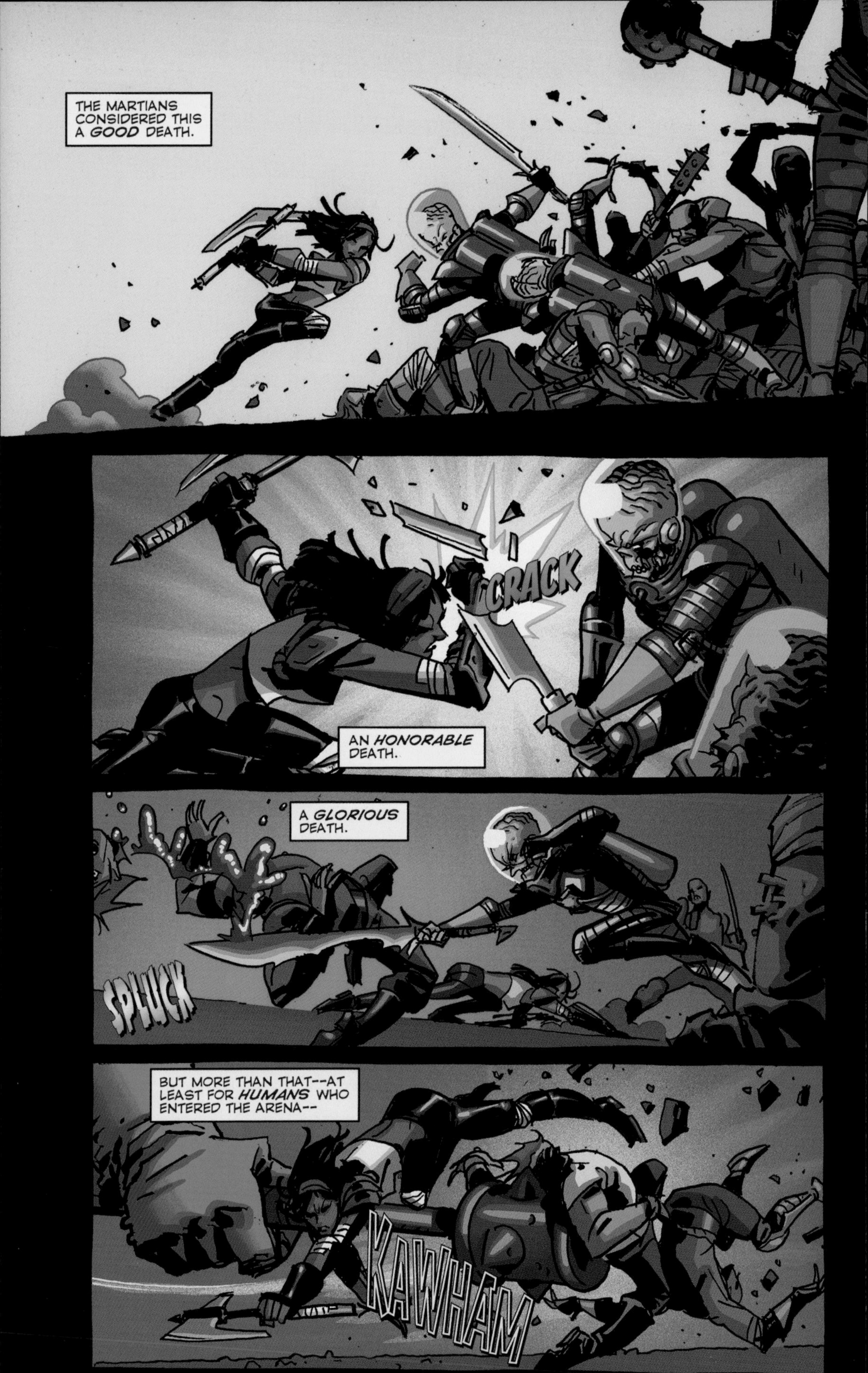
THE MARTIANS CONSIDERED THIS A GOOD DEATH.
CRACK
AN HONORABLE DEATH.
A GLORIOUS DEATH.
SPLUCK
BUT MORE THAN THAT--AT LEAST FOR HUMANS WHO ENTERED THE ARENA--
KAWHAM

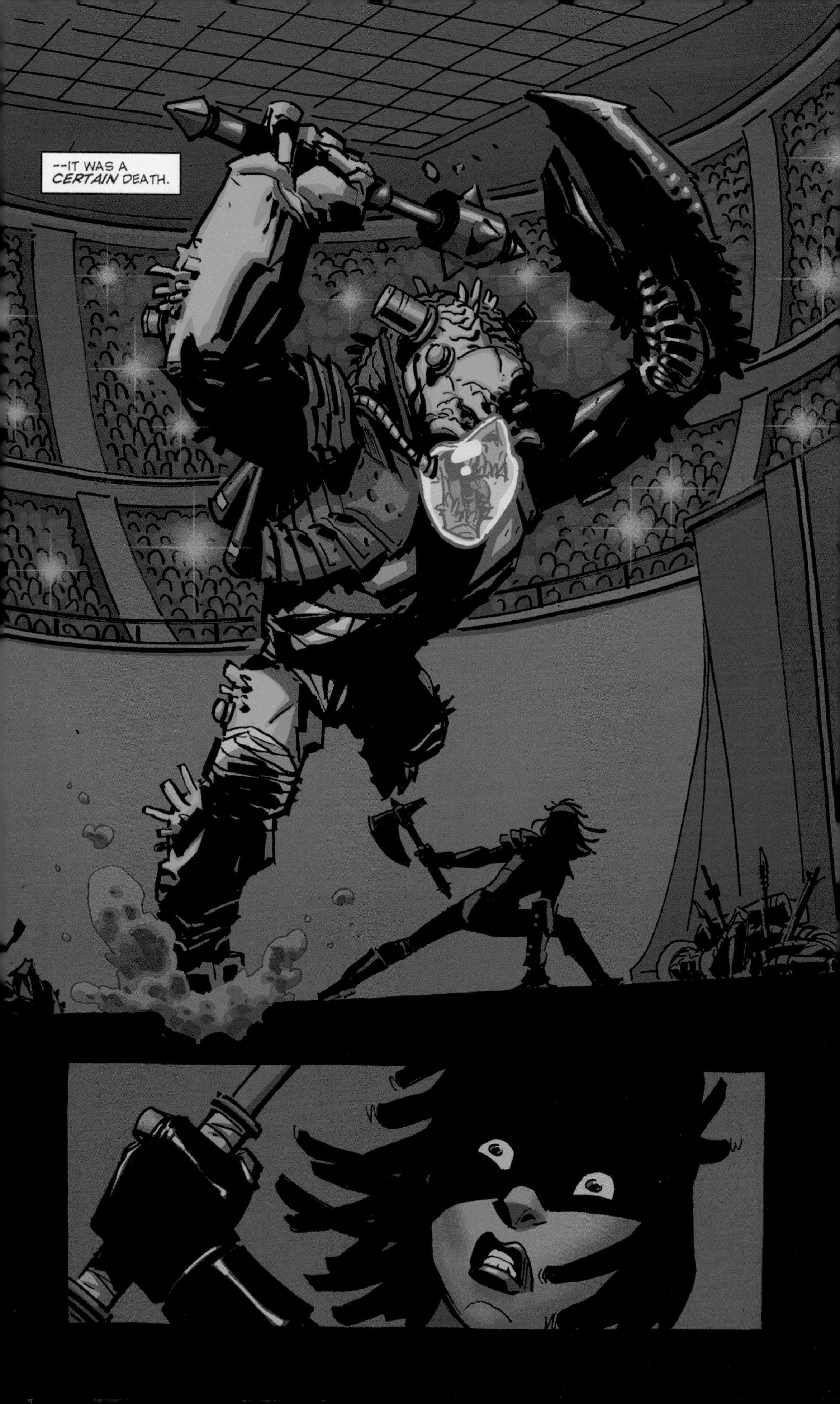
--IT WAS A *CERTAIN* DEATH.

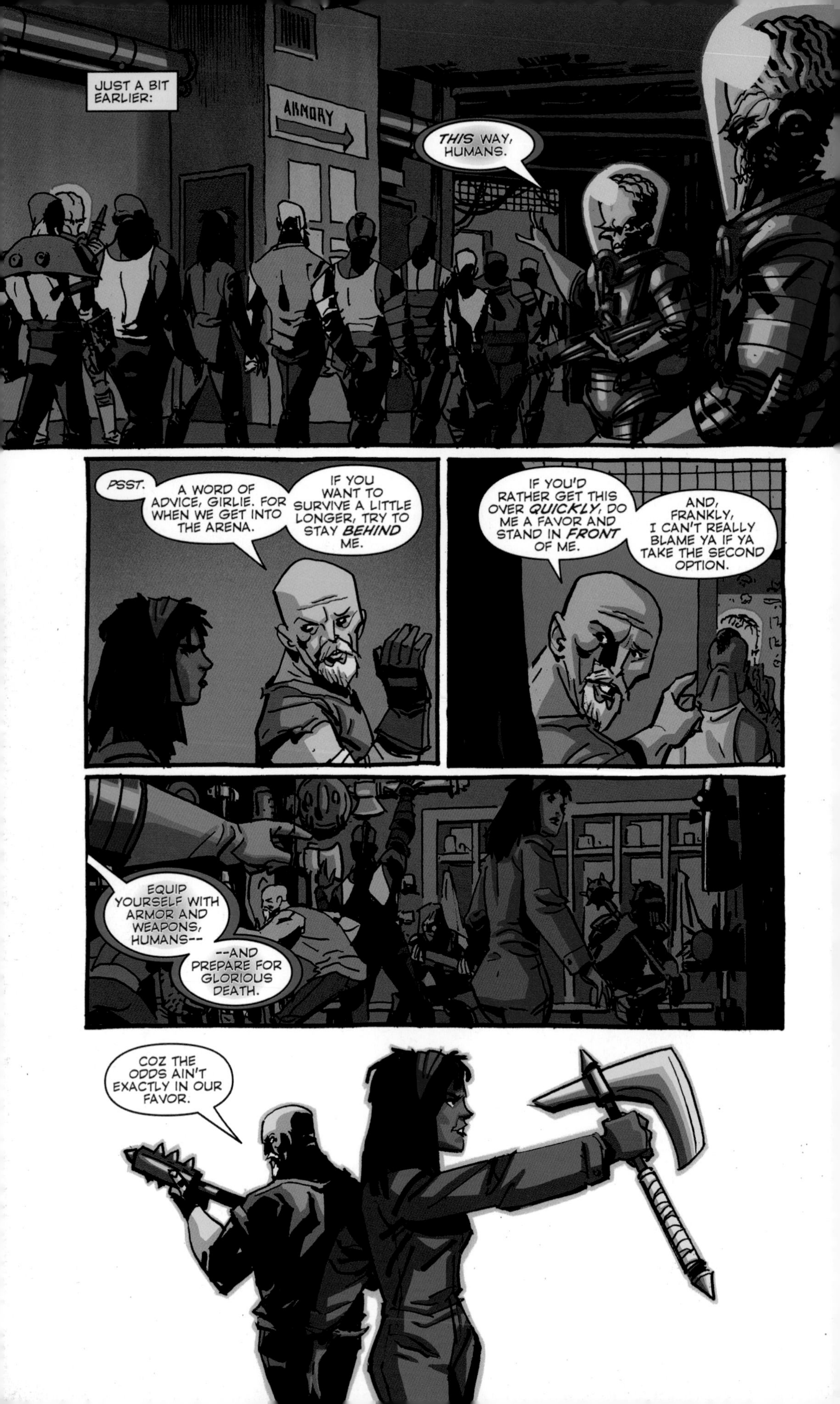

JUST A BIT EARLIER:
ARMORY
THIS WAY, HUMANS.
PSST.
A WORD OF ADVICE, GIRLIE. FOR WHEN WE GET INTO THE ARENA.
IF YOU WANT TO SURVIVE A LITTLE LONGER, TRY TO STAY BEHIND ME.
IF YOU'D RATHER GET THIS OVER QUICKLY, DO ME A FAVOR AND STAND IN FRONT OF ME.
AND, FRANKLY, I CAN'T REALLY BLAME YA IF YA TAKE THE SECOND OPTION.
EQUIP YOURSELF WITH ARMOR AND WEAPONS, HUMANS--
--AND PREPARE FOR GLORIOUS DEATH.
COZ THE ODDS AIN'T EXACTLY IN OUR FAVOR.

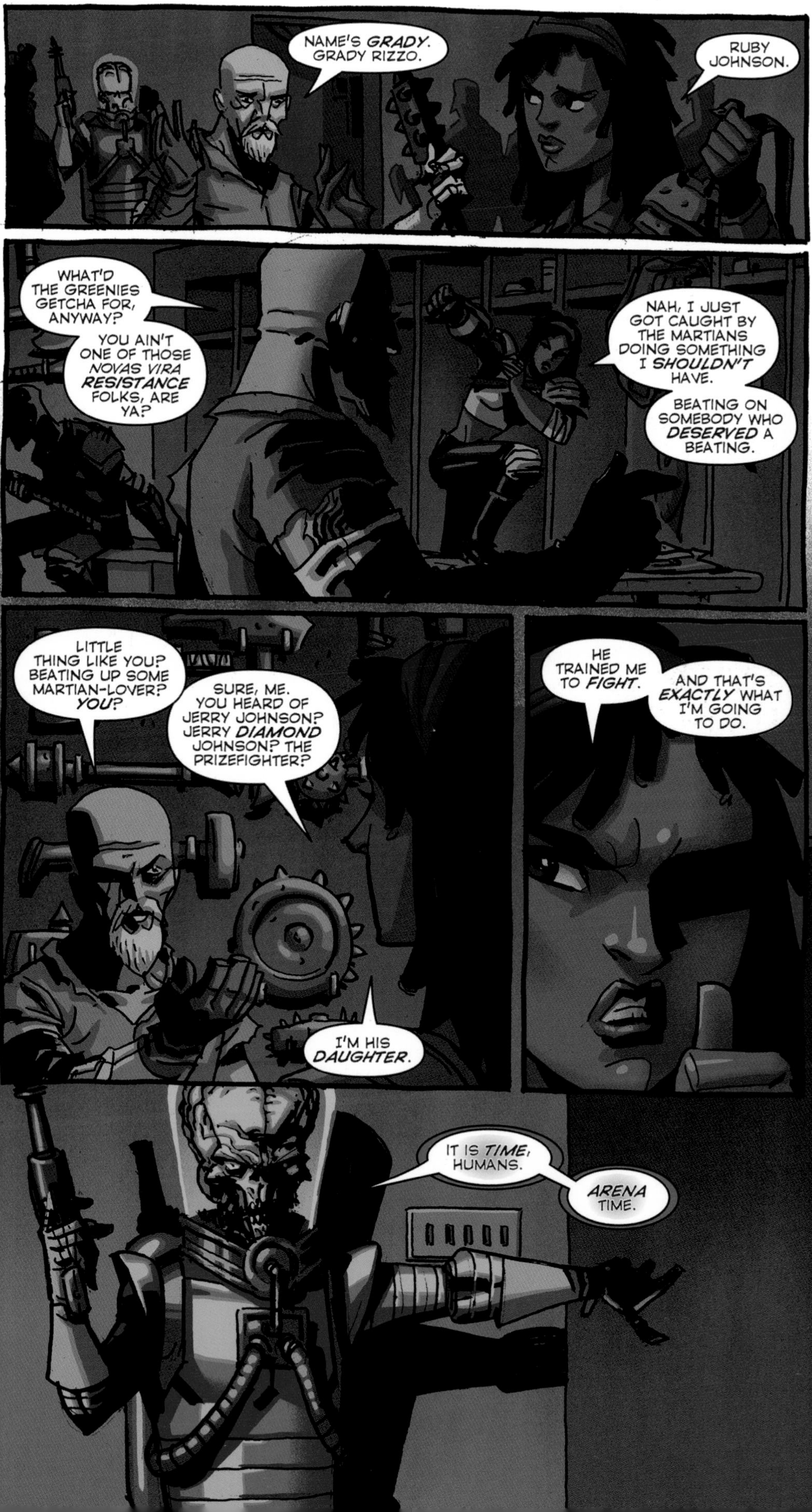
NAME'S GRADY. GRADY RIZZO.
RUBY JOHNSON.
WHAT'D THE GREENIES GETCHA FOR, ANYWAY?
YOU AIN'T ONE OF THOSE NOVAS VIRA RESISTANCE FOLKS, ARE YA?
NAH, I JUST GOT CAUGHT BY THE MARTIANS DOING SOMETHING I SHOULDN'T HAVE.
BEATING ON SOMEBODY WHO DESERVED A BEATING.
LITTLE THING LIKE YOU? BEATING UP SOME MARTIAN-LOVER? YOU?
SURE, ME. YOU HEARD OF JERRY JOHNSON? JERRY DIAMOND JOHNSON? THE PRIZEFIGHTER?
I'M HIS DAUGHTER.
HE TRAINED ME TO FIGHT.
AND THAT'S EXACTLY WHAT I'M GOING TO DO.
IT IS TIME, HUMANS.
ARENA TIME.

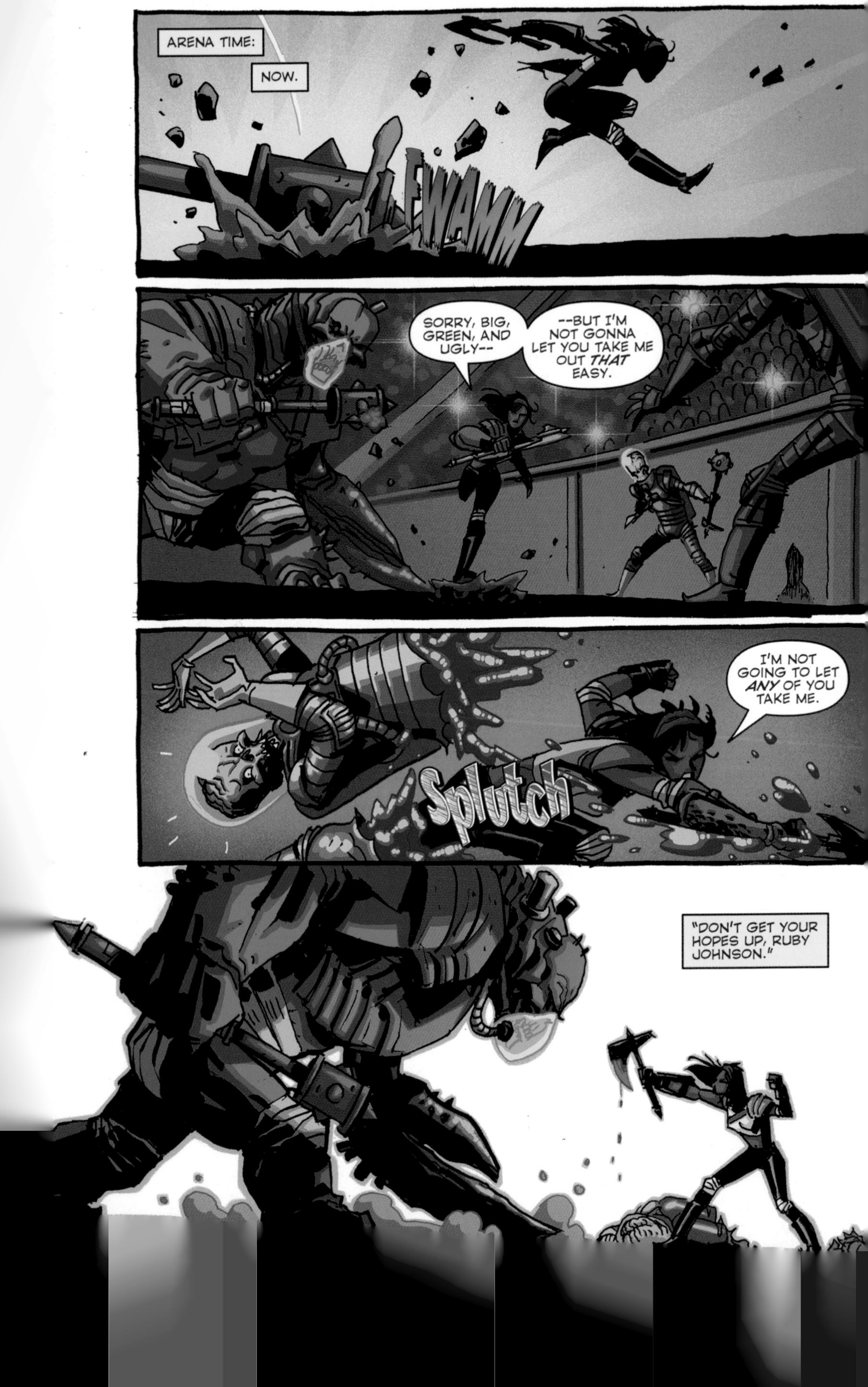
ARENA TIME:
NOW.
FWAMM
SORRY, BIG, GREEN, AND UGLY--
--BUT I'M NOT GONNA LET YOU TAKE ME OUT *THAT* EASY.
I'M NOT GOING TO LET *ANY* OF YOU TAKE ME.
Splutch
"DON'T GET YOUR HOPES UP, RUBY JOHNSON."

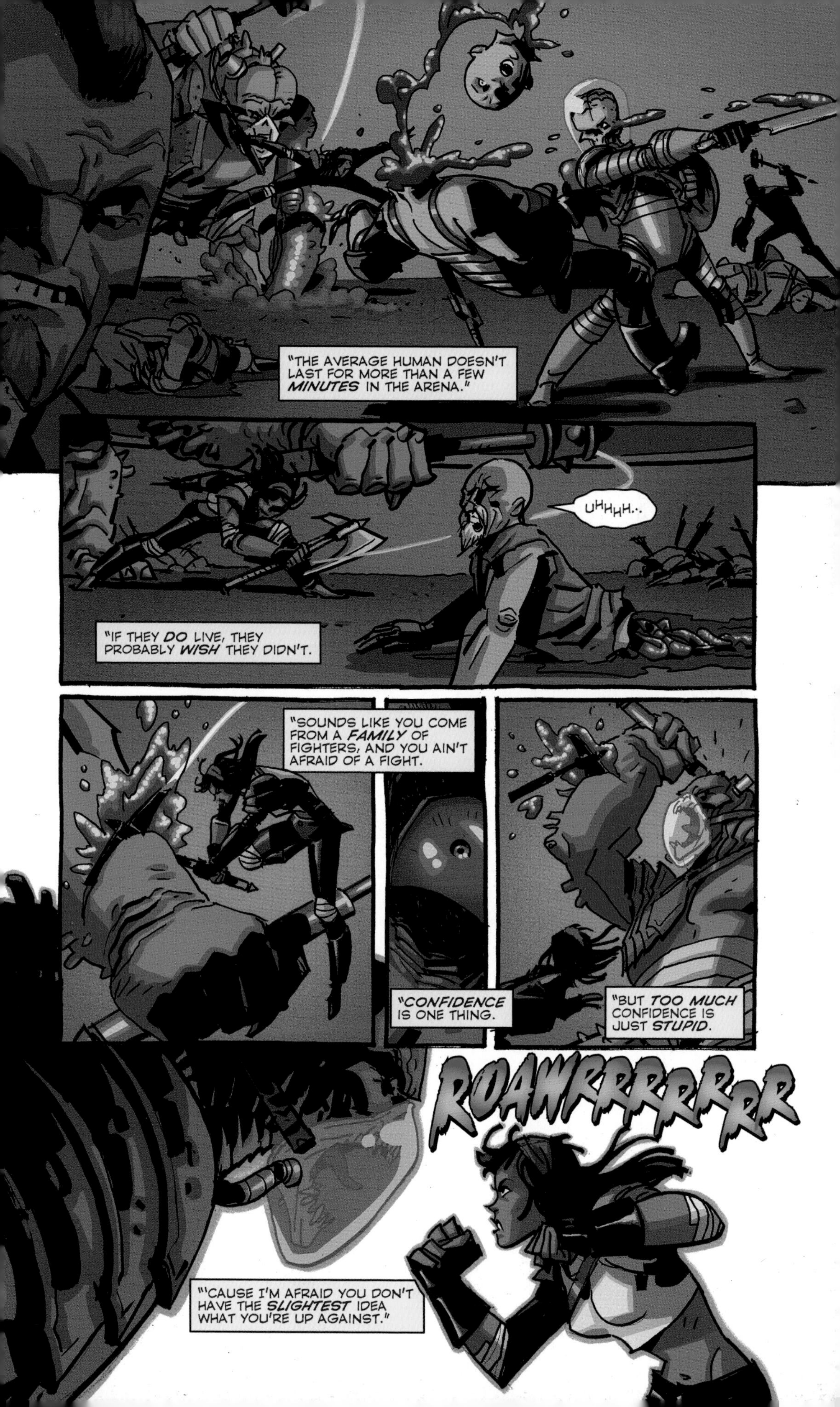
"THE AVERAGE HUMAN DOESN'T LAST FOR MORE THAN A FEW *MINUTES* IN THE ARENA."
UHHHH...
"IF THEY *DO* LIVE, THEY PROBABLY *WISH* THEY DIDN'T.
"SOUNDS LIKE YOU COME FROM A *FAMILY* OF FIGHTERS, AND YOU AIN'T AFRAID OF A FIGHT.
"*CONFIDENCE* IS ONE THING.
"BUT *TOO MUCH* CONFIDENCE IS JUST *STUPID*.
ROAWRRRRRRR
"'CAUSE I'M AFRAID YOU DON'T HAVE THE *SLIGHTEST* IDEA WHAT YOU'RE UP AGAINST."

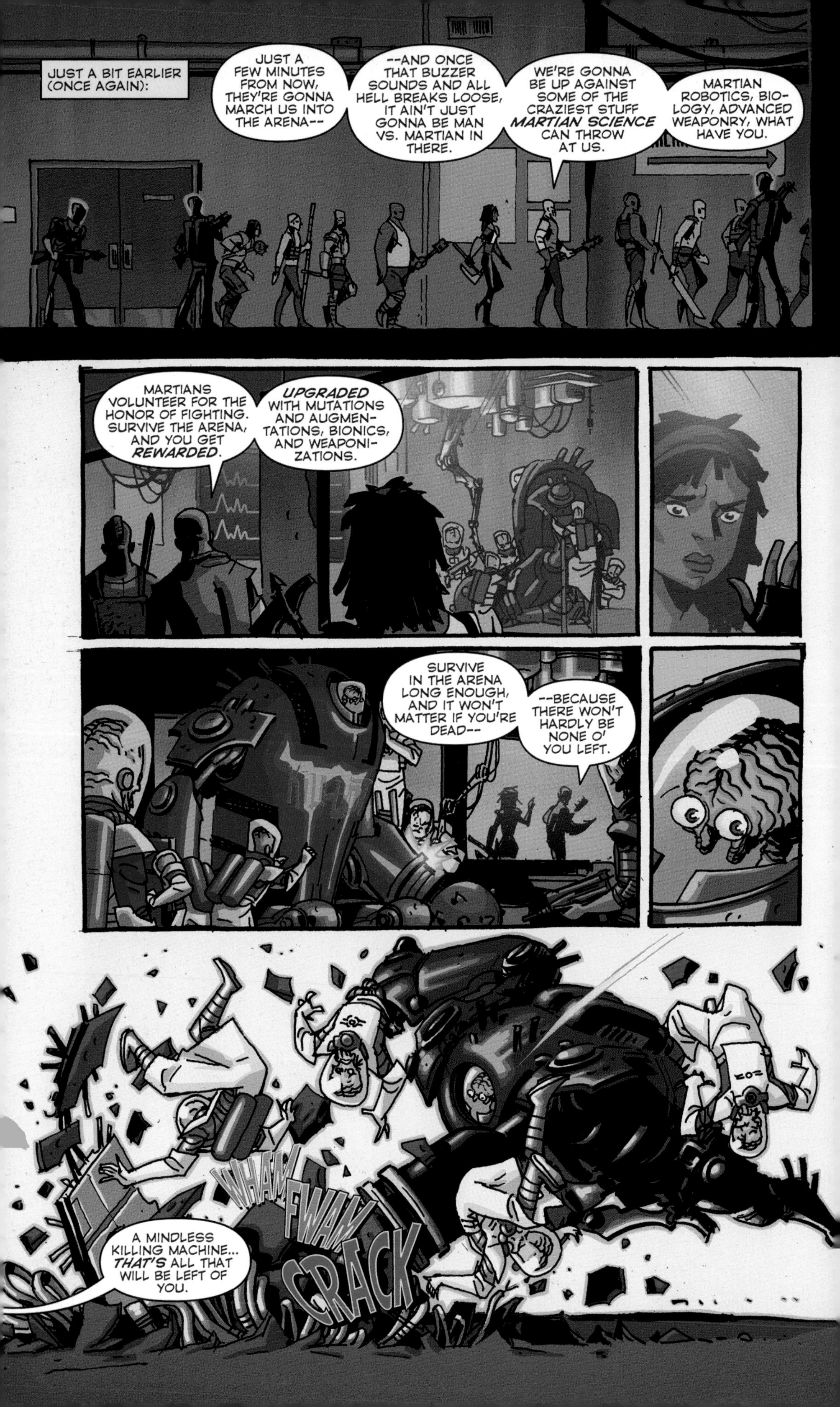

JUST A BIT EARLIER (ONCE AGAIN):
JUST A FEW MINUTES FROM NOW, THEY'RE GONNA MARCH US INTO THE ARENA--
--AND ONCE THAT BUZZER SOUNDS AND ALL HELL BREAKS LOOSE, IT AIN'T JUST GONNA BE MAN VS. MARTIAN IN THERE.
WE'RE GONNA BE UP AGAINST SOME OF THE CRAZIEST STUFF *MARTIAN SCIENCE* CAN THROW AT US.
MARTIAN ROBOTICS, BIOLOGY, ADVANCED WEAPONRY, WHAT HAVE YOU.
MARTIANS VOLUNTEER FOR THE HONOR OF FIGHTING. SURVIVE THE ARENA, AND YOU GET *REWARDED*.
UPGRADED WITH MUTATIONS AND AUGMENTATIONS, BIONICS, AND WEAPONIZATIONS.
SURVIVE IN THE ARENA LONG ENOUGH, AND IT WON'T MATTER IF YOU'RE DEAD--
--BECAUSE THERE WON'T HARDLY BE NONE O' YOU LEFT.
WHAM
FWAM
CRACK
A MINDLESS KILLING MACHINE... *THAT'S* ALL THAT WILL BE LEFT OF YOU.

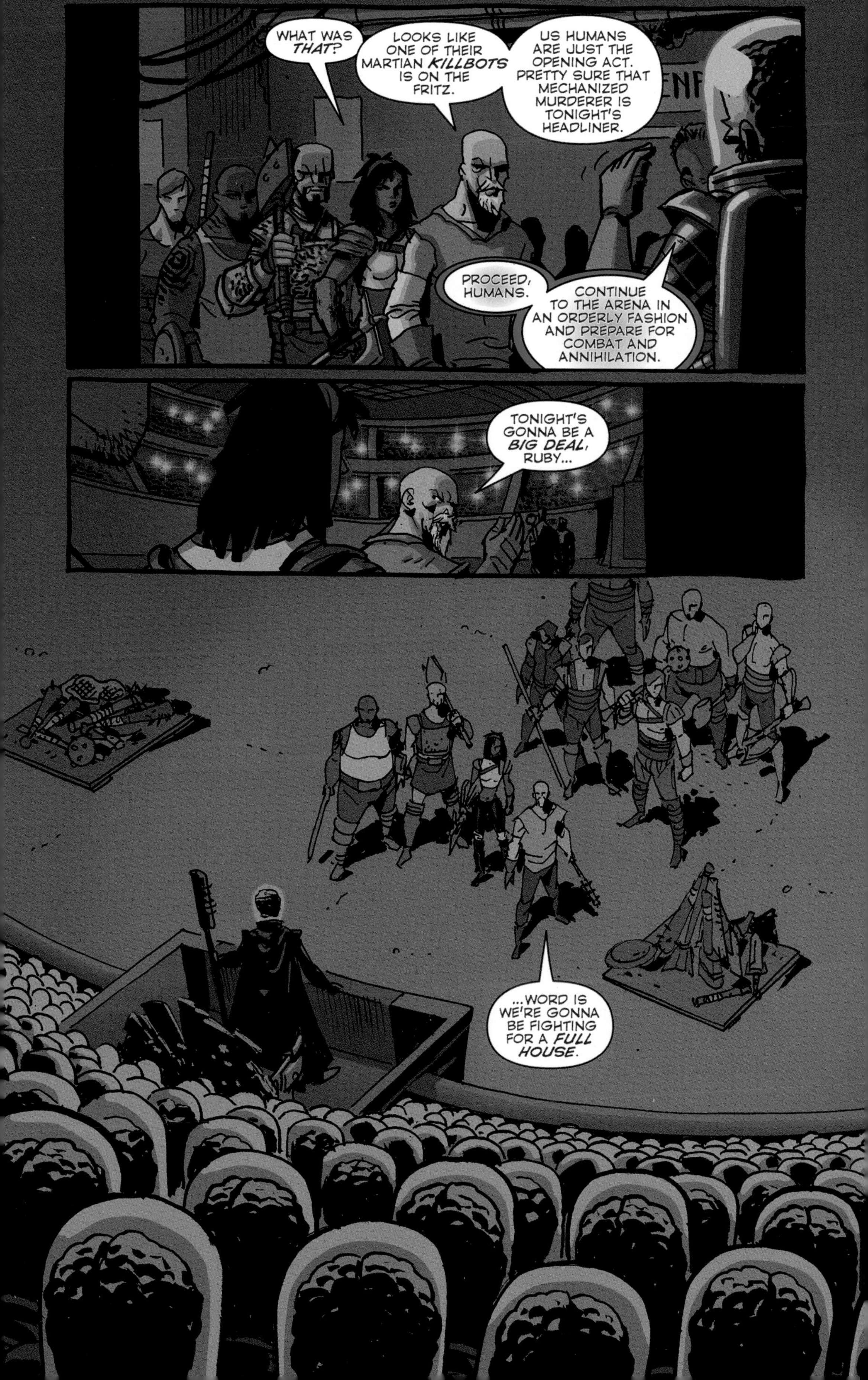
WHAT WAS THAT?
LOOKS LIKE ONE OF THEIR MARTIAN KILLBOTS IS ON THE FRITZ.
US HUMANS ARE JUST THE OPENING ACT. PRETTY SURE THAT MECHANIZED MURDERER IS TONIGHT'S HEADLINER.
PROCEED, HUMANS.
CONTINUE TO THE ARENA IN AN ORDERLY FASHION AND PREPARE FOR COMBAT AND ANNIHILATION.
TONIGHT'S GONNA BE A BIG DEAL, RUBY...
...WORD IS WE'RE GONNA BE FIGHTING FOR A FULL HOUSE.

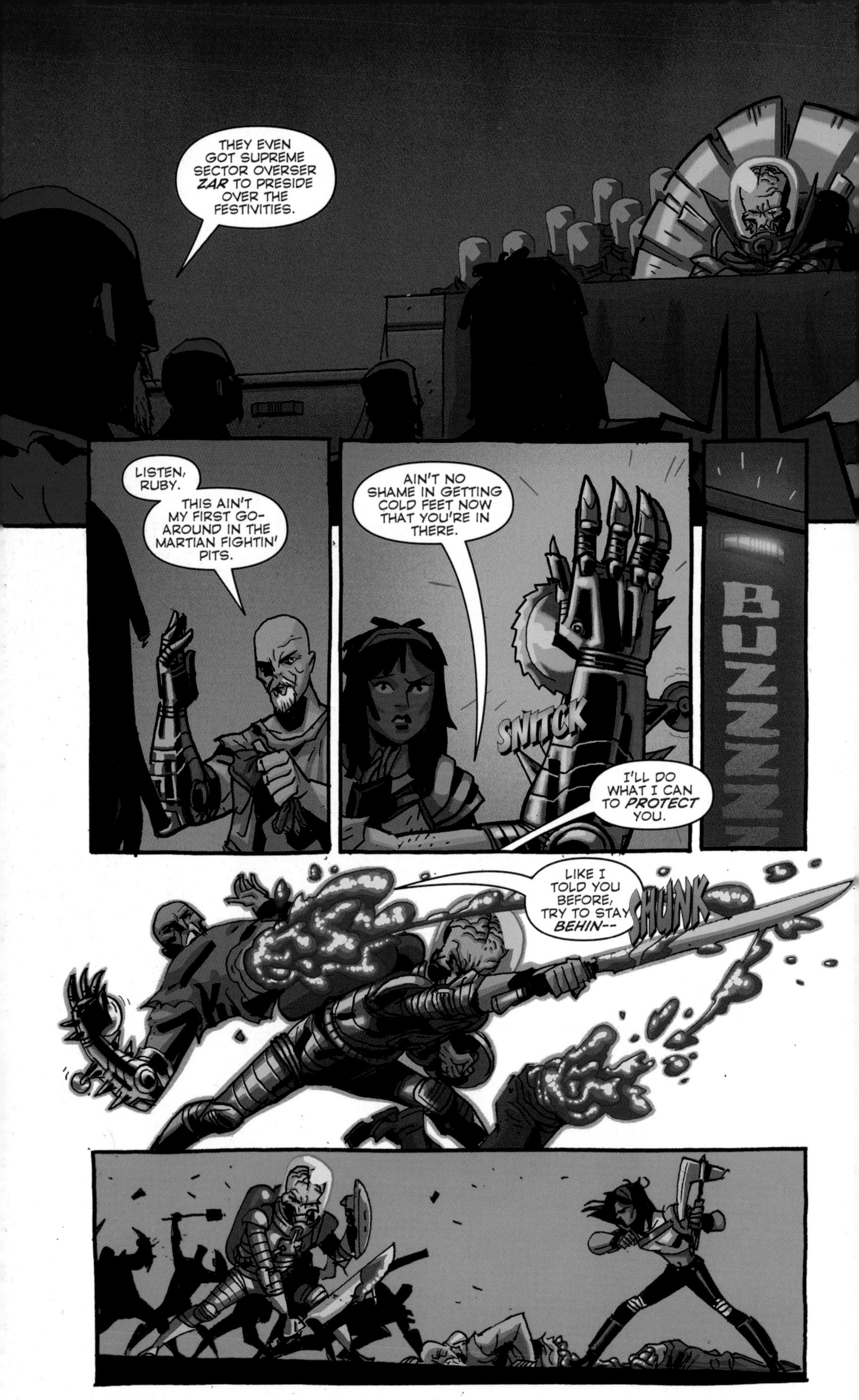
THEY EVEN GOT SUPREME SECTOR OVERSER *ZAR* TO PRESIDE OVER THE FESTIVITIES.
LISTEN, RUBY.
THIS AIN'T MY FIRST GO-AROUND IN THE MARTIAN FIGHTIN' PITS.
AIN'T NO SHAME IN GETTING COLD FEET NOW THAT YOU'RE IN THERE.
SNITCK
I'LL DO WHAT I CAN TO *PROTECT* YOU.
BUZZZZ
LIKE I TOLD YOU BEFORE, TRY TO STAY *BEHIN--*
SHUNK

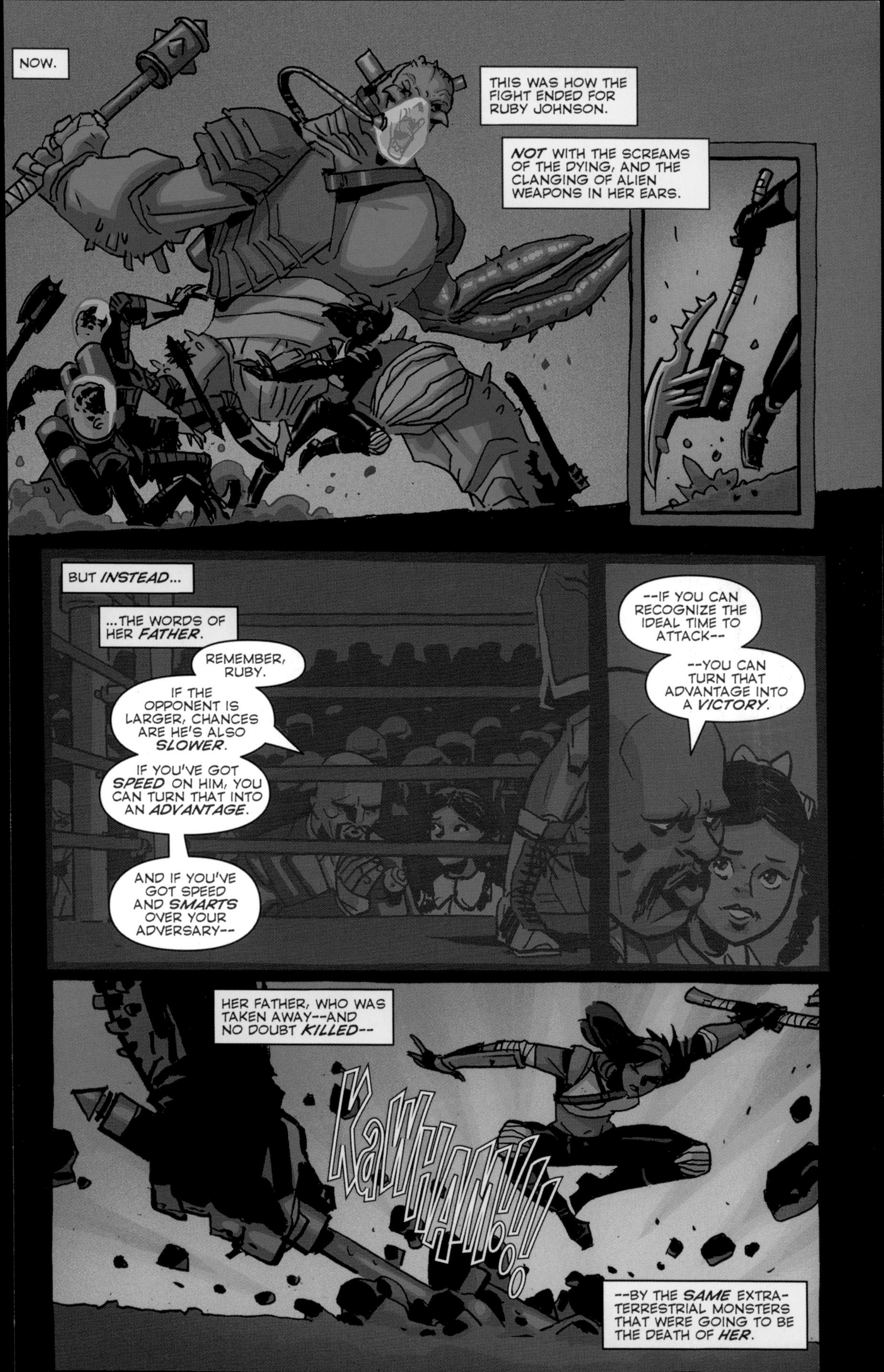
NOW.
THIS WAS HOW THE FIGHT ENDED FOR RUBY JOHNSON.
NOT WITH THE SCREAMS OF THE DYING, AND THE CLANGING OF ALIEN WEAPONS IN HER EARS.
BUT INSTEAD...
...THE WORDS OF HER FATHER.
REMEMBER, RUBY.
IF THE OPPONENT IS LARGER, CHANCES ARE HE'S ALSO SLOWER.
IF YOU'VE GOT SPEED ON HIM, YOU CAN TURN THAT INTO AN ADVANTAGE.
AND IF YOU'VE GOT SPEED AND SMARTS OVER YOUR ADVERSARY--
--IF YOU CAN RECOGNIZE THE IDEAL TIME TO ATTACK--
--YOU CAN TURN THAT ADVANTAGE INTO A VICTORY.
HER FATHER, WHO WAS TAKEN AWAY--AND NO DOUBT KILLED--
KaWHAMooo!!
--BY THE SAME EXTRA-TERRESTRIAL MONSTERS THAT WERE GOING TO BE THE DEATH OF HER.

HER FATHER, WHO INSISTED SHE TRAINED *EVERY* DAY.

UHH?

SHE WAS A *JOHNSON*, AFTER ALL, HE TOLD HER.

AND JOHNSONS WERE *FIGHTERS*.

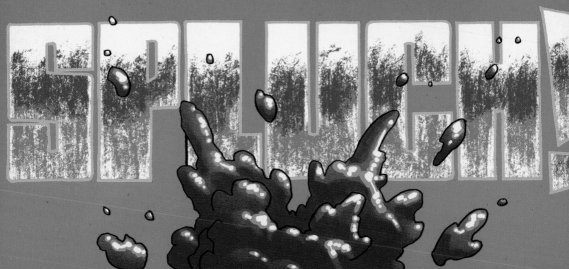

SPLUCH!

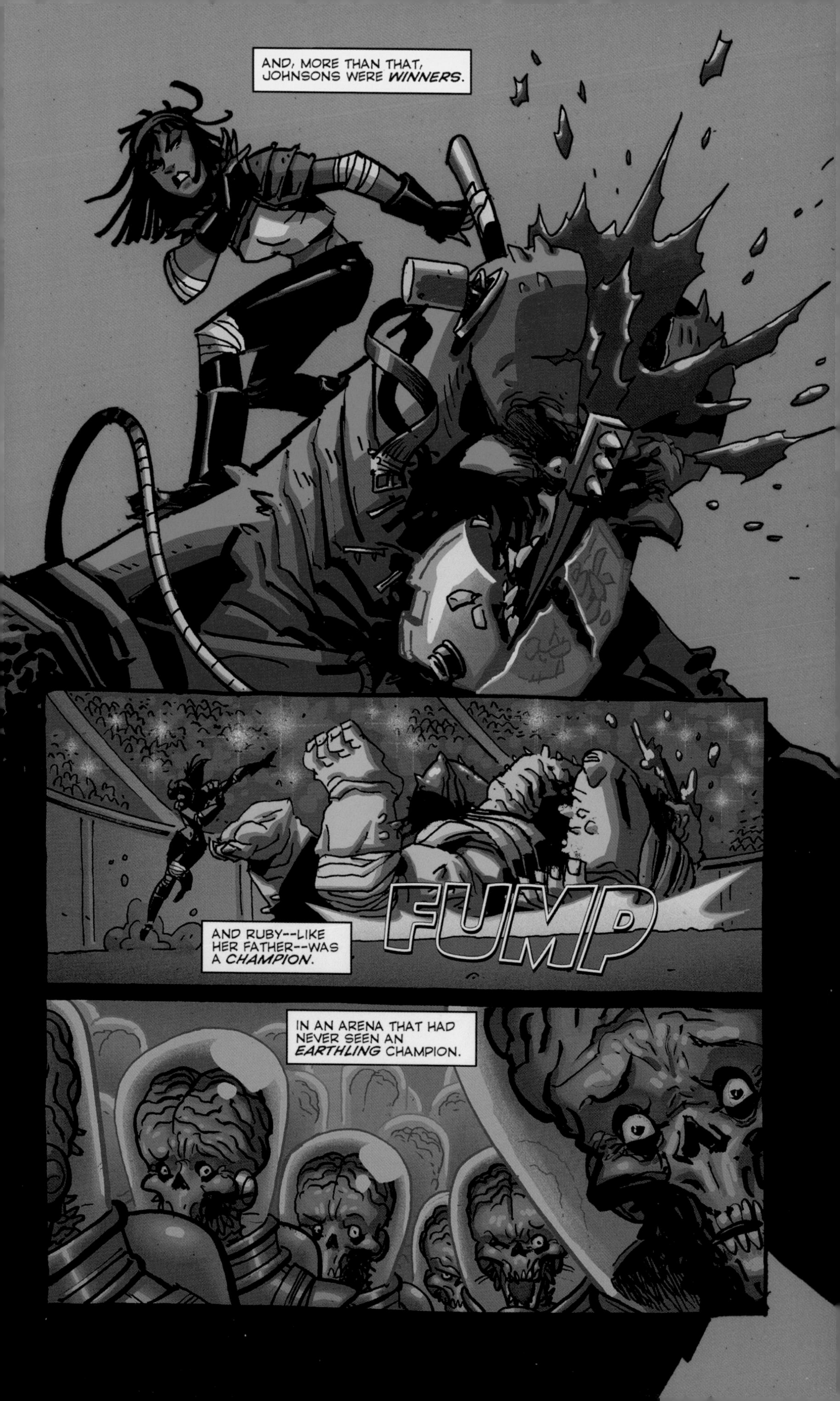
AND, MORE THAN THAT, JOHNSONS WERE *WINNERS*.
FUMP
AND RUBY--LIKE HER FATHER--WAS A *CHAMPION*.
IN AN ARENA THAT HAD NEVER SEEN AN *EARTHLING* CHAMPION.

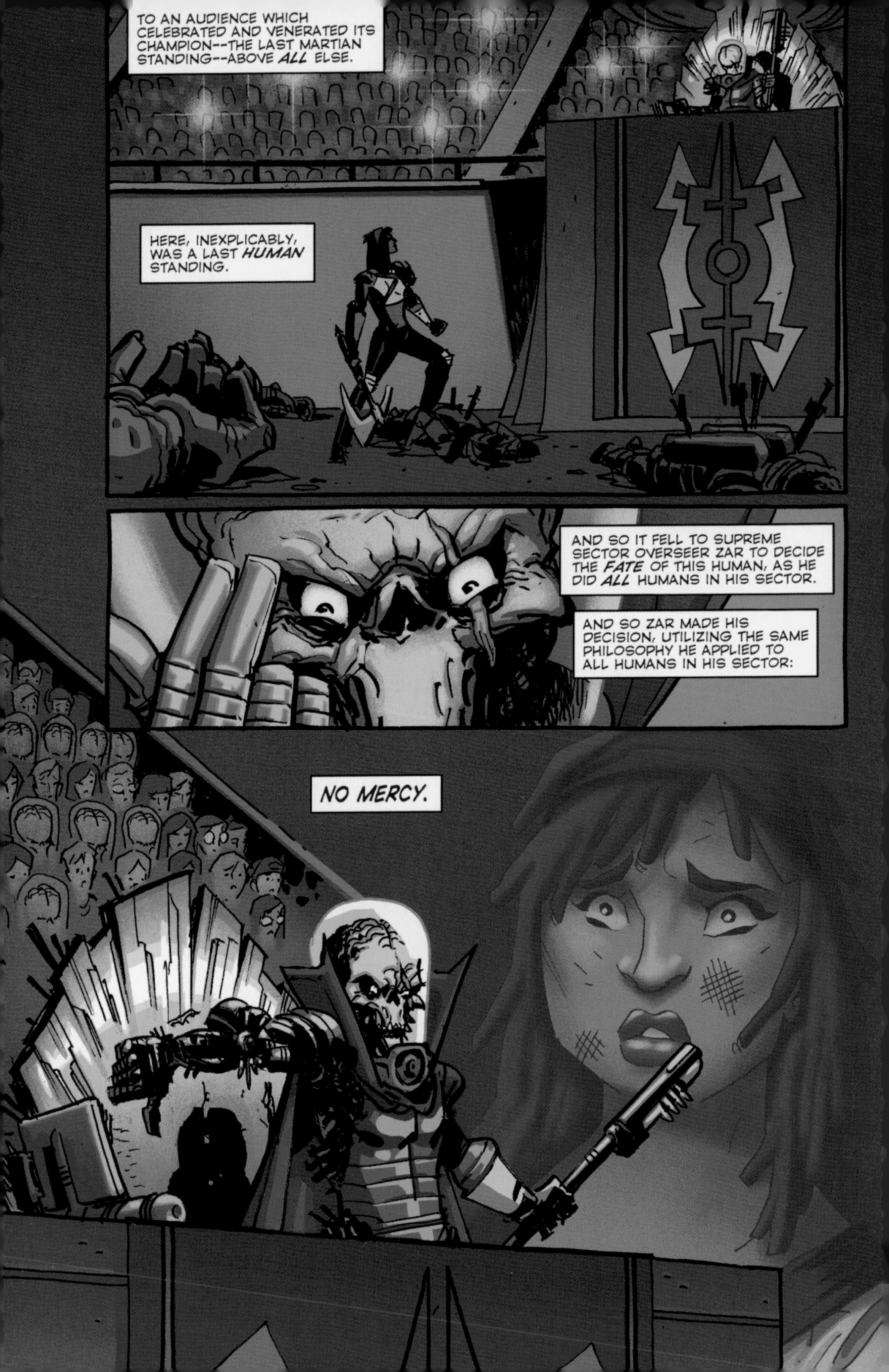

TO AN AUDIENCE WHICH CELEBRATED AND VENERATED ITS CHAMPION--THE LAST MARTIAN STANDING--ABOVE *ALL* ELSE.
HERE, INEXPLICABLY, WAS A LAST *HUMAN* STANDING.
AND SO IT FELL TO SUPREME SECTOR OVERSEER ZAR TO DECIDE THE *FATE* OF THIS HUMAN, AS HE DID *ALL* HUMANS IN HIS SECTOR.
AND SO ZAR MADE HIS DECISION, UTILIZING THE SAME PHILOSOPHY HE APPLIED TO ALL HUMANS IN HIS SECTOR:
NO MERCY.

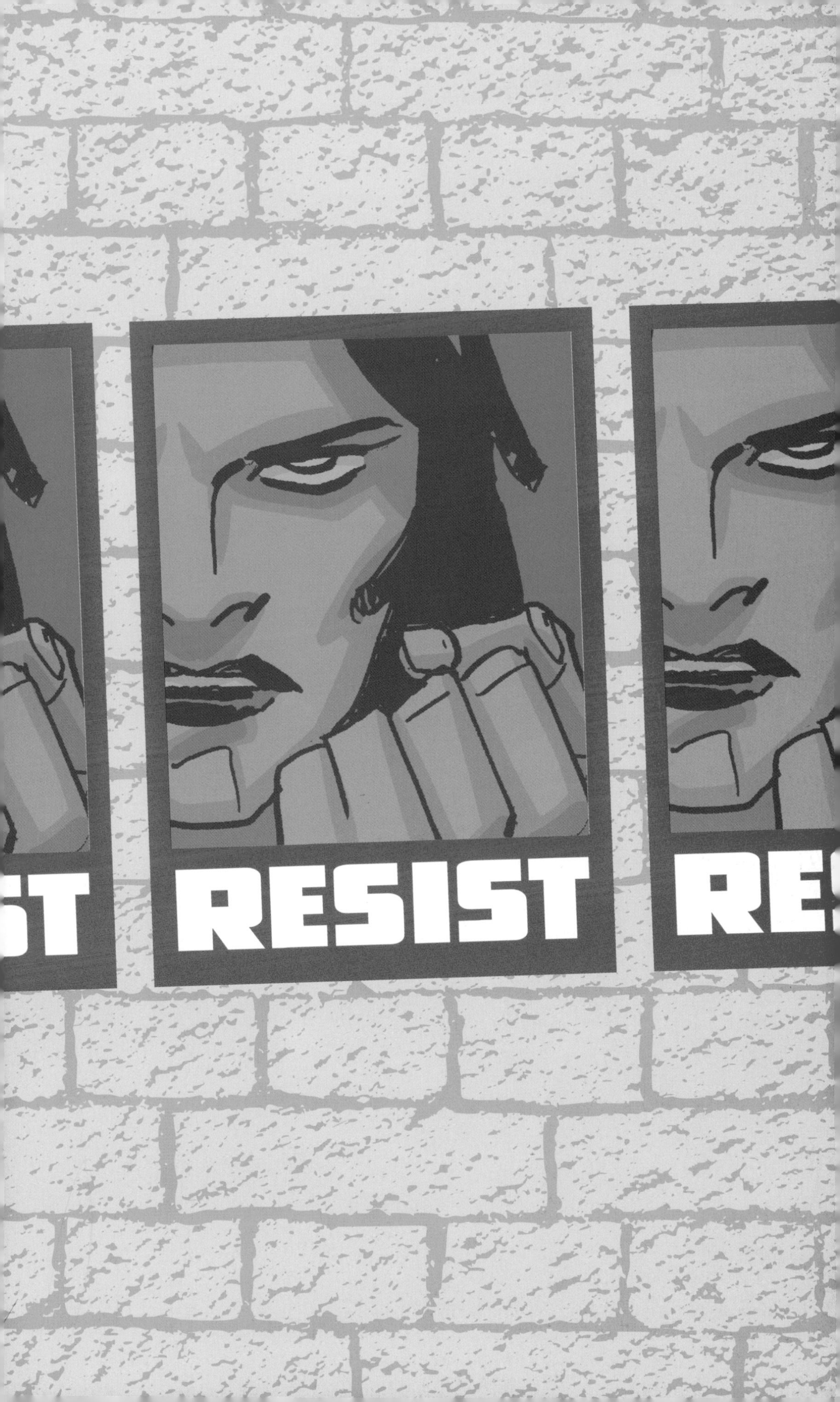

ST
RESIST
RE

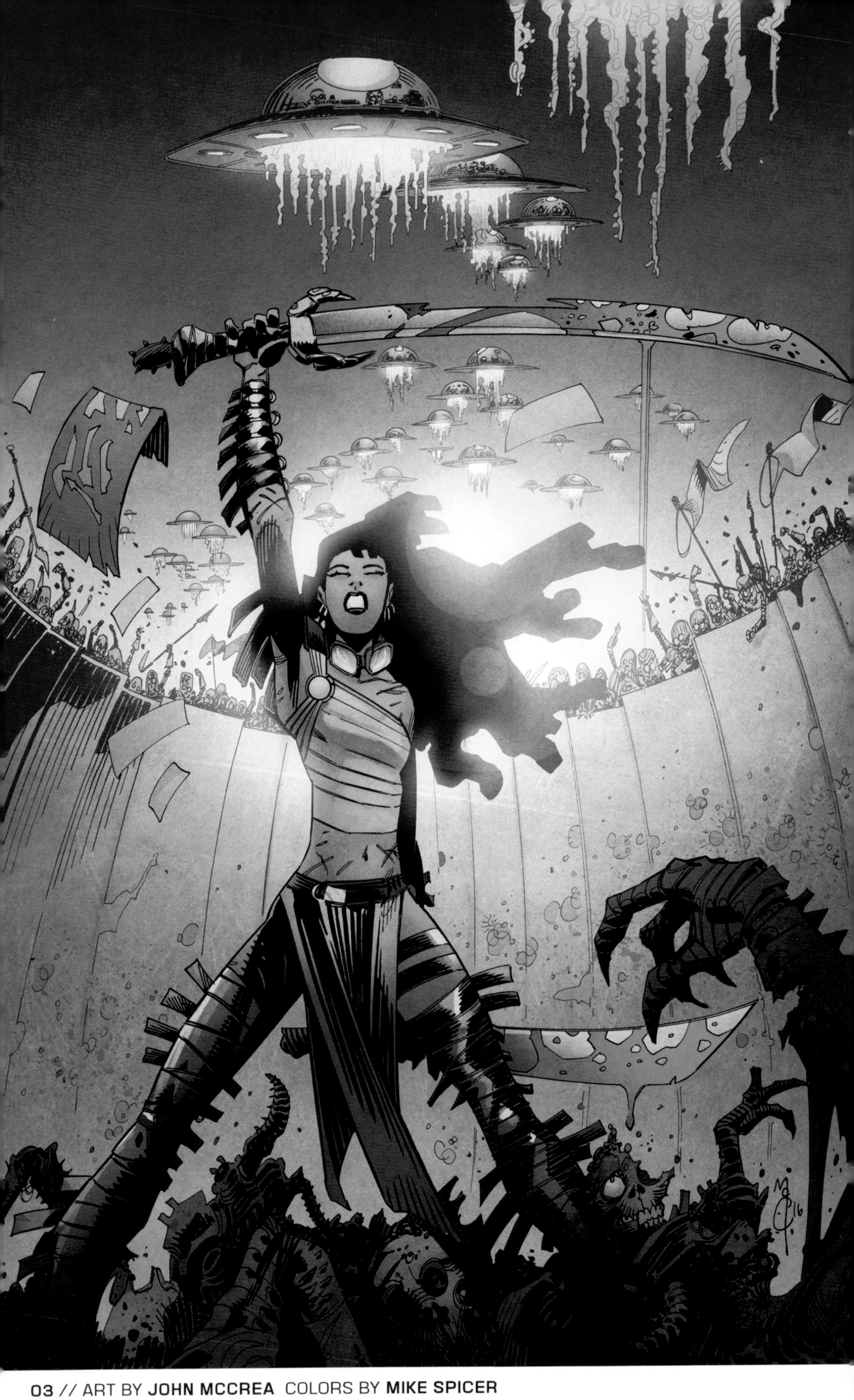

03 // ART BY **JOHN MCCREA** COLORS BY **MIKE SPICER**

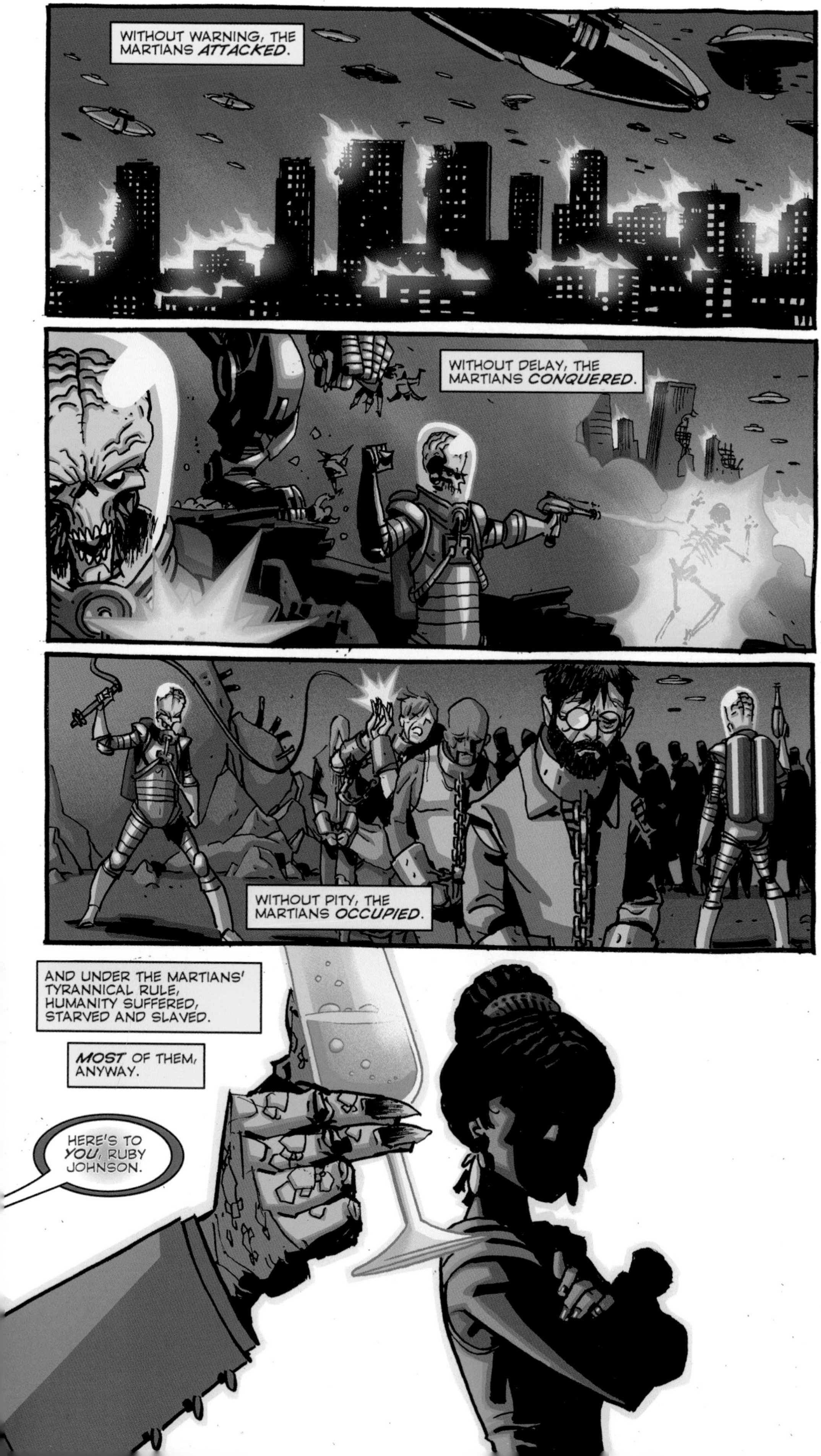

WITHOUT WARNING, THE MARTIANS ATTACKED.
WITHOUT DELAY, THE MARTIANS CONQUERED.
WITHOUT PITY, THE MARTIANS OCCUPIED.
AND UNDER THE MARTIANS' TYRANNICAL RULE, HUMANITY SUFFERED, STARVED AND SLAVED.
MOST OF THEM, ANYWAY.
HERE'S TO YOU, RUBY JOHNSON.

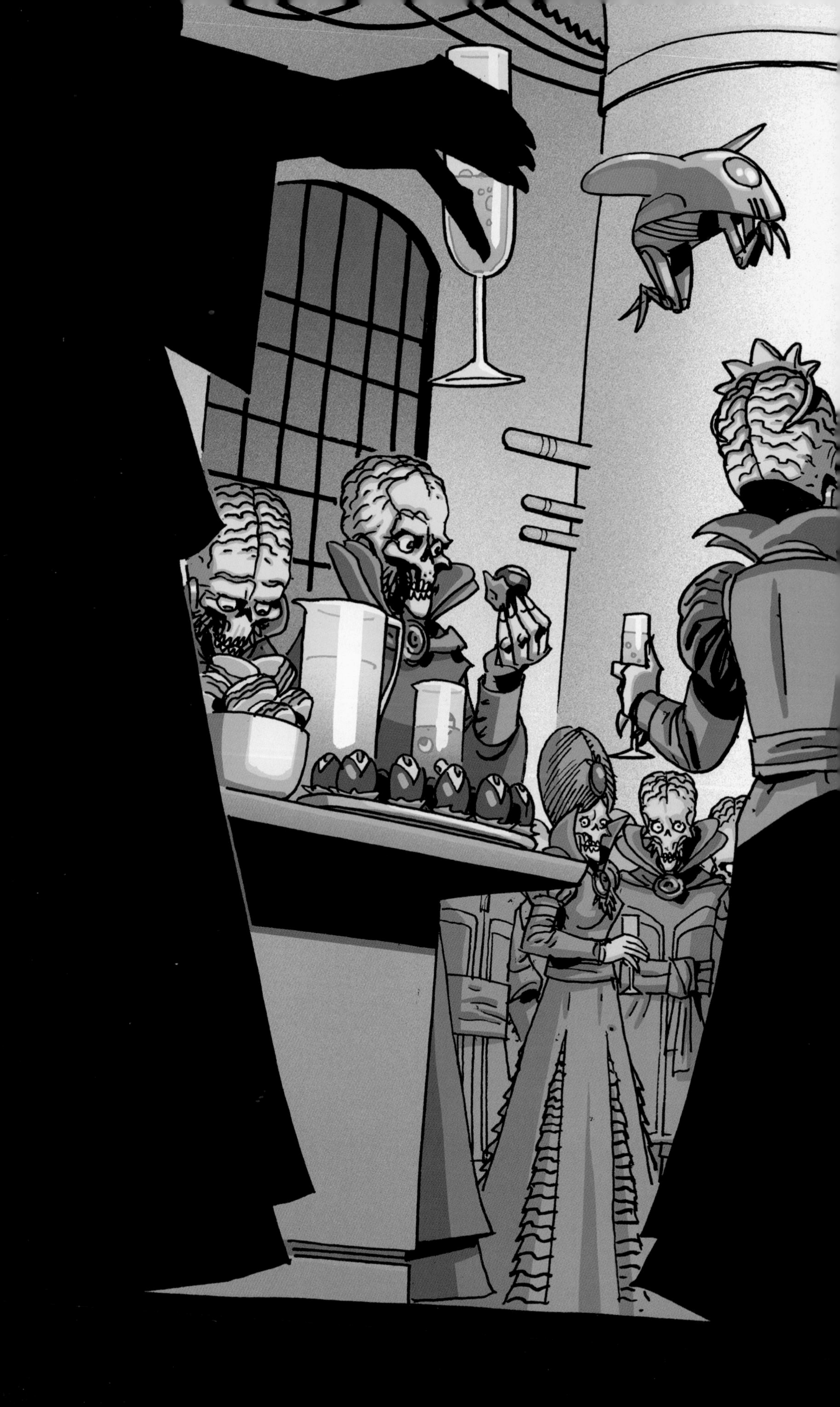

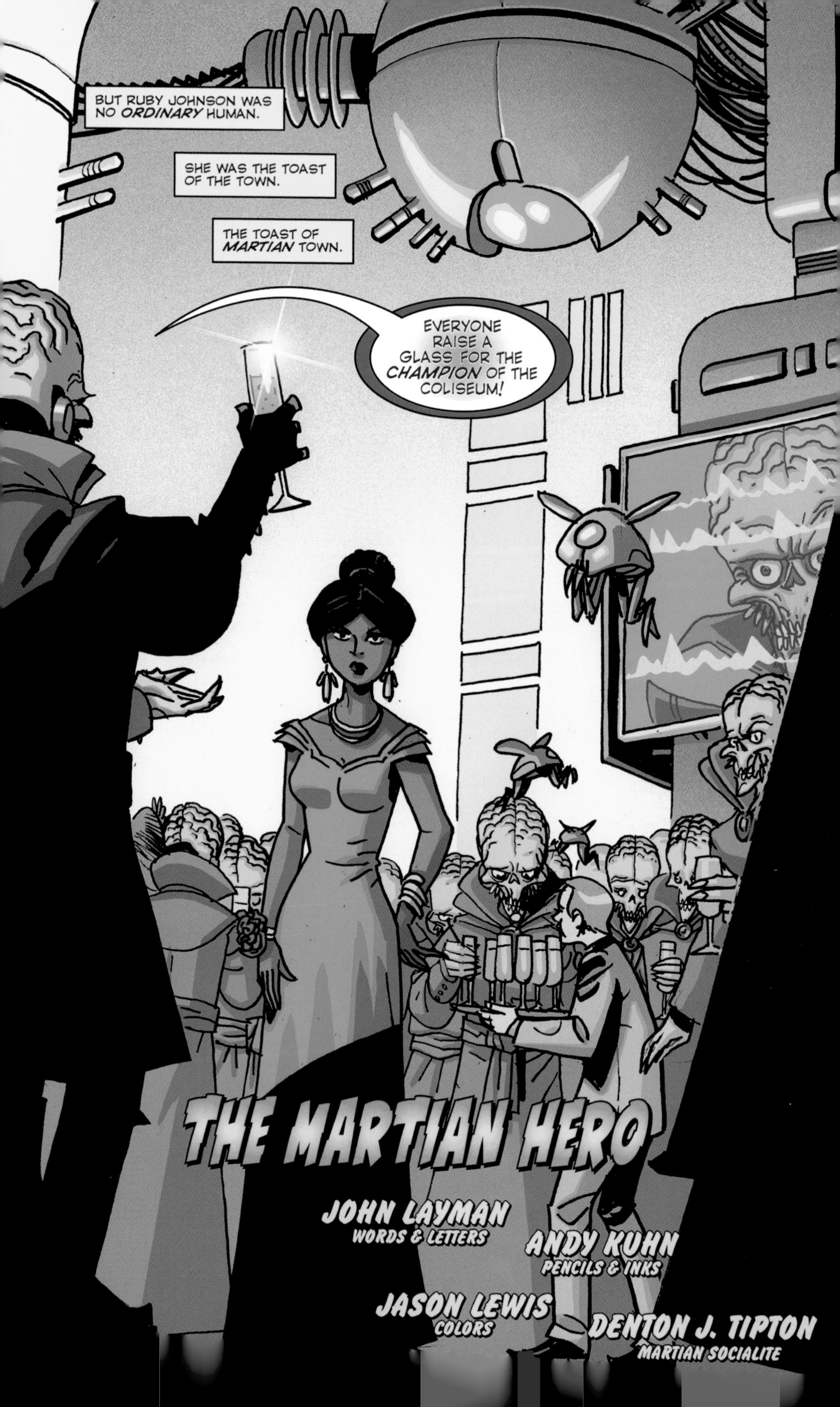
BUT RUBY JOHNSON WAS NO ORDINARY HUMAN.
SHE WAS THE TOAST OF THE TOWN.
THE TOAST OF MARTIAN TOWN.
EVERYONE RAISE A GLASS FOR THE CHAMPION OF THE COLISEUM!
THE MARTIAN HERO
JOHN LAYMAN WORDS & LETTERS
ANDY KUHN PENCILS & INKS
JASON LEWIS COLORS
DENTON J. TIPTON MARTIAN SOCIALITE

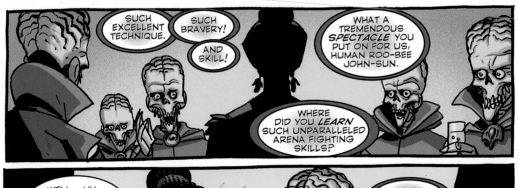

SUCH EXCELLENT TECHNIQUE.

SUCH BRAVERY!

AND SKILL!

WHAT A TREMENDOUS *SPECTACLE* YOU PUT ON FOR US, HUMAN ROO-BEE JOHN-SUN.

WHERE DID YOU *LEARN* SUCH UNPARALLELED ARENA FIGHTING SKILLS?

WELL... UH... MY FATHER... HE... HE USED TO BE A *BOXER*... AND HE TAUG--

NEVER MIND THAT.

WOULD YOU CARE FOR SOME *XYPZLURP*? A FINE VINTAGE--

--SECRETED BY SABAUES BEETLES THAT NEST UNDER THE MARTIAN SAND DUNES AT COPRATES.

PERHAPS SOME FOOD, THEN?

YOU'LL NEED YOUR STRENGTH FOR THIS WEEKEND'S BIG FIGHT.

I... I...

OH, I SEE.

IT'S *HUMAN* FOOD YOU DESIRE.

YOU! SLAVE! FETCH SOME *HUMAN* FOOD FOR OUR FRIEND.

FWAP

"FRIEND"?

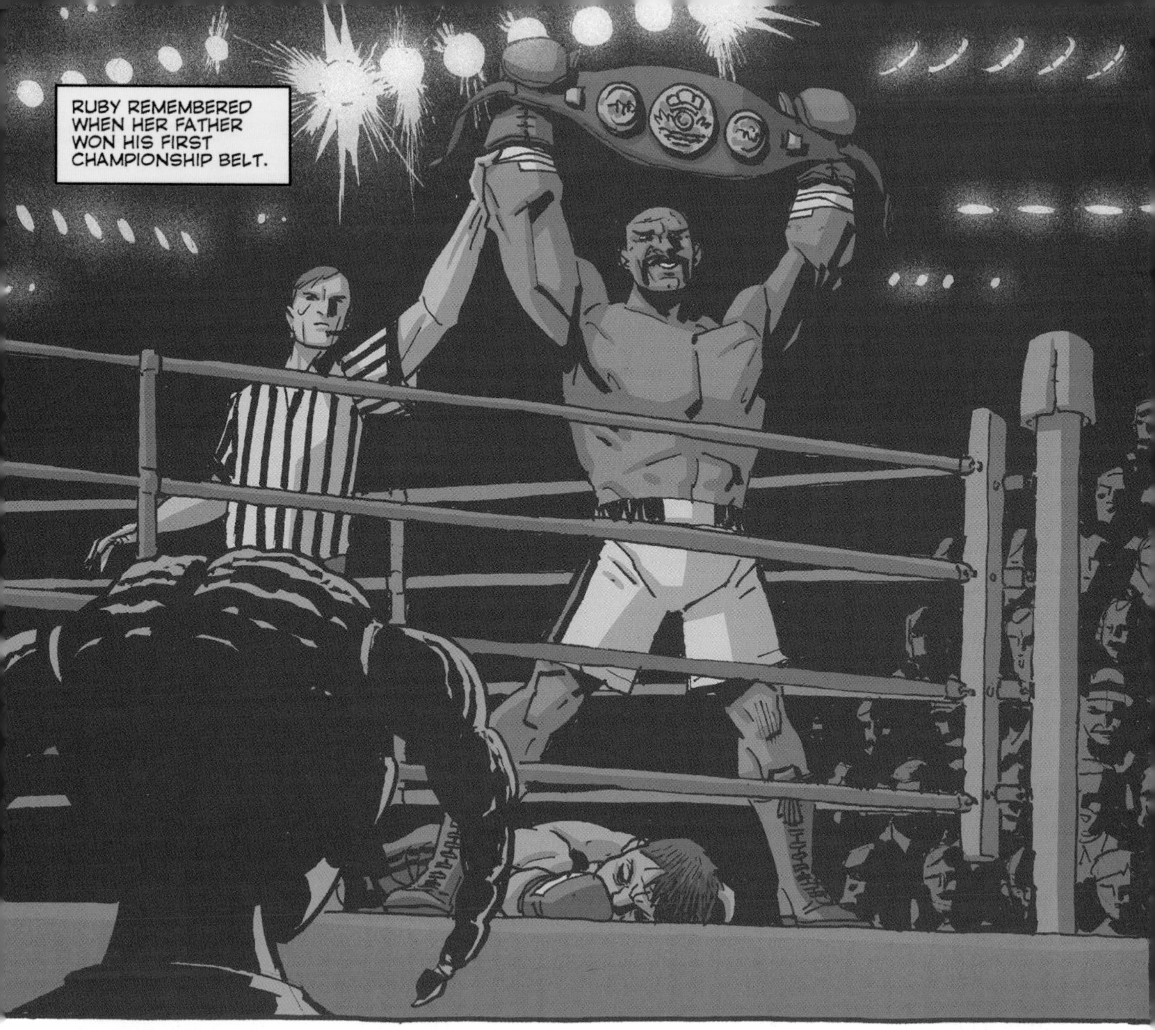
RUBY REMEMBERED WHEN HER FATHER WON HIS FIRST CHAMPIONSHIP BELT.

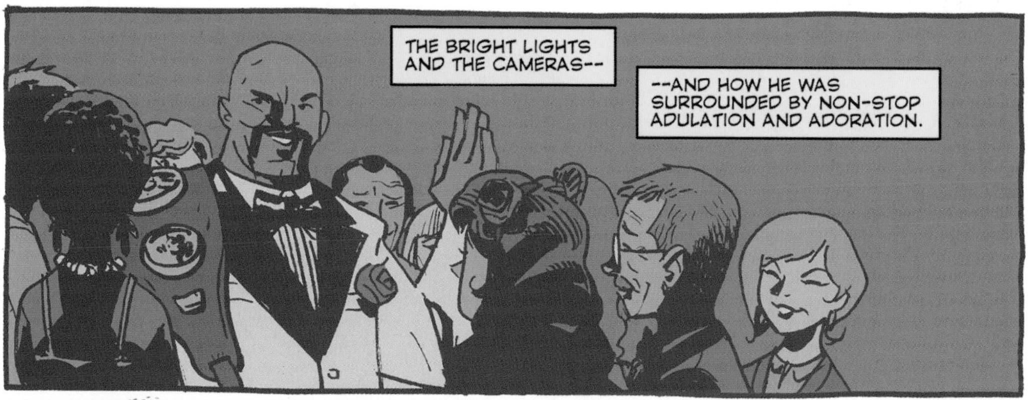
THE BRIGHT LIGHTS AND THE CAMERAS--
--AND HOW HE WAS SURROUNDED BY NON-STOP ADULATION AND ADORATION.

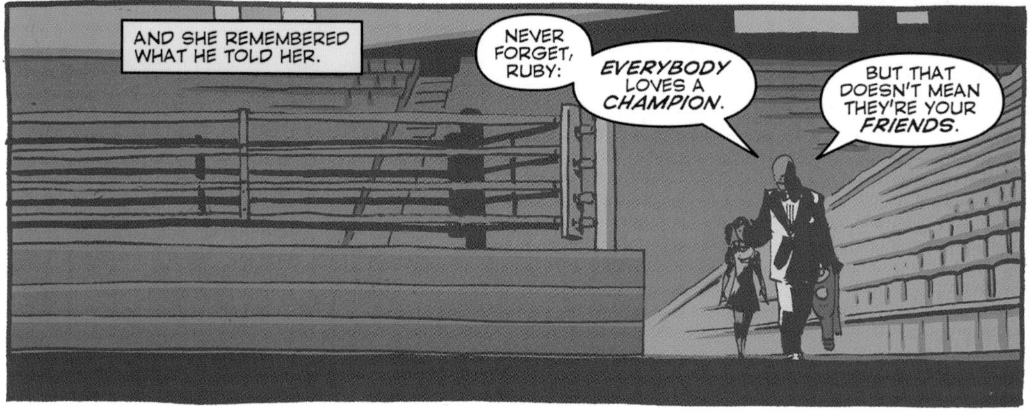
AND SHE REMEMBERED WHAT HE TOLD HER.
NEVER FORGET, RUBY: *EVERYBODY* LOVES A *CHAMPION*.
BUT THAT DOESN'T MEAN THEY'RE YOUR *FRIENDS*.

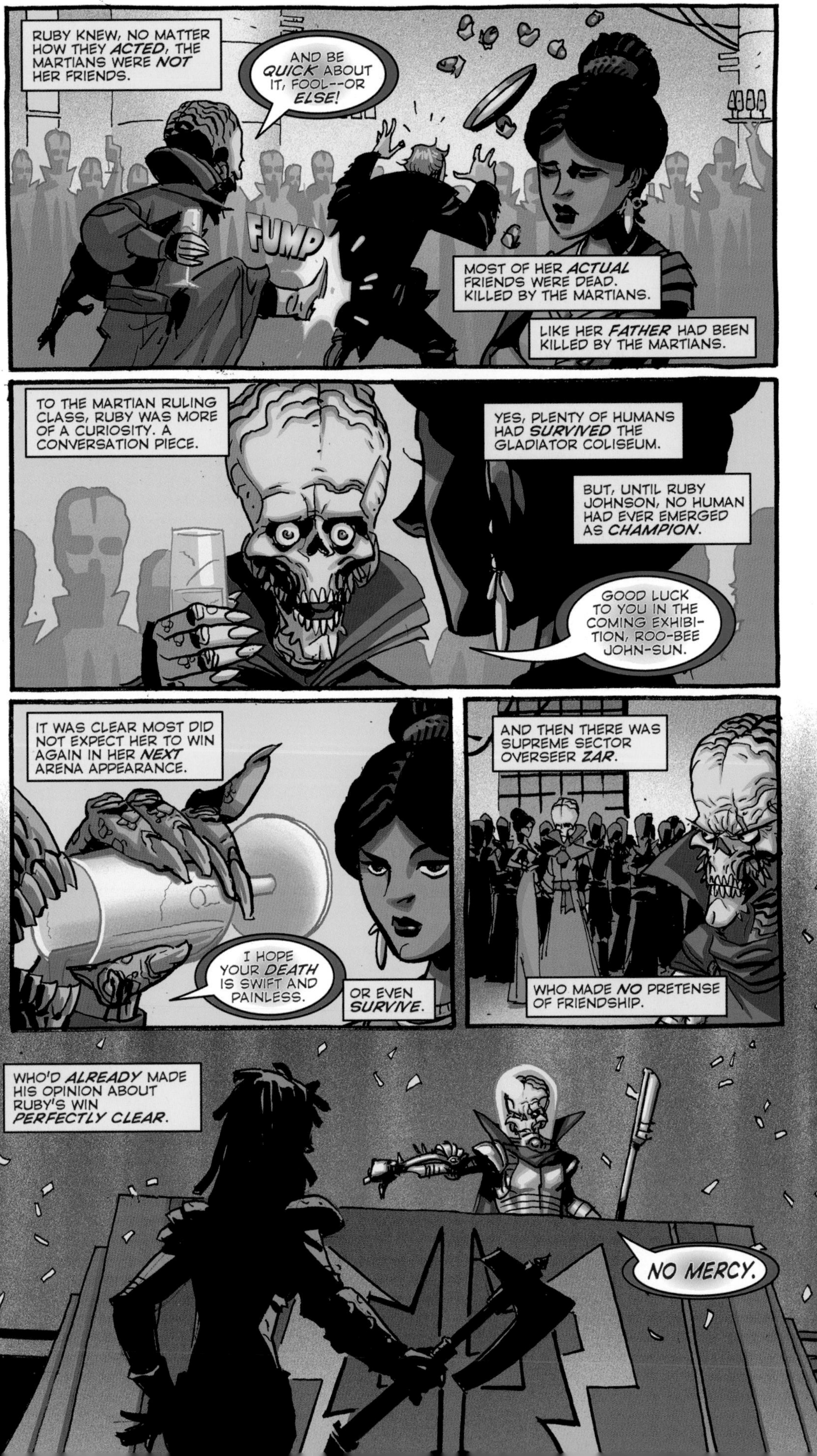
RUBY KNEW, NO MATTER HOW THEY ACTED, THE MARTIANS WERE NOT HER FRIENDS.
AND BE QUICK ABOUT IT, FOOL--OR ELSE!
FUMP
MOST OF HER ACTUAL FRIENDS WERE DEAD. KILLED BY THE MARTIANS.
LIKE HER FATHER HAD BEEN KILLED BY THE MARTIANS.
TO THE MARTIAN RULING CLASS, RUBY WAS MORE OF A CURIOSITY. A CONVERSATION PIECE.
YES, PLENTY OF HUMANS HAD SURVIVED THE GLADIATOR COLISEUM.
BUT, UNTIL RUBY JOHNSON, NO HUMAN HAD EVER EMERGED AS CHAMPION.
GOOD LUCK TO YOU IN THE COMING EXHIBITION, ROO-BEE JOHN-SUN.
IT WAS CLEAR MOST DID NOT EXPECT HER TO WIN AGAIN IN HER NEXT ARENA APPEARANCE.
I HOPE YOUR DEATH IS SWIFT AND PAINLESS.
OR EVEN SURVIVE.
AND THEN THERE WAS SUPREME SECTOR OVERSEER ZAR.
WHO MADE NO PRETENSE OF FRIENDSHIP.
WHO'D ALREADY MADE HIS OPINION ABOUT RUBY'S WIN PERFECTLY CLEAR.
NO MERCY.

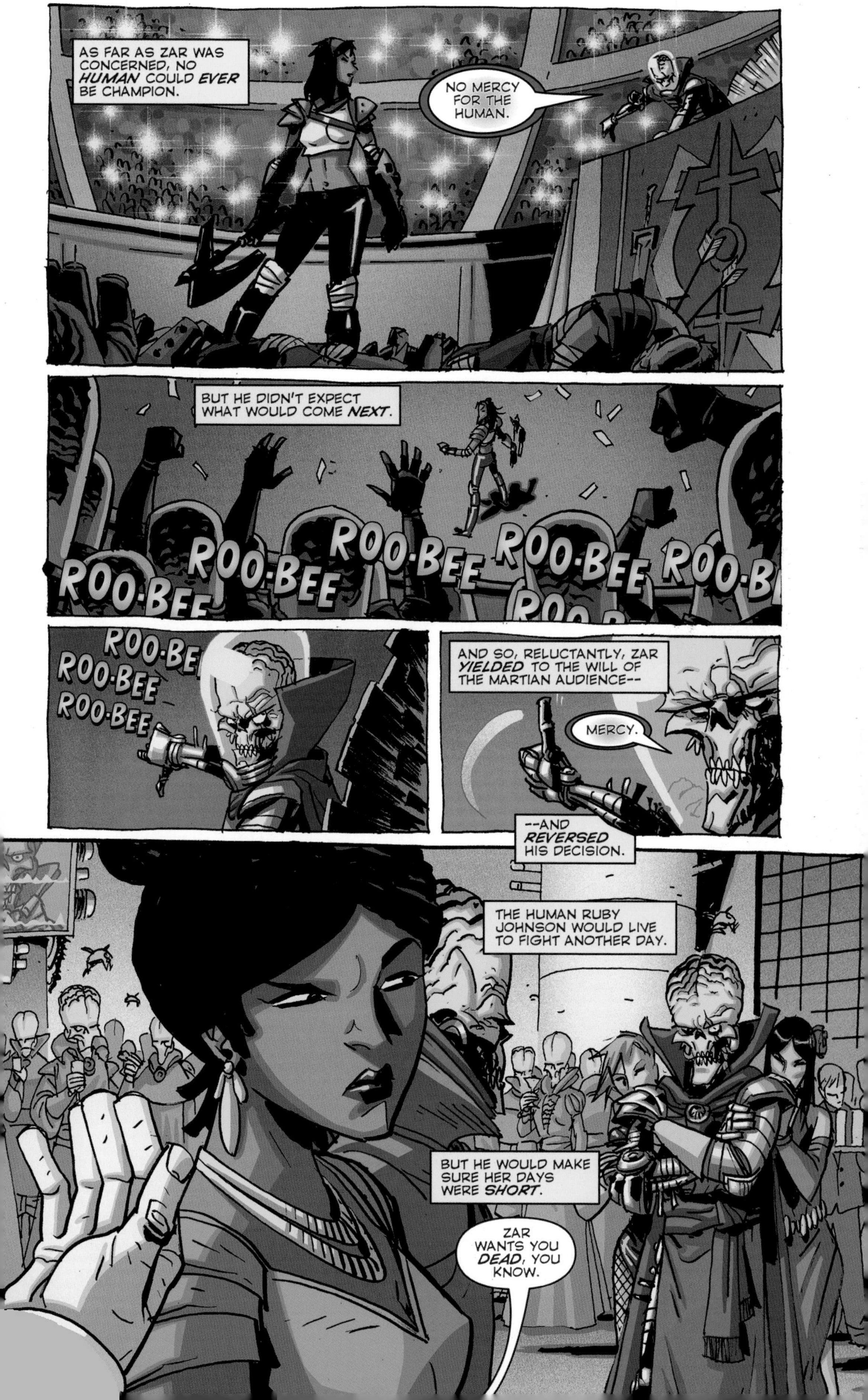
AS FAR AS ZAR WAS CONCERNED, NO HUMAN COULD EVER BE CHAMPION.
NO MERCY FOR THE HUMAN.
BUT HE DIDN'T EXPECT WHAT WOULD COME NEXT.
ROO-BEE ROO-BEE ROO-BEE ROO-BEE
ROO-BEE ROO-BEE ROO-BEE
AND SO, RELUCTANTLY, ZAR YIELDED TO THE WILL OF THE MARTIAN AUDIENCE--
MERCY.
--AND REVERSED HIS DECISION.
THE HUMAN RUBY JOHNSON WOULD LIVE TO FIGHT ANOTHER DAY.
BUT HE WOULD MAKE SURE HER DAYS WERE SHORT.
ZAR WANTS YOU DEAD, YOU KNOW.

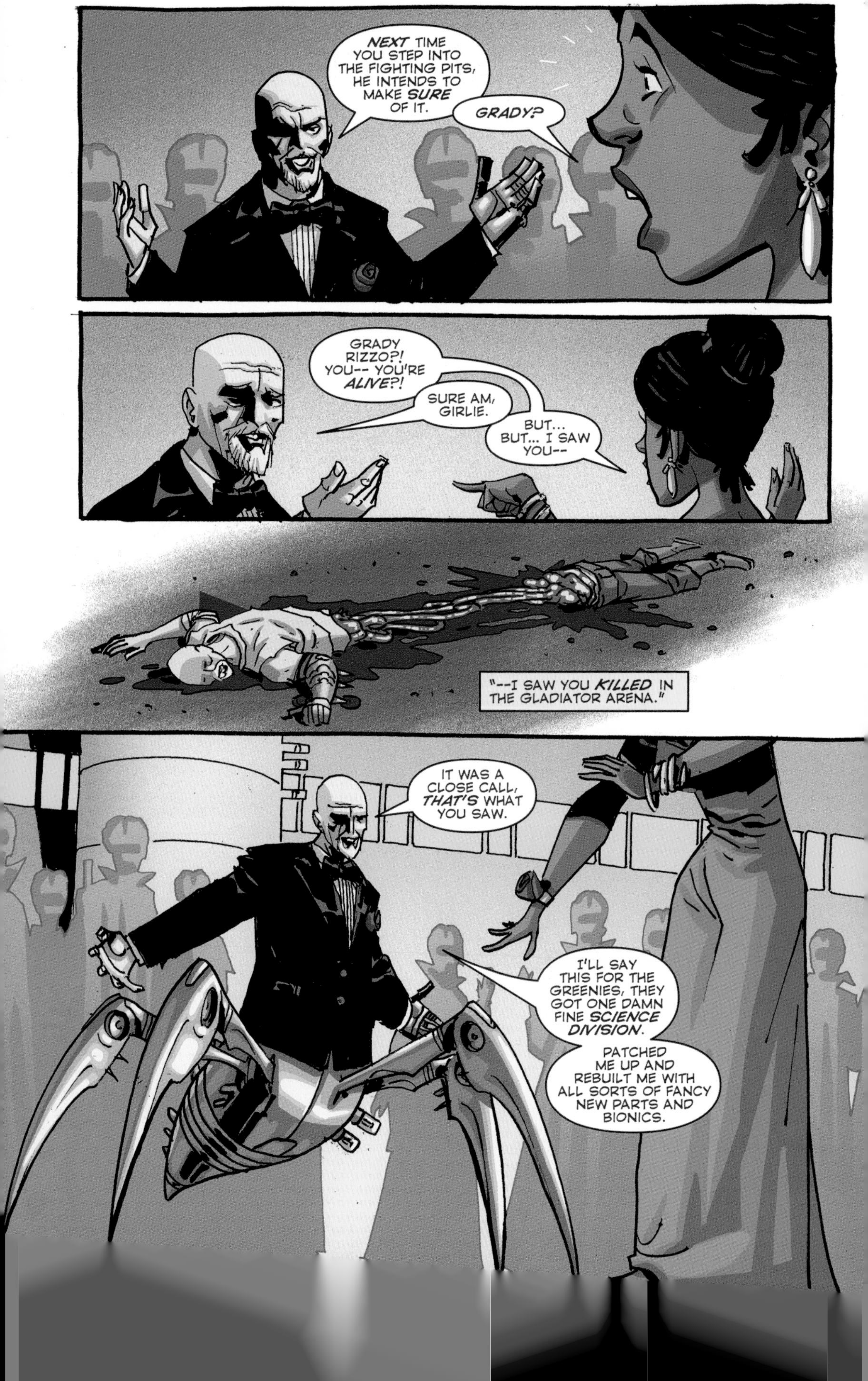

NEXT TIME YOU STEP INTO THE FIGHTING PITS, HE INTENDS TO MAKE SURE OF IT.
GRADY?
GRADY RIZZO?! YOU-- YOU'RE ALIVE?!
SURE AM, GIRLIE.
BUT... BUT... I SAW YOU--
"--I SAW YOU KILLED IN THE GLADIATOR ARENA."
IT WAS A CLOSE CALL, THAT'S WHAT YOU SAW.
I'LL SAY THIS FOR THE GREENIES, THEY GOT ONE DAMN FINE SCIENCE DIVISION.
PATCHED ME UP AND REBUILT ME WITH ALL SORTS OF FANCY NEW PARTS AND BIONICS.

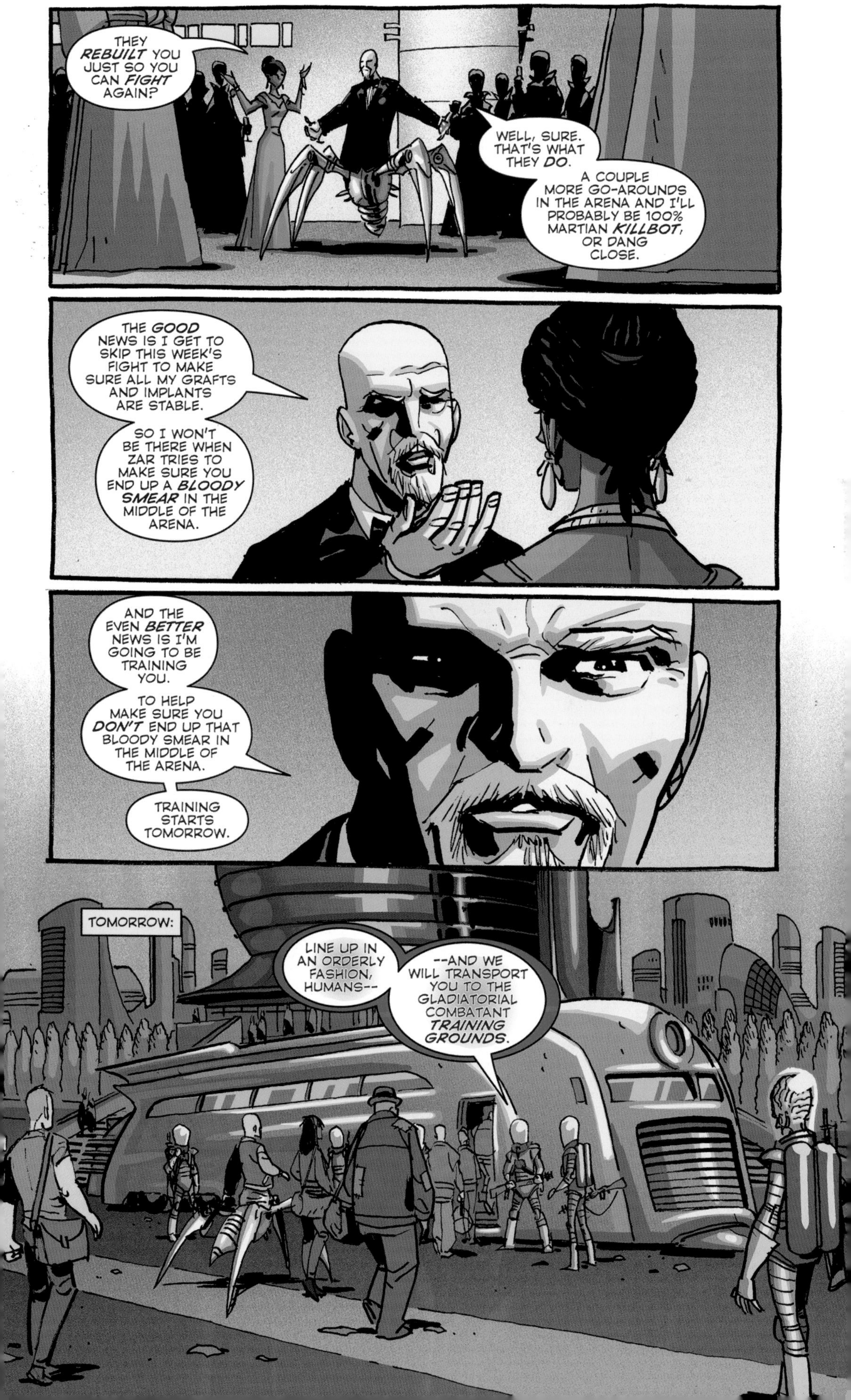
THEY *REBUILT* YOU JUST SO YOU CAN *FIGHT* AGAIN?
WELL, SURE. THAT'S WHAT THEY *DO*.
A COUPLE MORE GO-AROUNDS IN THE ARENA AND I'LL PROBABLY BE 100% MARTIAN *KILLBOT*, OR DANG CLOSE.
THE *GOOD* NEWS IS I GET TO SKIP THIS WEEK'S FIGHT TO MAKE SURE ALL MY GRAFTS AND IMPLANTS ARE STABLE.
SO I WON'T BE THERE WHEN ZAR TRIES TO MAKE SURE YOU END UP A *BLOODY SMEAR* IN THE MIDDLE OF THE ARENA.
AND THE EVEN *BETTER* NEWS IS I'M GOING TO BE TRAINING YOU.
TO HELP MAKE SURE YOU *DON'T* END UP THAT BLOODY SMEAR IN THE MIDDLE OF THE ARENA.
TRAINING STARTS TOMORROW.
TOMORROW:
LINE UP IN AN ORDERLY FASHION, HUMANS--
--AND WE WILL TRANSPORT YOU TO THE GLADIATORIAL COMBATANT *TRAINING GROUNDS*.

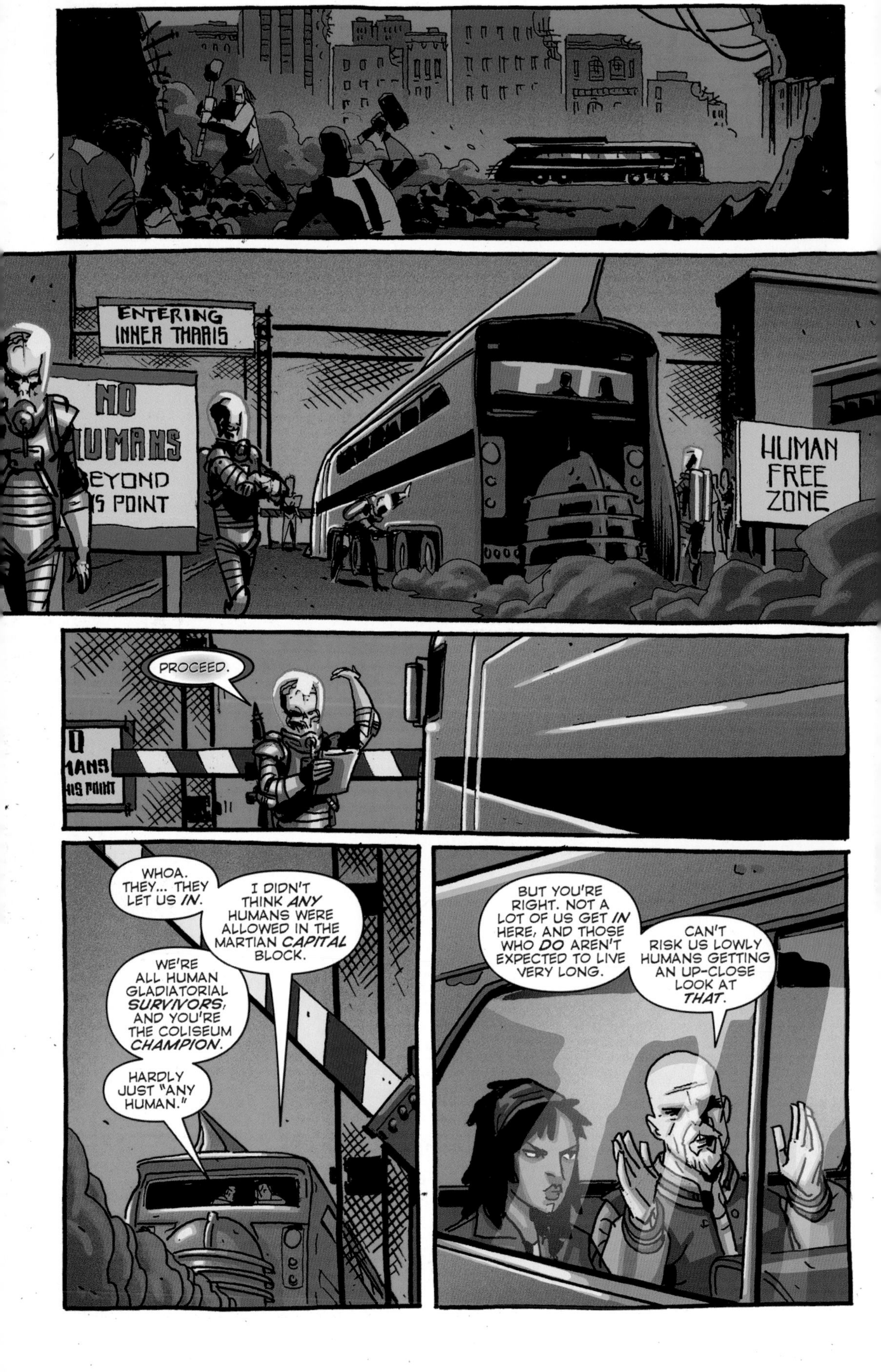
ENTERING
INNER THARIS
NO HUMANS BEYOND THIS POINT
HUMAN FREE ZONE
PROCEED.
WHOA. THEY... THEY LET US IN.
I DIDN'T THINK ANY HUMANS WERE ALLOWED IN THE MARTIAN CAPITAL BLOCK.
WE'RE ALL HUMAN GLADIATORIAL SURVIVORS, AND YOU'RE THE COLISEUM CHAMPION.
HARDLY JUST "ANY HUMAN."
BUT YOU'RE RIGHT. NOT A LOT OF US GET IN HERE, AND THOSE WHO DO AREN'T EXPECTED TO LIVE VERY LONG.
CAN'T RISK US LOWLY HUMANS GETTING AN UP-CLOSE LOOK AT THAT.

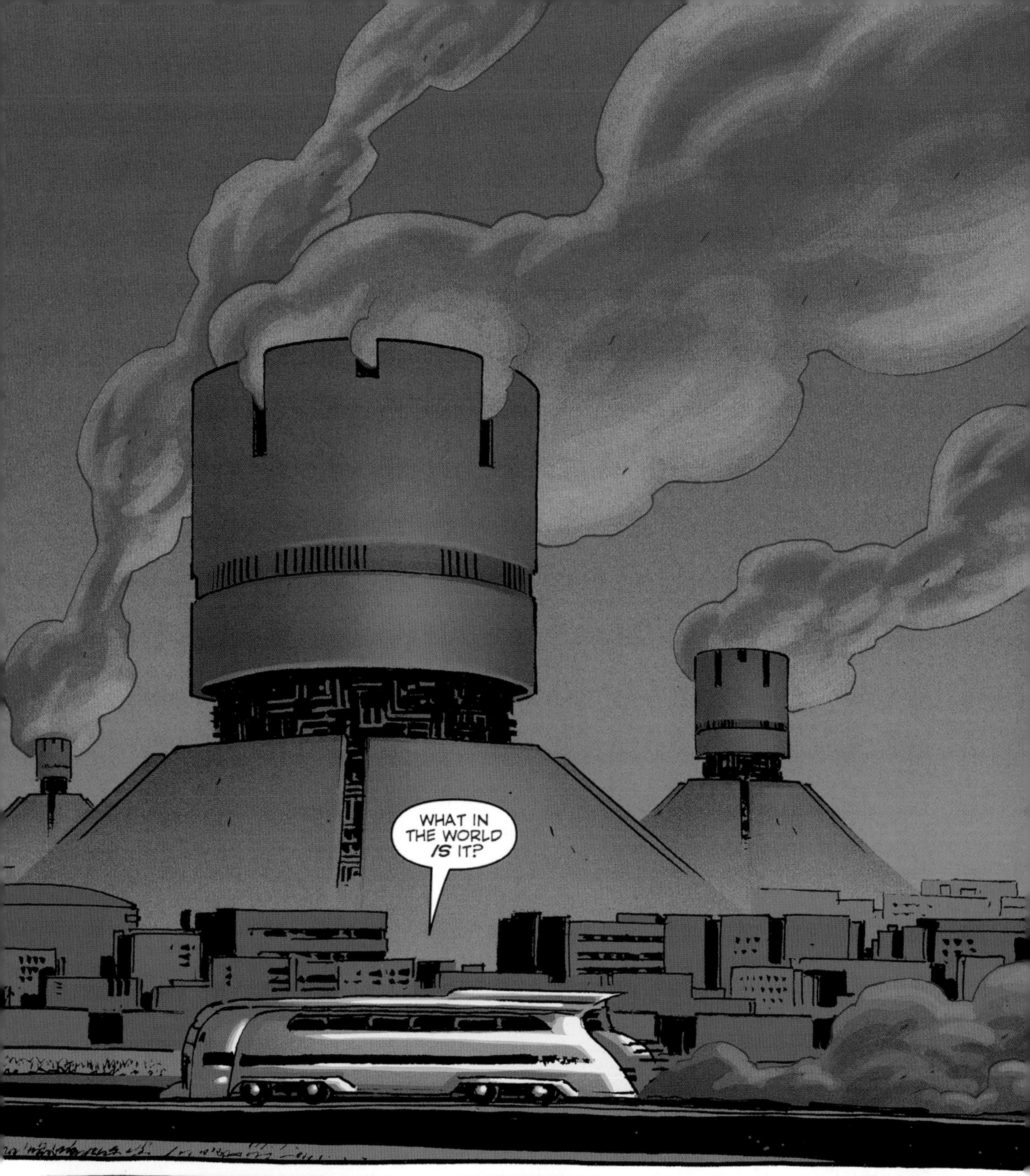
WHAT IN THE WORLD *IS* IT?

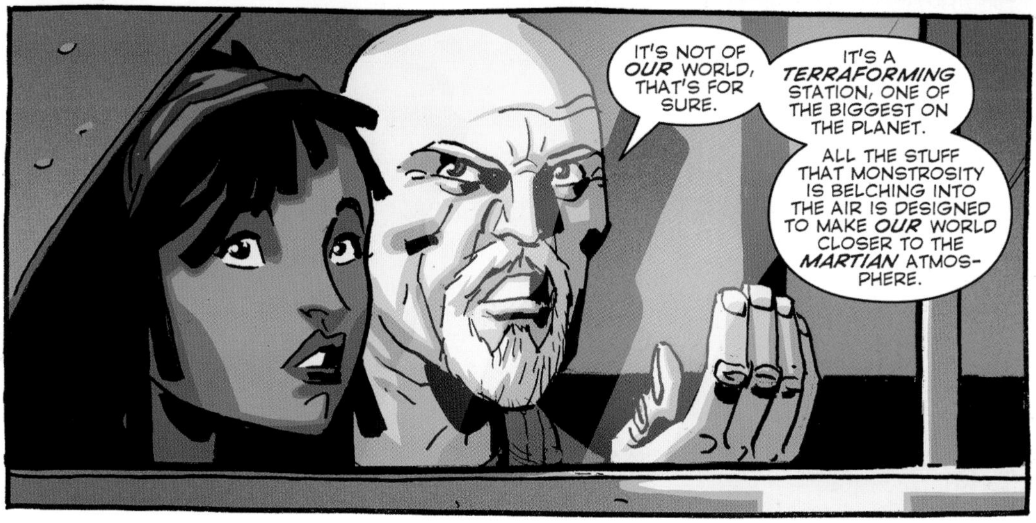
IT'S NOT OF *OUR* WORLD, THAT'S FOR SURE.
IT'S A *TERRAFORMING* STATION, ONE OF THE BIGGEST ON THE PLANET.
ALL THE STUFF THAT MONSTROSITY IS BELCHING INTO THE AIR IS DESIGNED TO MAKE *OUR* WORLD CLOSER TO THE *MARTIAN* ATMOS-PHERE.

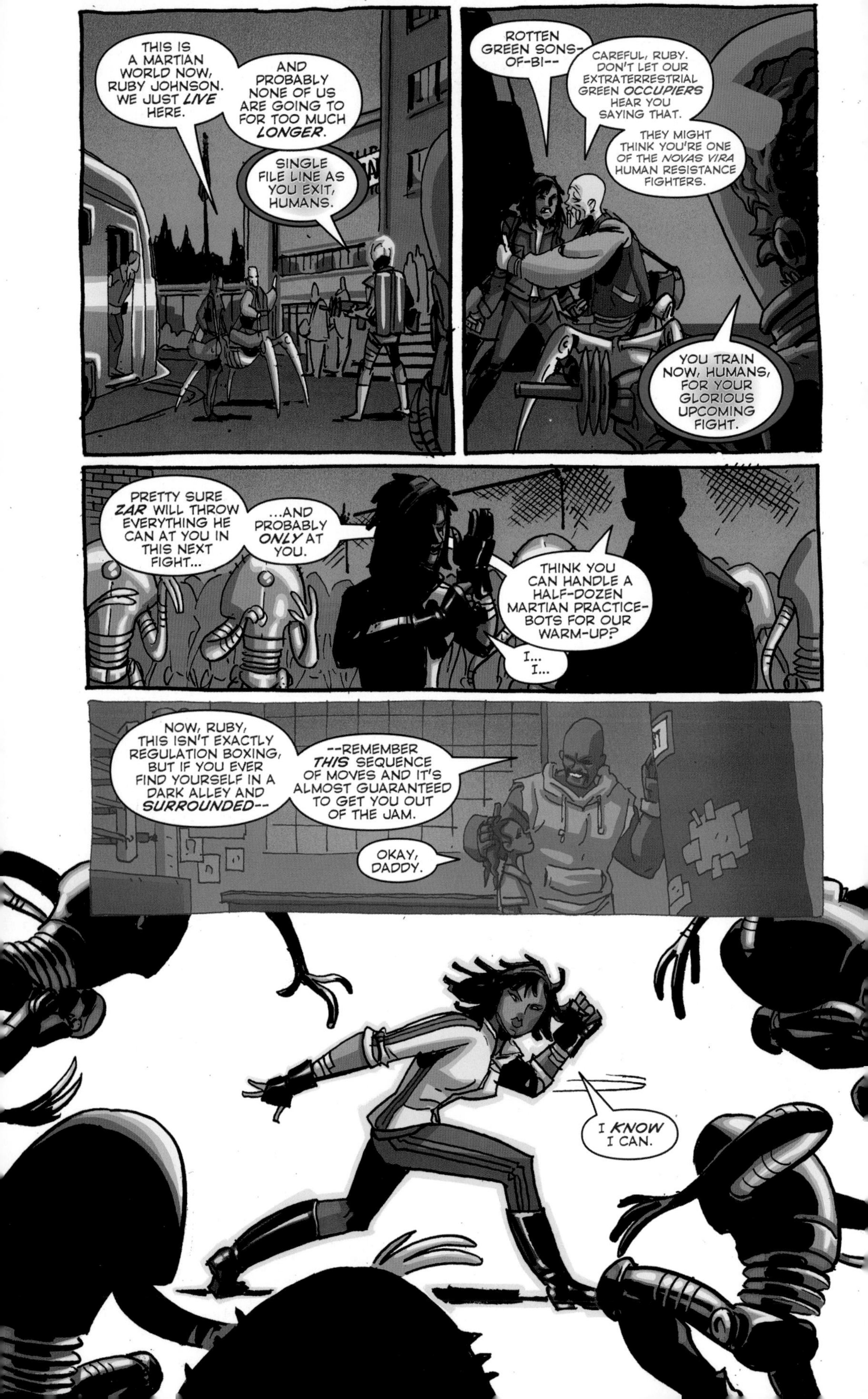
THIS IS A MARTIAN WORLD NOW, RUBY JOHNSON. WE JUST LIVE HERE.
AND PROBABLY NONE OF US ARE GOING TO FOR TOO MUCH LONGER.
SINGLE FILE LINE AS YOU EXIT, HUMANS.
ROTTEN GREEN SONS-OF-BI--
CAREFUL, RUBY. DON'T LET OUR EXTRATERRESTRIAL GREEN OCCUPIERS HEAR YOU SAYING THAT.
THEY MIGHT THINK YOU'RE ONE OF THE NOVAS VIRA HUMAN RESISTANCE FIGHTERS.
YOU TRAIN NOW, HUMANS, FOR YOUR GLORIOUS UPCOMING FIGHT.
PRETTY SURE ZAR WILL THROW EVERYTHING HE CAN AT YOU IN THIS NEXT FIGHT...
...AND PROBABLY ONLY AT YOU.
THINK YOU CAN HANDLE A HALF-DOZEN MARTIAN PRACTICE-BOTS FOR OUR WARM-UP?
I... I...
NOW, RUBY, THIS ISN'T EXACTLY REGULATION BOXING, BUT IF YOU EVER FIND YOURSELF IN A DARK ALLEY AND SURROUNDED--
--REMEMBER THIS SEQUENCE OF MOVES AND IT'S ALMOST GUARANTEED TO GET YOU OUT OF THE JAM.
OKAY, DADDY.
I KNOW I CAN.

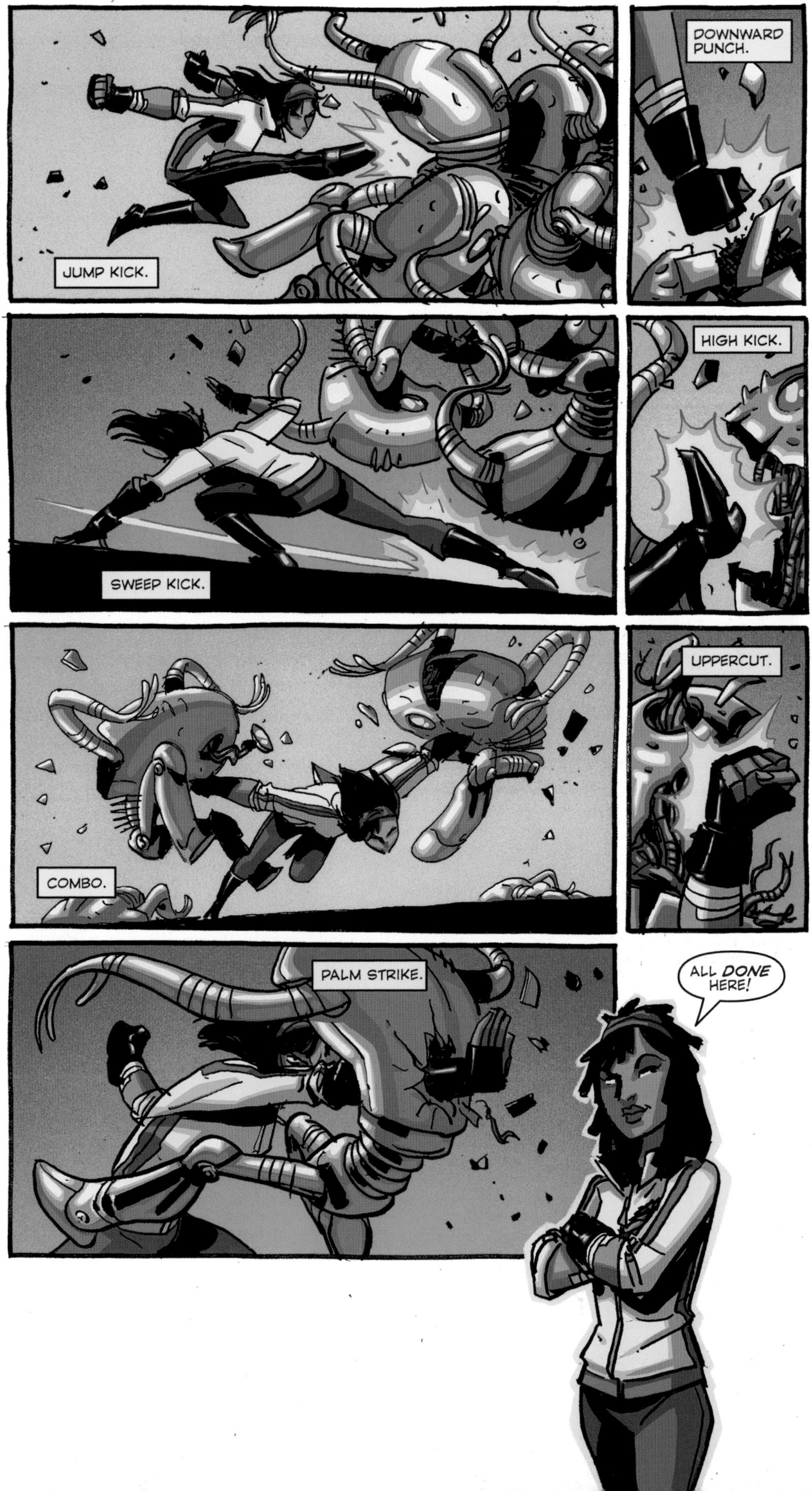
JUMP KICK.
DOWNWARD PUNCH.
SWEEP KICK.
HIGH KICK.
COMBO.
UPPERCUT.
PALM STRIKE.
ALL *DONE* HERE!

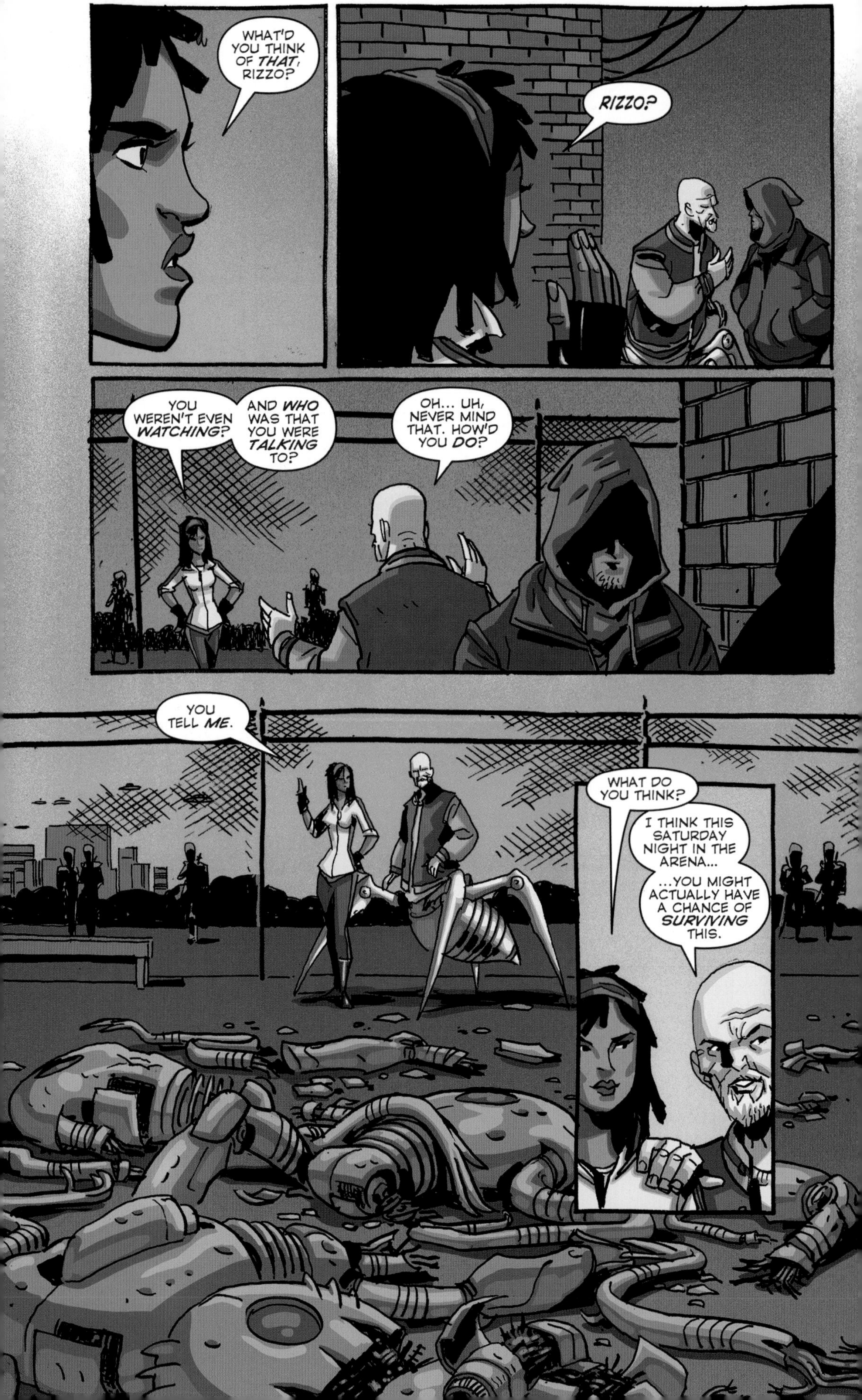

WHAT'D YOU THINK OF *THAT*, RIZZO?
RIZZO?
YOU WEREN'T EVEN *WATCHING*?
AND *WHO* WAS THAT YOU WERE *TALKING* TO?
OH... UH, NEVER MIND THAT. HOW'D YOU *DO*?
YOU TELL *ME*.
WHAT DO YOU THINK?
I THINK THIS SATURDAY NIGHT IN THE ARENA...
...YOU MIGHT ACTUALLY HAVE A CHANCE OF *SURVIVING* THIS.

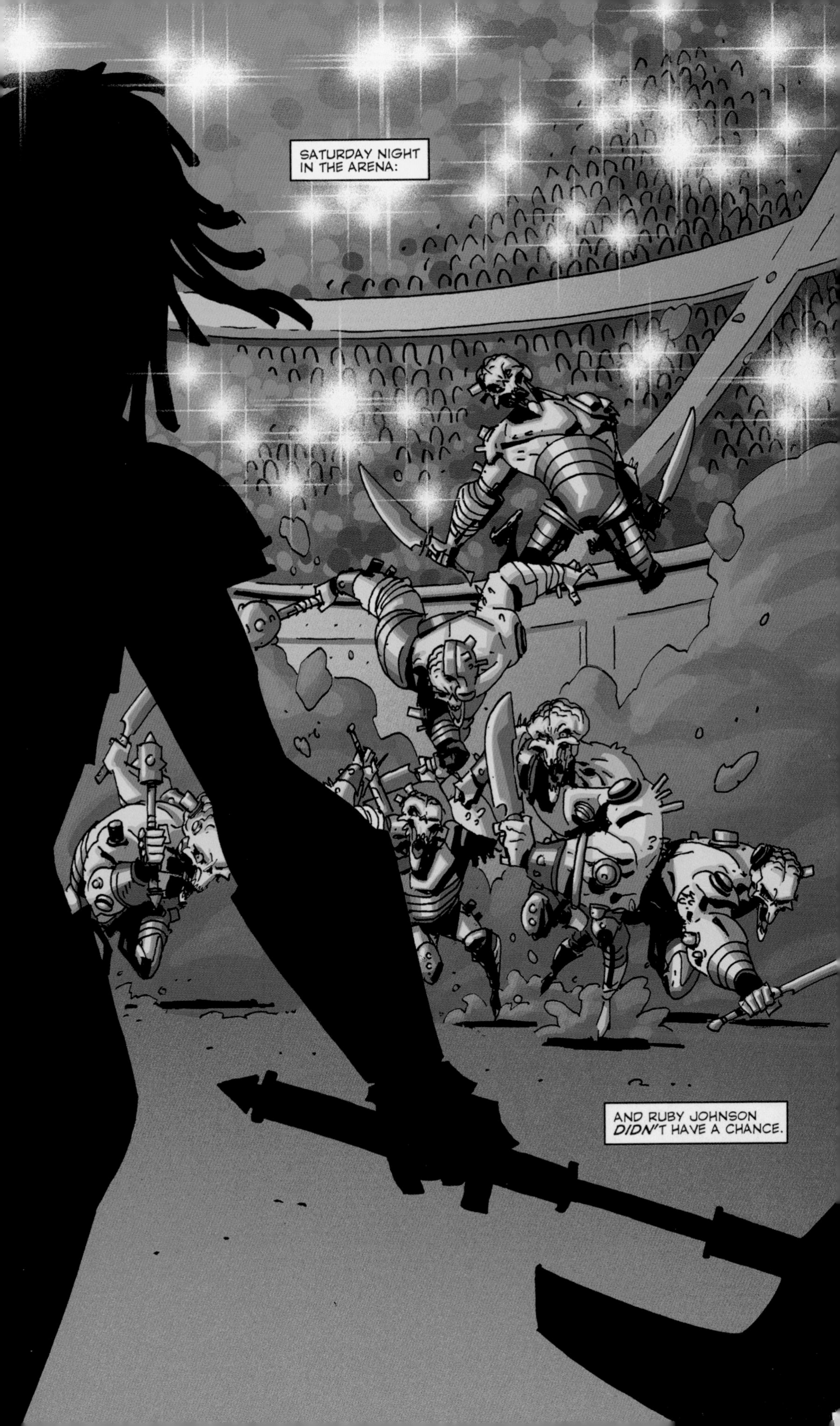
SATURDAY NIGHT IN THE ARENA:
AND RUBY JOHNSON *DIDN'T* HAVE A CHANCE.

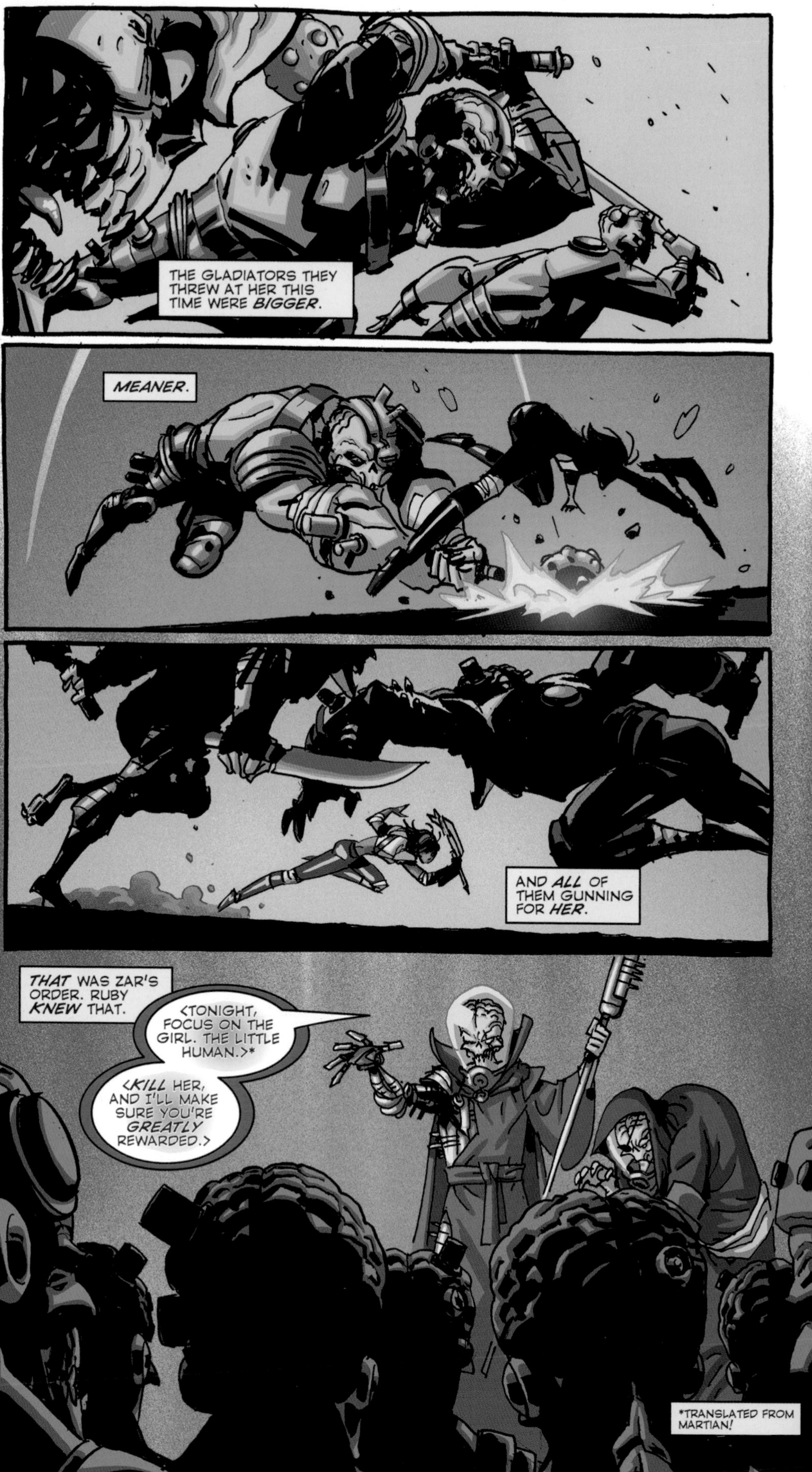
THE GLADIATORS THEY THREW AT HER THIS TIME WERE *BIGGER*.
MEANER.
AND *ALL* OF THEM GUNNING FOR *HER*.
THAT WAS ZAR'S ORDER. RUBY *KNEW* THAT.
<TONIGHT, FOCUS ON THE GIRL. THE LITTLE HUMAN.>*
<*KILL* HER, AND I'LL MAKE SURE YOU'RE *GREATLY* REWARDED.>
*TRANSLATED FROM MARTIAN!

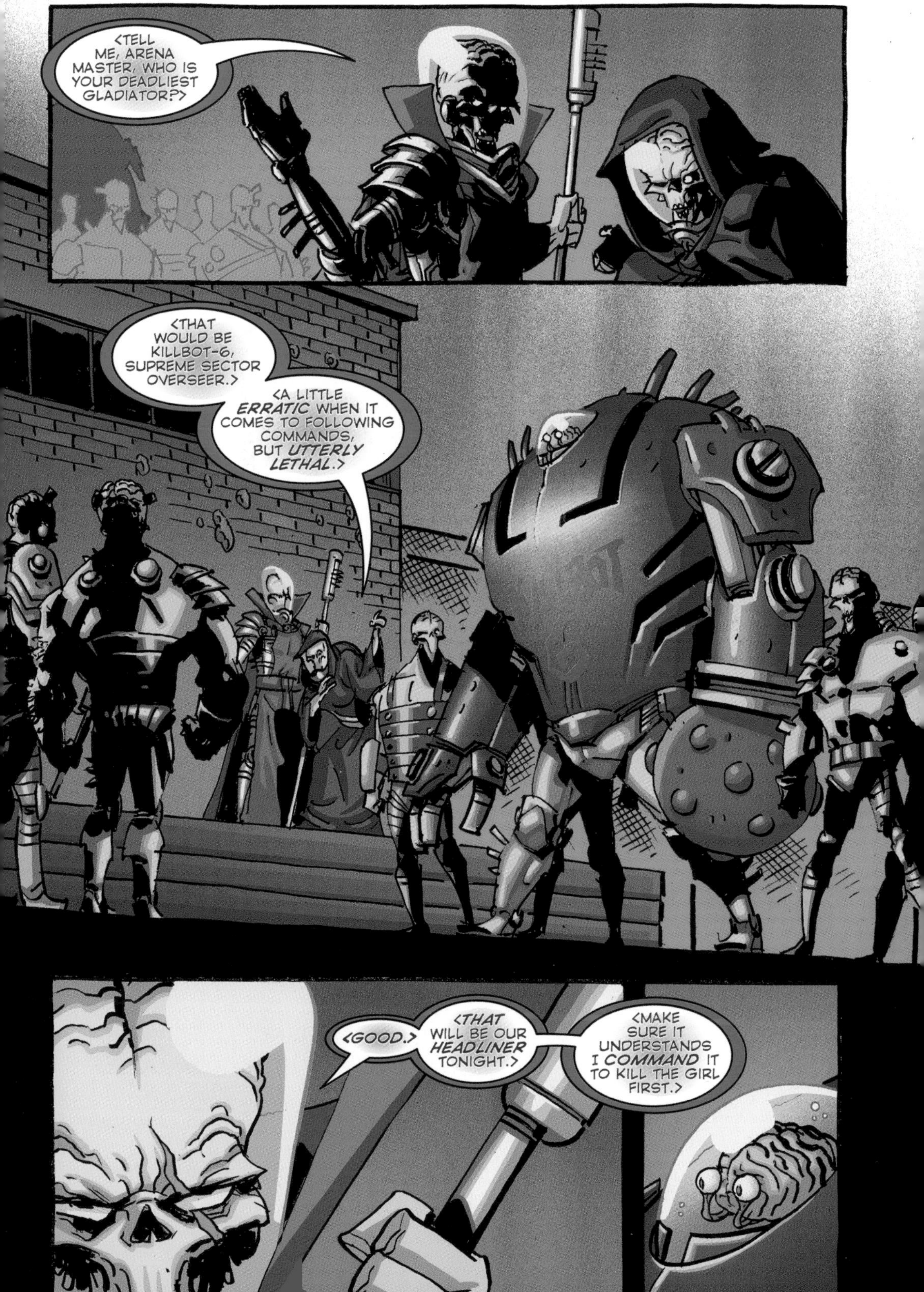
<TELL ME, ARENA MASTER, WHO IS YOUR DEADLIEST GLADIATOR?>
<THAT WOULD BE KILLBOT-6, SUPREME SECTOR OVERSEER.>
<A LITTLE *ERRATIC* WHEN IT COMES TO FOLLOWING COMMANDS, BUT *UTTERLY LETHAL*.>
<GOOD.>
<*THAT* WILL BE OUR *HEADLINER* TONIGHT.>
<MAKE SURE IT UNDERSTANDS I *COMMAND* IT TO KILL THE GIRL FIRST.>

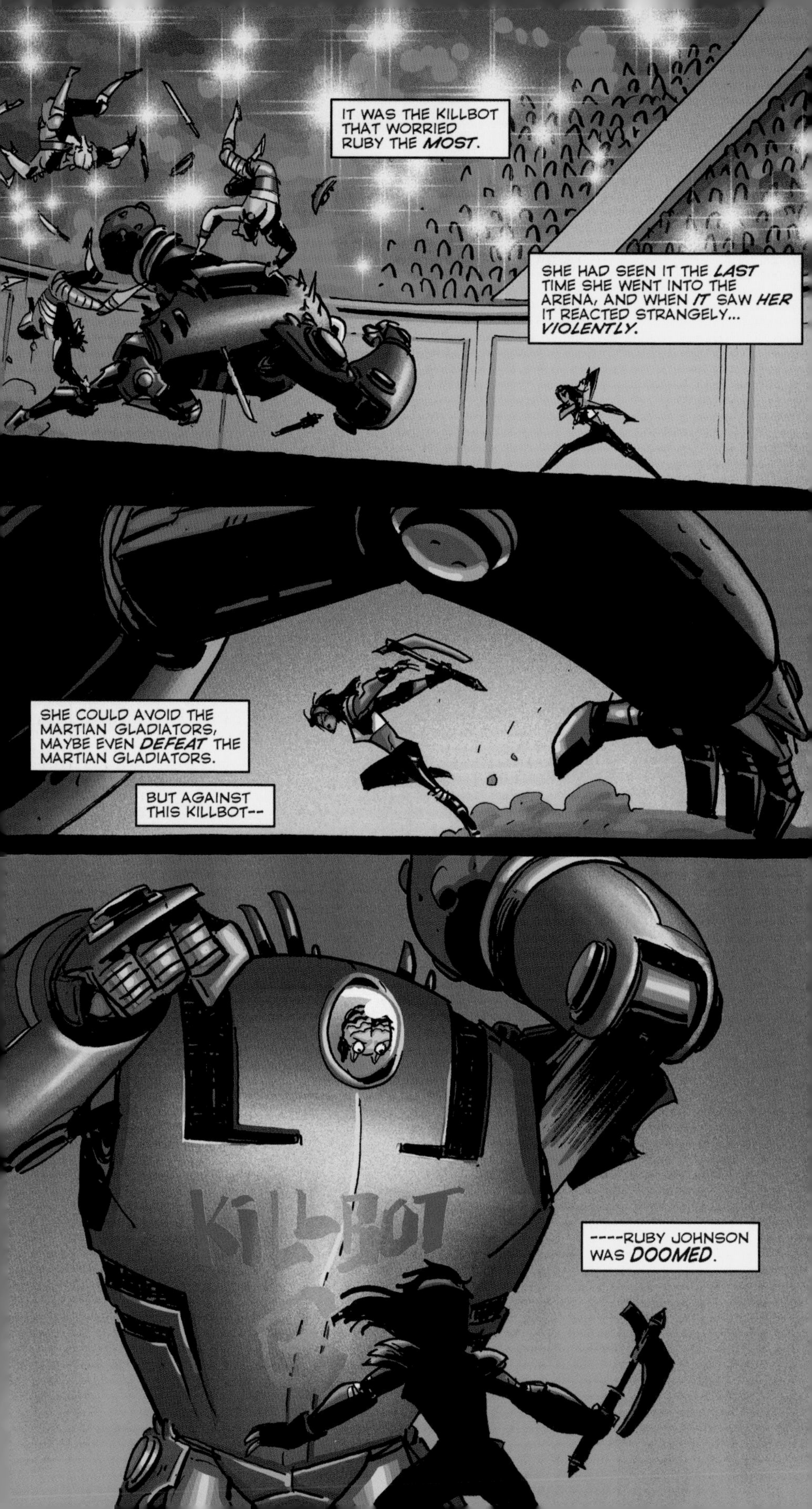

IT WAS THE KILLBOT THAT WORRIED RUBY THE *MOST*.
SHE HAD SEEN IT THE *LAST* TIME SHE WENT INTO THE ARENA, AND WHEN *IT* SAW *HER* IT REACTED STRANGELY... *VIOLENTLY*.
SHE COULD AVOID THE MARTIAN GLADIATORS, MAYBE EVEN *DEFEAT* THE MARTIAN GLADIATORS.
BUT AGAINST THIS KILLBOT--
KILLBOT
----RUBY JOHNSON WAS *DOOMED*.

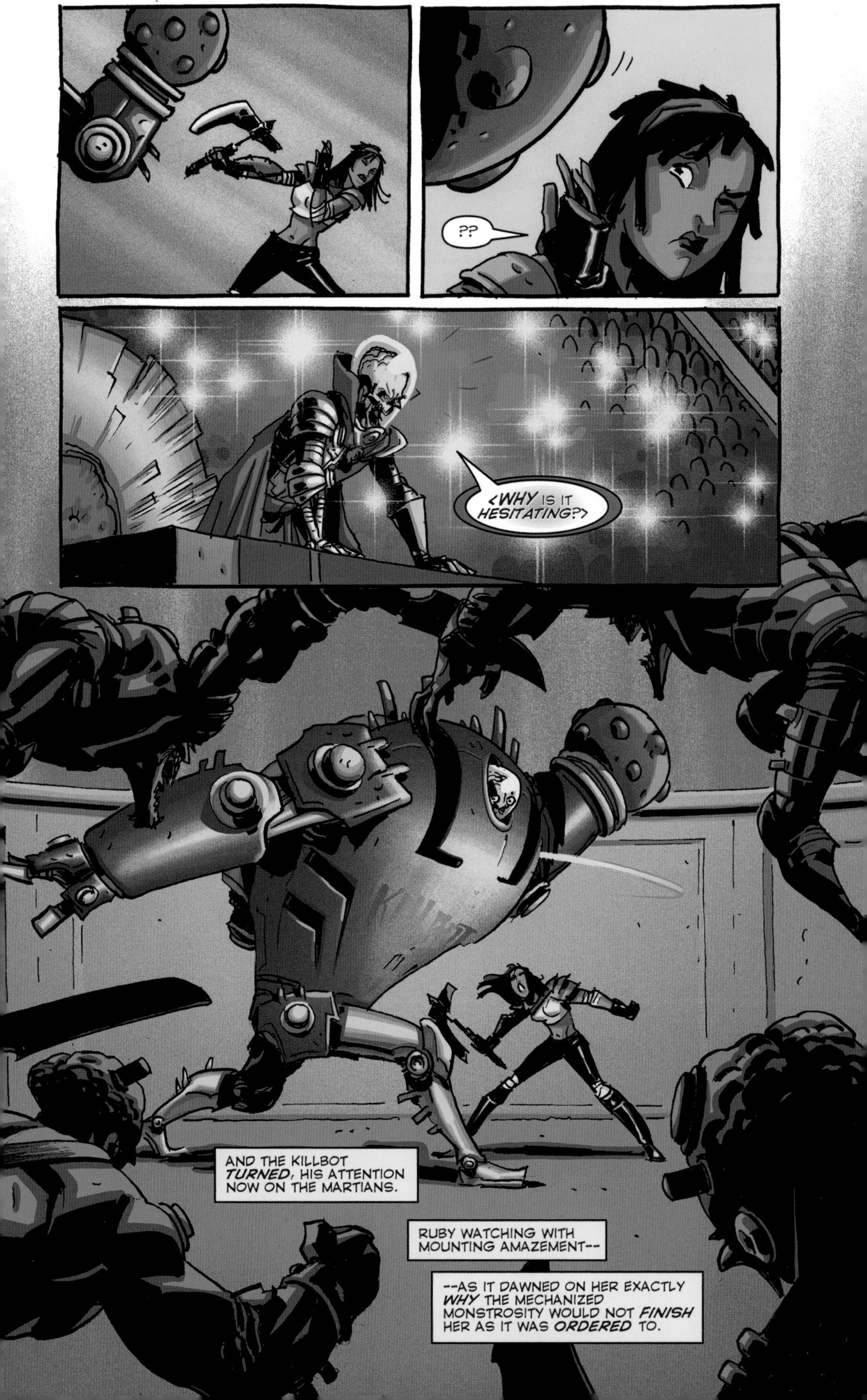

??
<WHY IS IT HESITATING?>
AND THE KILLBOT TURNED, HIS ATTENTION NOW ON THE MARTIANS.
RUBY WATCHING WITH MOUNTING AMAZEMENT--
--AS IT DAWNED ON HER EXACTLY WHY THE MECHANIZED MONSTROSITY WOULD NOT FINISH HER AS IT WAS ORDERED TO.

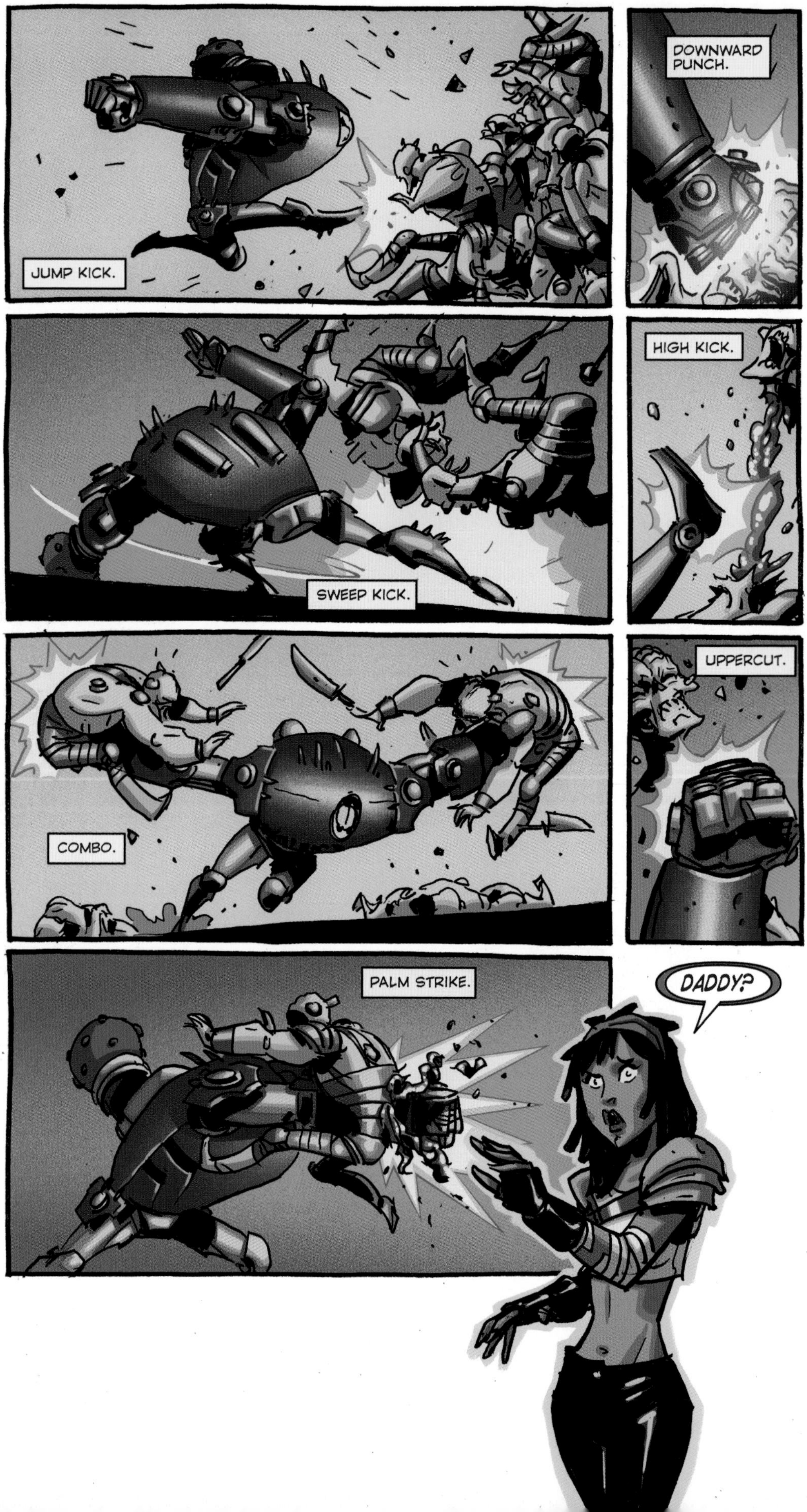
JUMP KICK.
DOWNWARD PUNCH.
SWEEP KICK.
HIGH KICK.
COMBO.
UPPERCUT.
PALM STRIKE.
DADDY?

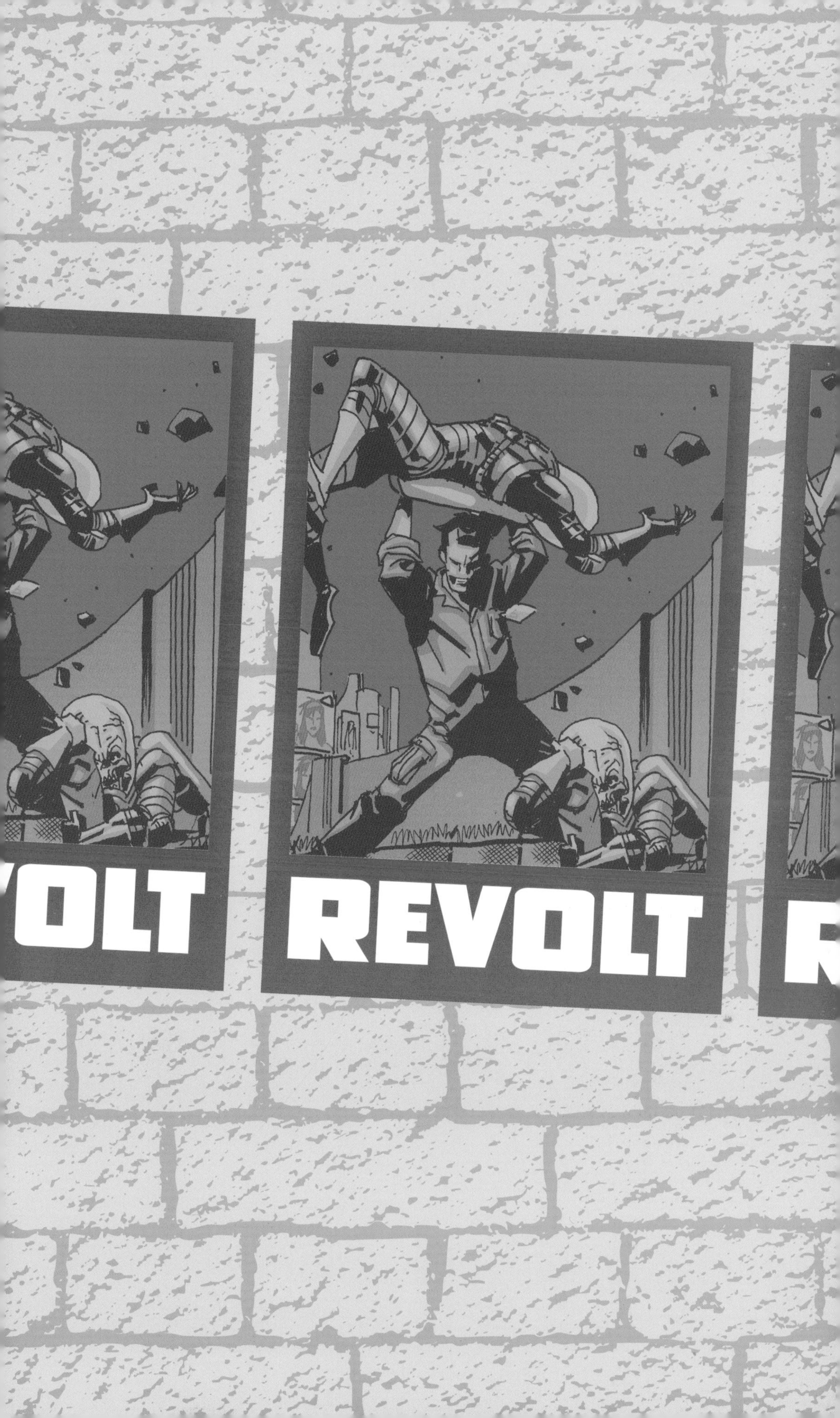

VOLT
REVOLT
R

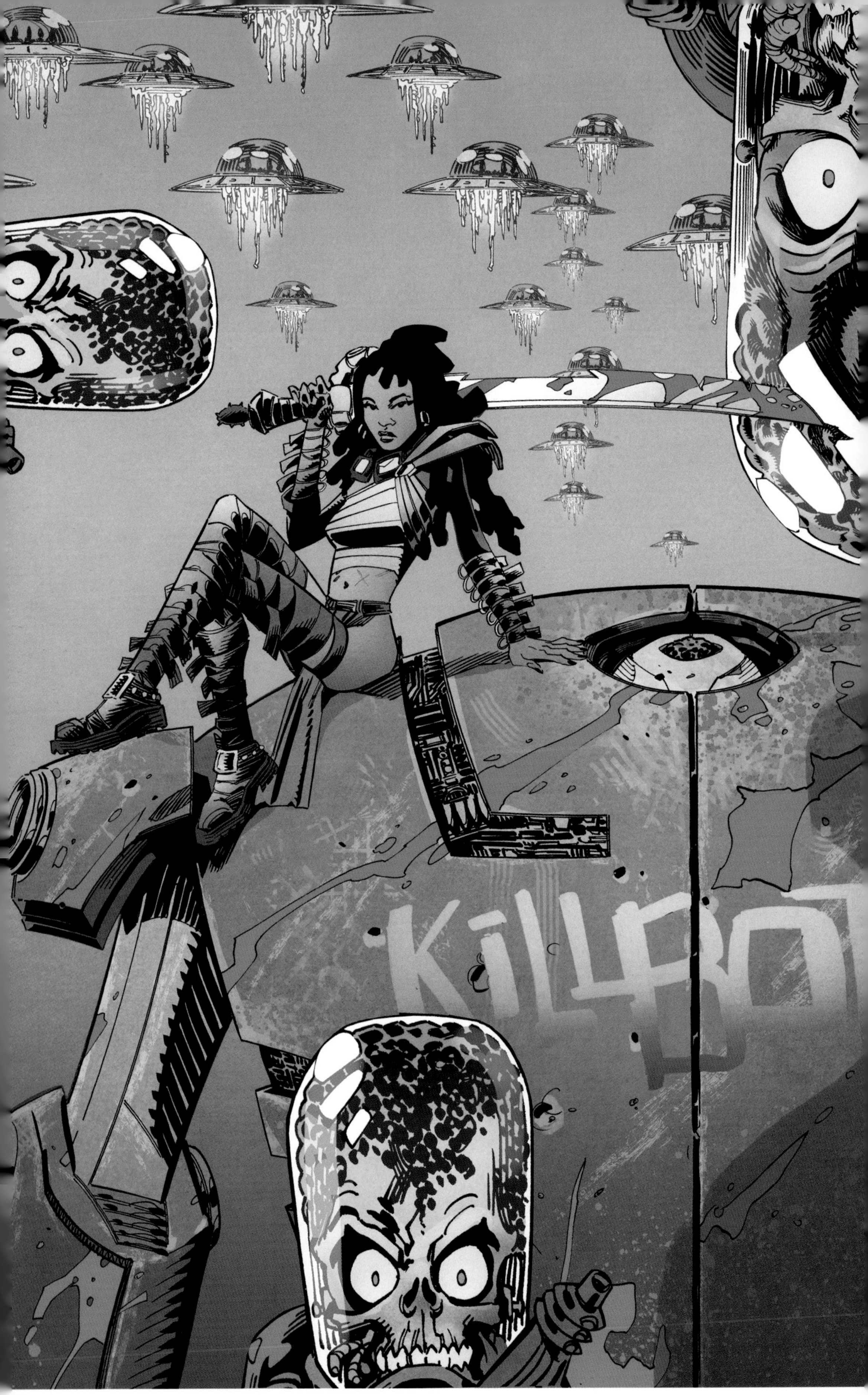
KILLBOT

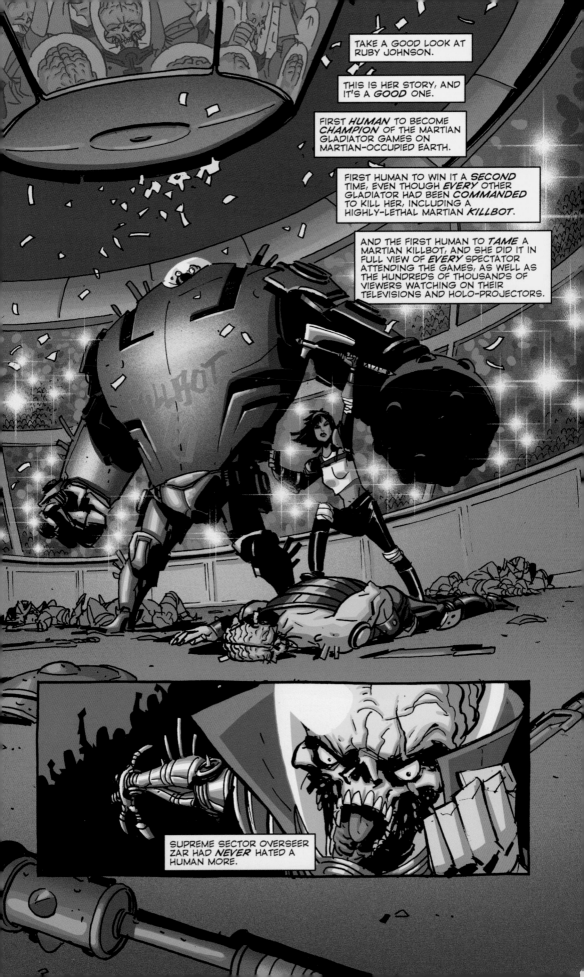

TAKE A GOOD LOOK AT RUBY JOHNSON.

THIS IS HER STORY, AND IT'S A *GOOD* ONE.

FIRST *HUMAN* TO BECOME *CHAMPION* OF THE MARTIAN GLADIATOR GAMES ON MARTIAN-OCCUPIED EARTH.

FIRST HUMAN TO WIN IT A *SECOND* TIME, EVEN THOUGH *EVERY* OTHER GLADIATOR HAD BEEN *COMMANDED* TO KILL HER, INCLUDING A HIGHLY-LETHAL MARTIAN *KILLBOT.*

AND THE FIRST HUMAN TO *TAME* A MARTIAN KILLBOT, AND SHE DID IT IN FULL VIEW OF *EVERY* SPECTATOR ATTENDING THE GAMES, AS WELL AS THE HUNDREDS OF THOUSANDS OF VIEWERS WATCHING ON THEIR TELEVISIONS AND HOLO-PROJECTORS.

SUPREME SECTOR OVERSEER ZAR HAD *NEVER* HATED A HUMAN MORE.

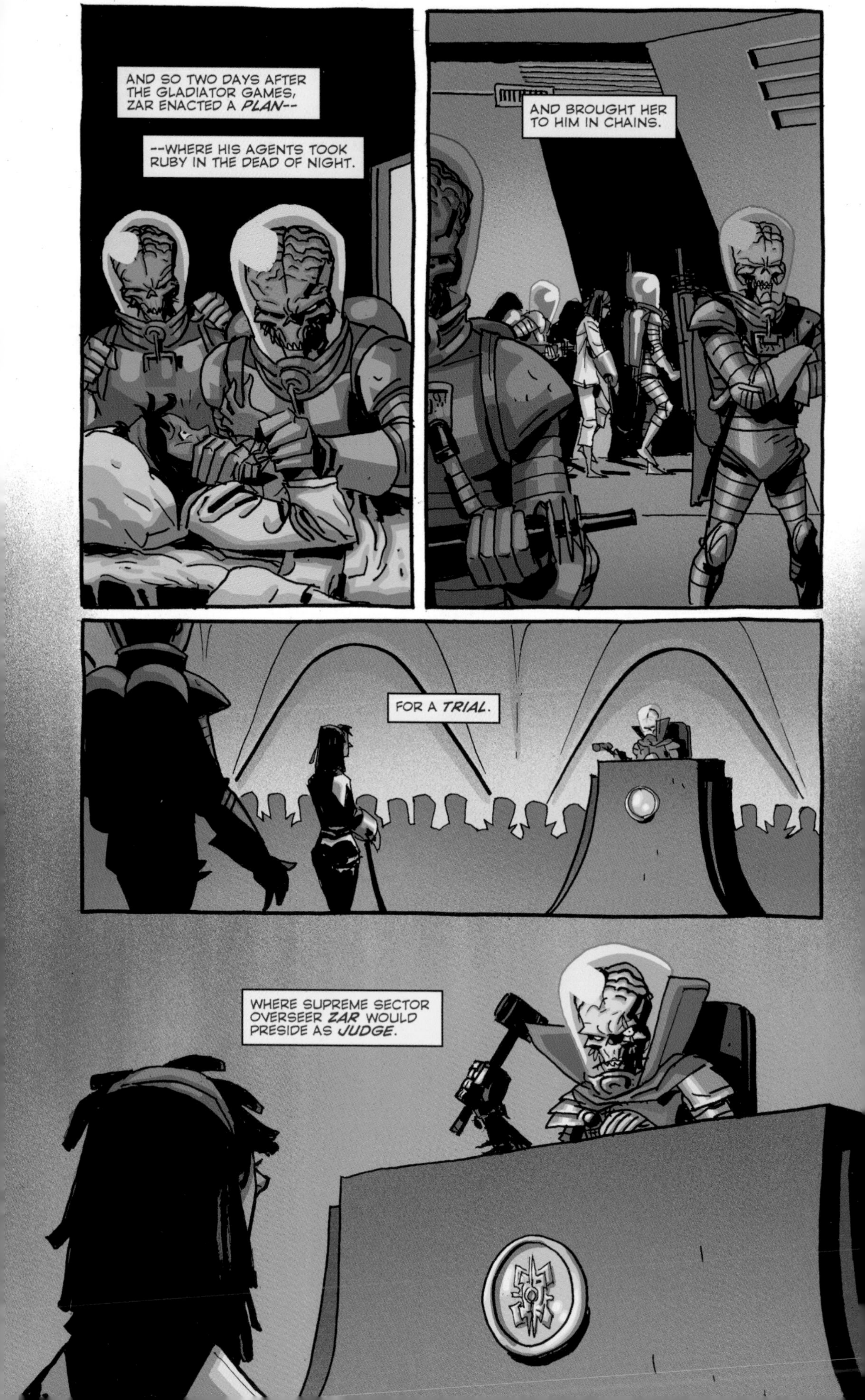
AND SO TWO DAYS AFTER THE GLADIATOR GAMES, ZAR ENACTED A *PLAN*--
--WHERE HIS AGENTS TOOK RUBY IN THE DEAD OF NIGHT.
AND BROUGHT HER TO HIM IN CHAINS.
FOR A *TRIAL*.
WHERE SUPREME SECTOR OVERSEER *ZAR* WOULD PRESIDE AS *JUDGE*.

ZAR OPENED THE TRIAL WITH A LIST OF ALL OF RUBY JOHNSON'S TRAITOROUS, TREACHEROUS, AND SEDITIOUS ACTS AGAINST THE MARTIAN EMPIRE.

(NONE OF WHICH WERE TRUE.)

HE NAMED HER A *SABOTEUR* AND A *SPY*, AND PRODUCED (FALSE) EVIDENCE THAT SHE WAS A MEMBER OF UNDERGROUND HUMAN REBEL GROUP KNOWN AS THE *NOVAS VIRA*.

HE DECLARED HER *GUILTY*--

(WHICH, OF COURSE, HE WAS ALWAYS *GOING* TO DO.)

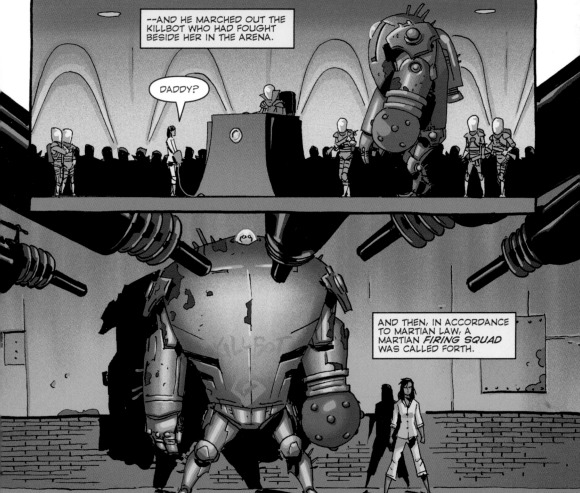

--AND HE MARCHED OUT THE KILLBOT WHO HAD FOUGHT BESIDE HER IN THE ARENA.

DADDY?

AND THEN, IN ACCORDANCE TO MARTIAN LAW, A MARTIAN *FIRING SQUAD* WAS CALLED FORTH.

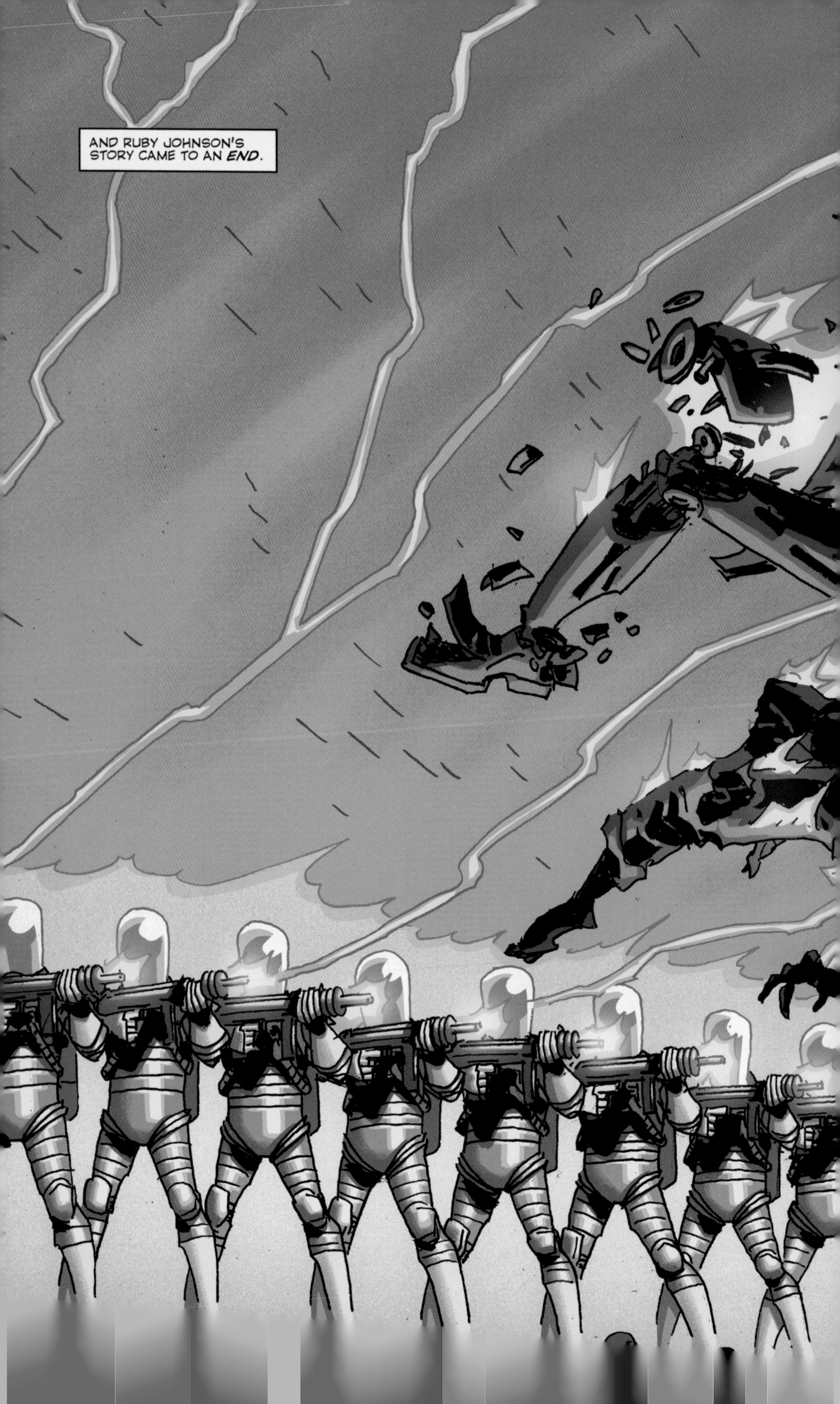
AND RUBY JOHNSON'S STORY CAME TO AN *END*.

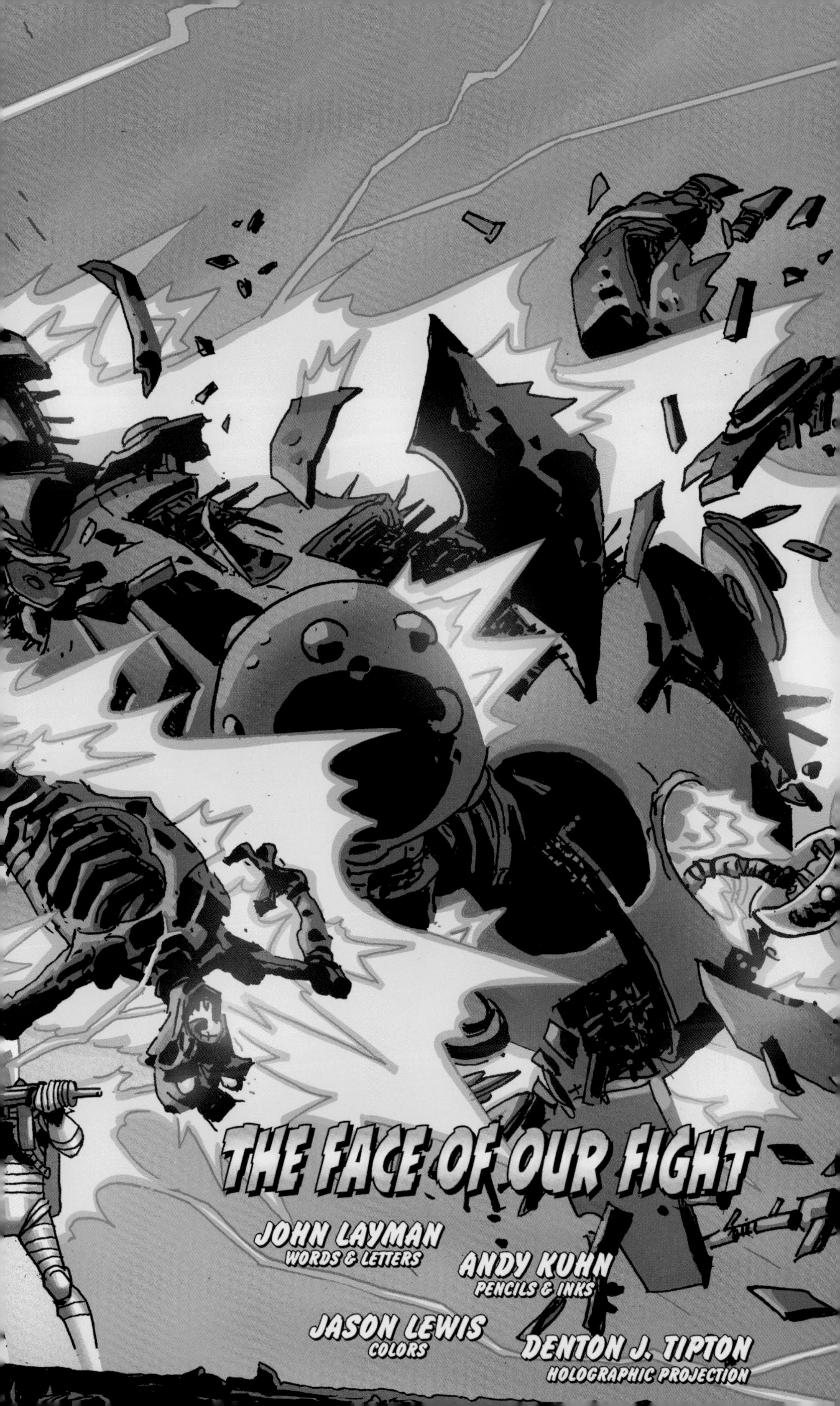
THE FACE OF OUR FIGHT
JOHN LAYMAN
WORDS & LETTERS
ANDY KUHN
PENCILS & INKS
JASON LEWIS
COLORS
DENTON J. TIPTON
HOLOGRAPHIC PROJECTION

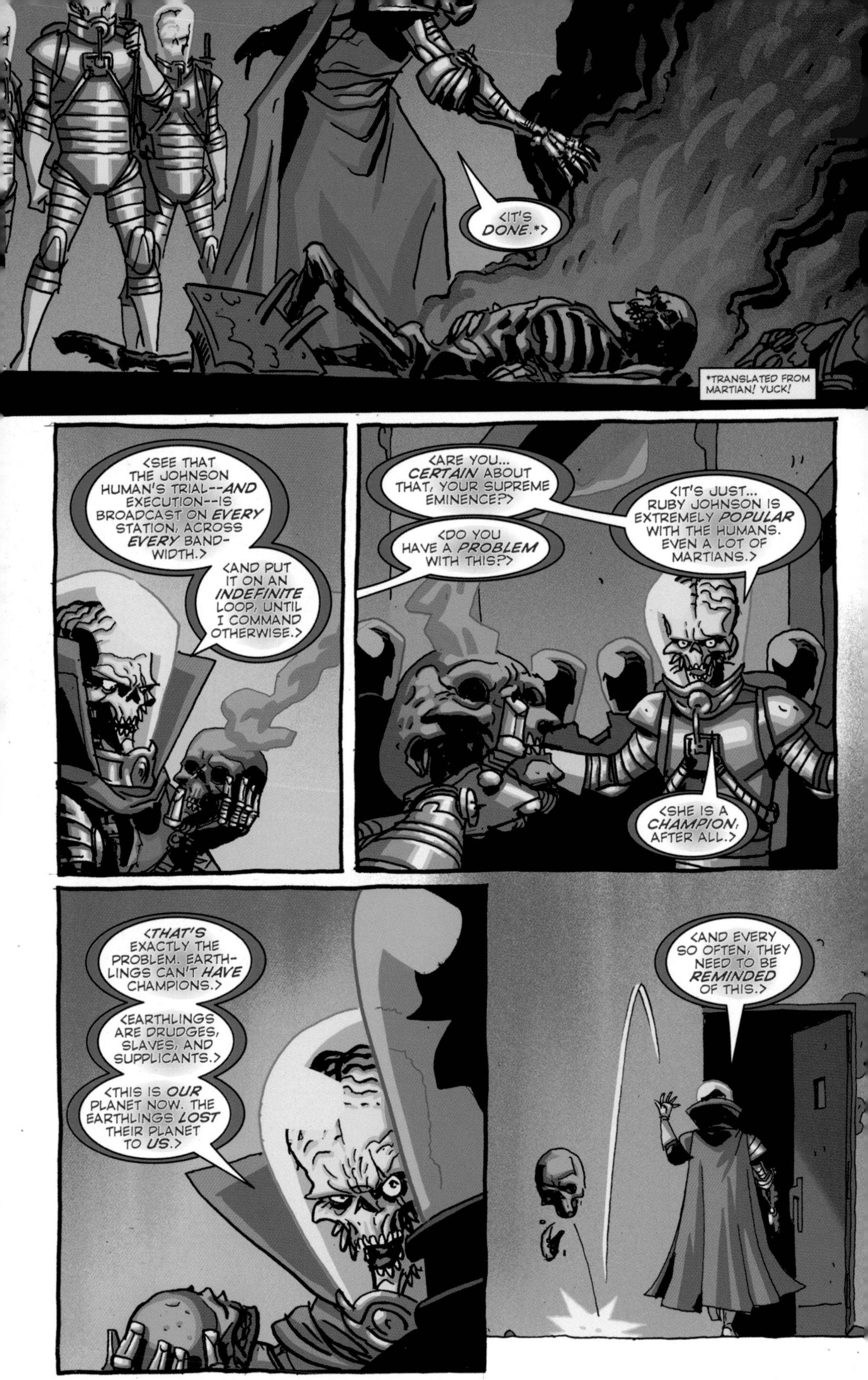
<IT'S DONE.*>
*TRANSLATED FROM MARTIAN! YUCK!
<SEE THAT THE JOHNSON HUMAN'S TRIAL--AND EXECUTION--IS BROADCAST ON EVERY STATION, ACROSS EVERY BANDWIDTH.>
<AND PUT IT ON AN INDEFINITE LOOP, UNTIL I COMMAND OTHERWISE.>
<ARE YOU... CERTAIN ABOUT THAT, YOUR SUPREME EMINENCE?>
<DO YOU HAVE A PROBLEM WITH THIS?>
<IT'S JUST... RUBY JOHNSON IS EXTREMELY POPULAR WITH THE HUMANS. EVEN A LOT OF MARTIANS.>
<SHE IS A CHAMPION, AFTER ALL.>
<THAT'S EXACTLY THE PROBLEM. EARTHLINGS CAN'T HAVE CHAMPIONS.>
<EARTHLINGS ARE DRUDGES, SLAVES, AND SUPPLICANTS.>
<THIS IS OUR PLANET NOW. THE EARTHLINGS LOST THEIR PLANET TO US.>
<AND EVERY SO OFTEN, THEY NEED TO BE REMINDED OF THIS.>

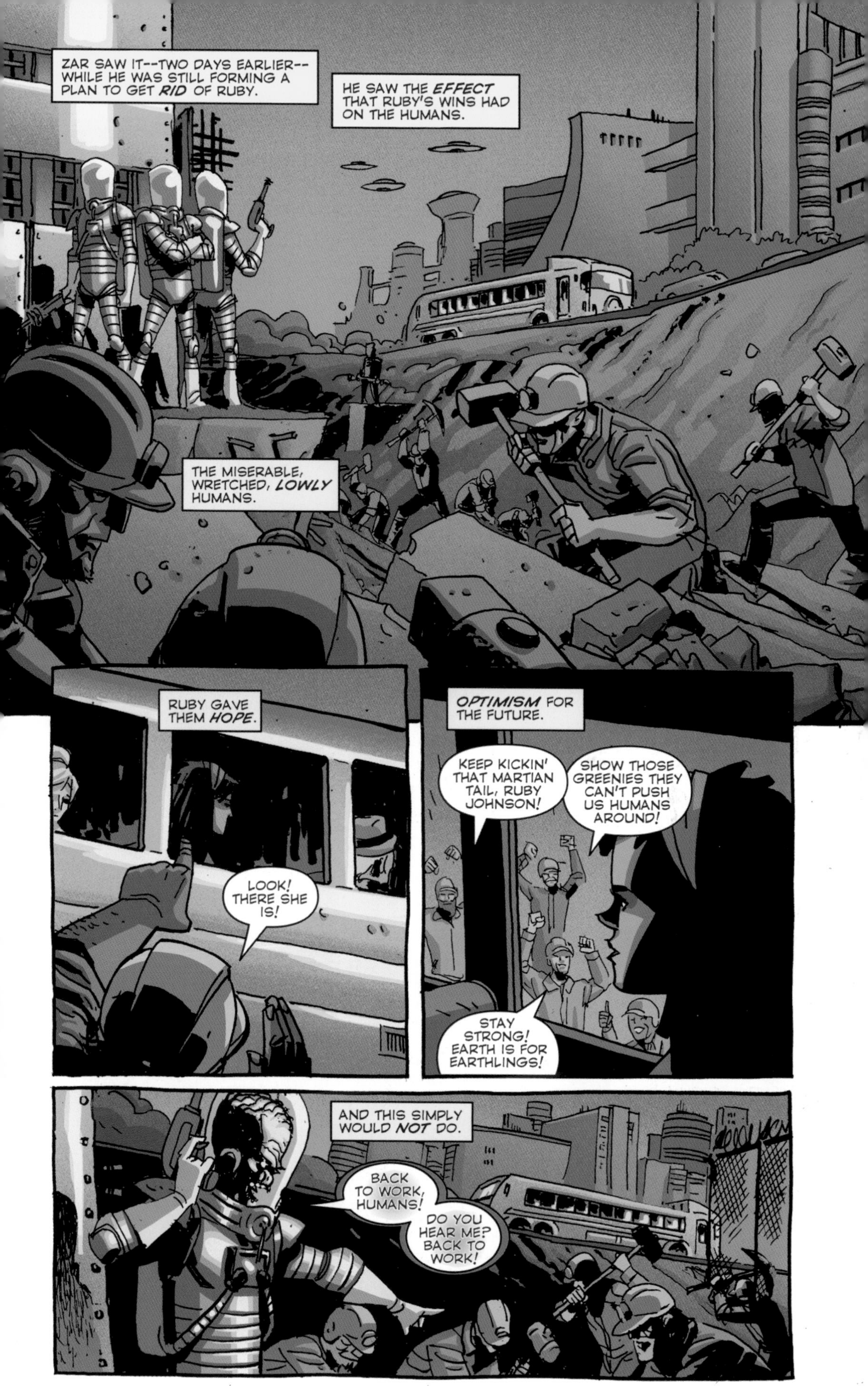
ZAR SAW IT--TWO DAYS EARLIER--WHILE HE WAS STILL FORMING A PLAN TO GET *RID* OF RUBY.
HE SAW THE *EFFECT* THAT RUBY'S WINS HAD ON THE HUMANS.
THE MISERABLE, WRETCHED, *LOWLY* HUMANS.
RUBY GAVE THEM *HOPE*.
LOOK! THERE SHE IS!
OPTIMISM FOR THE FUTURE.
KEEP KICKIN' THAT MARTIAN TAIL, RUBY JOHNSON!
SHOW THOSE GREENIES THEY CAN'T PUSH US HUMANS AROUND!
STAY STRONG! EARTH IS FOR EARTHLINGS!
AND THIS SIMPLY WOULD *NOT* DO.
BACK TO WORK, HUMANS!
DO YOU HEAR ME? BACK TO WORK!

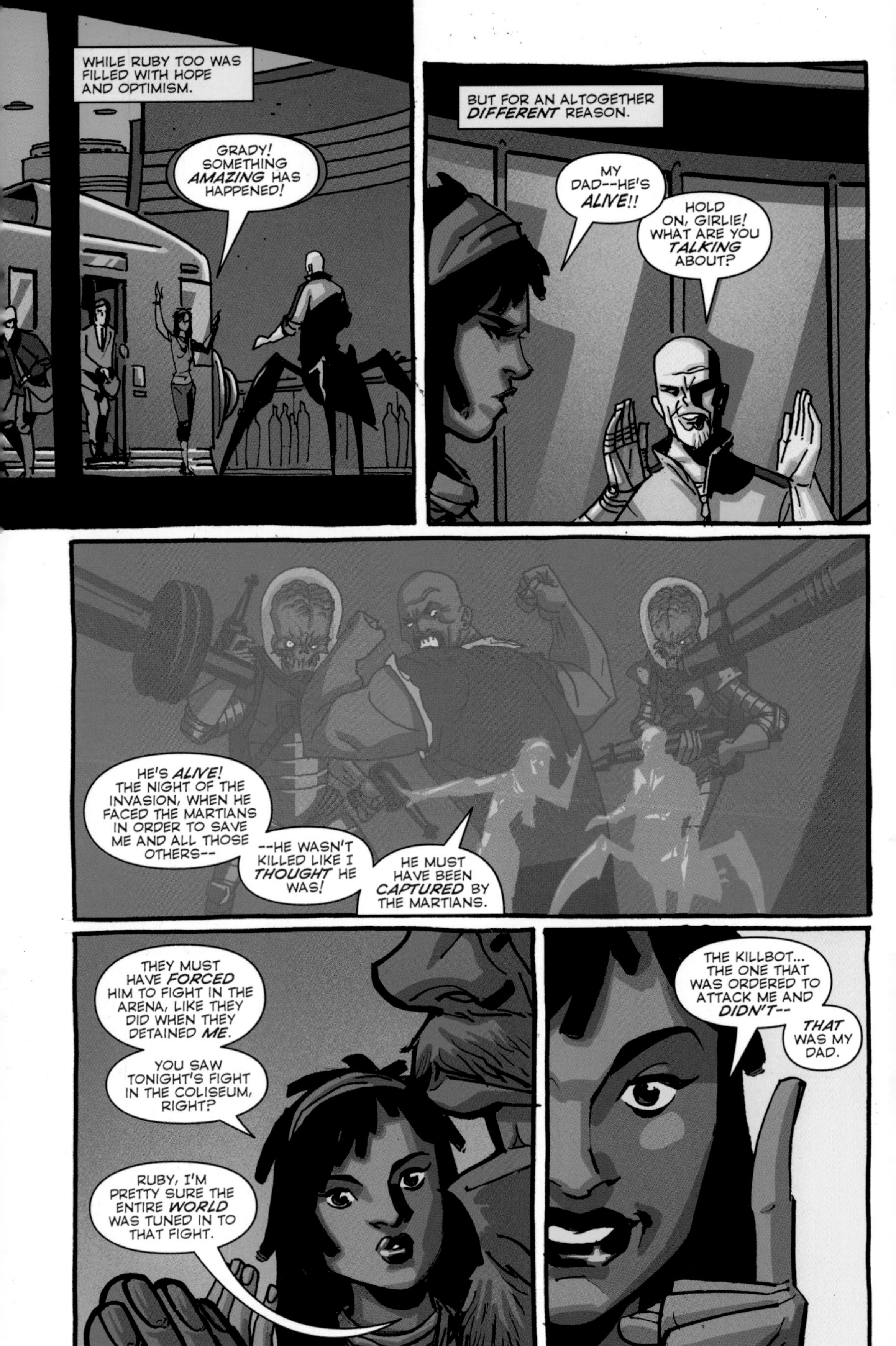
WHILE RUBY TOO WAS FILLED WITH HOPE AND OPTIMISM.
GRADY! SOMETHING AMAZING HAS HAPPENED!
BUT FOR AN ALTOGETHER DIFFERENT REASON.
MY DAD--HE'S ALIVE!!
HOLD ON, GIRLIE! WHAT ARE YOU TALKING ABOUT?
HE'S ALIVE! THE NIGHT OF THE INVASION, WHEN HE FACED THE MARTIANS IN ORDER TO SAVE ME AND ALL THOSE OTHERS--
--HE WASN'T KILLED LIKE I THOUGHT HE WAS!
HE MUST HAVE BEEN CAPTURED BY THE MARTIANS.
THEY MUST HAVE FORCED HIM TO FIGHT IN THE ARENA, LIKE THEY DID WHEN THEY DETAINED ME.
YOU SAW TONIGHT'S FIGHT IN THE COLISEUM, RIGHT?
RUBY, I'M PRETTY SURE THE ENTIRE WORLD WAS TUNED IN TO THAT FIGHT.
THE KILLBOT... THE ONE THAT WAS ORDERED TO ATTACK ME AND DIDN'T--
THAT WAS MY DAD.

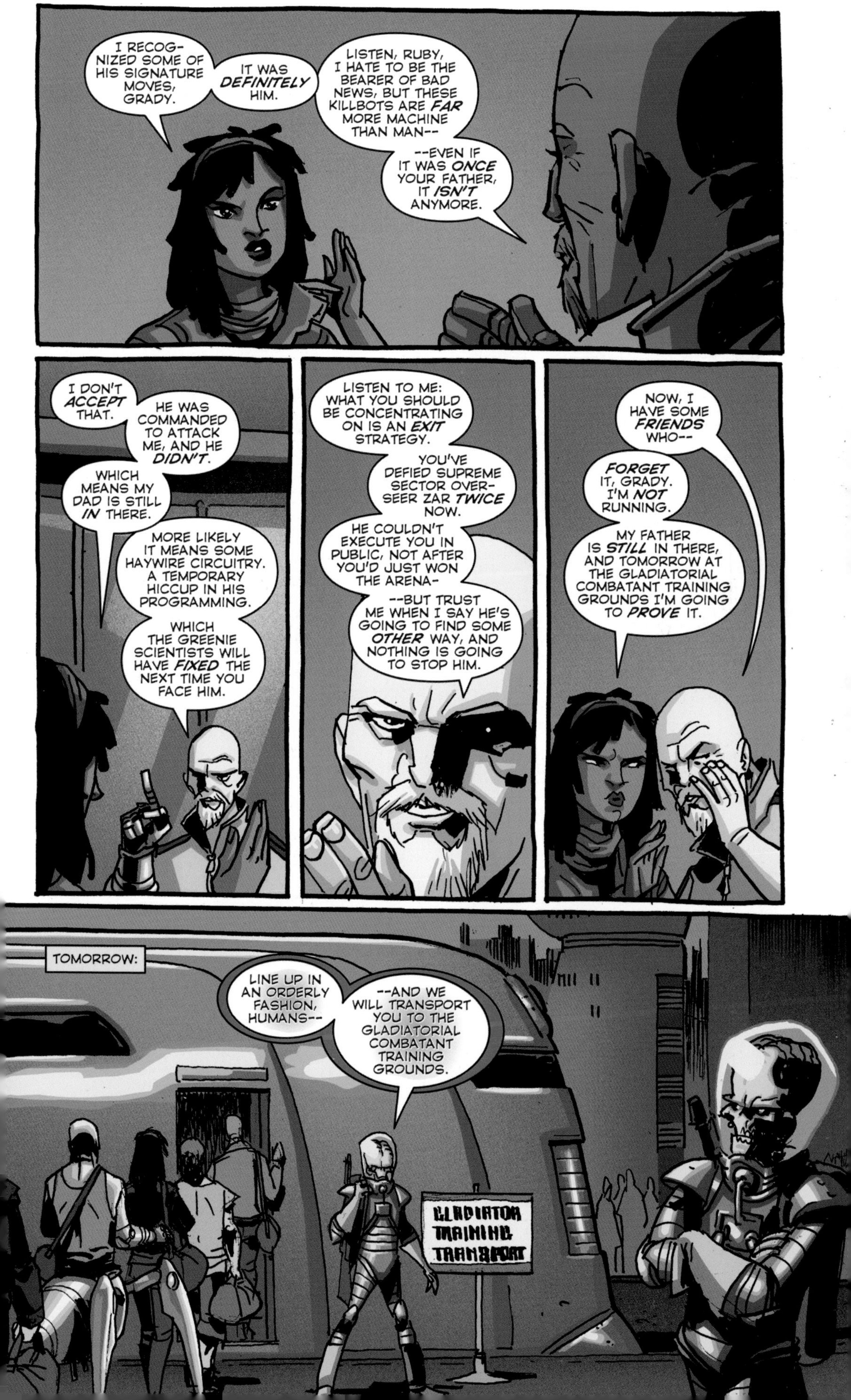
I RECOGNIZED SOME OF HIS SIGNATURE MOVES, GRADY.
IT WAS DEFINITELY HIM.
LISTEN, RUBY, I HATE TO BE THE BEARER OF BAD NEWS, BUT THESE KILLBOTS ARE FAR MORE MACHINE THAN MAN--
--EVEN IF IT WAS ONCE YOUR FATHER, IT ISN'T ANYMORE.
I DON'T ACCEPT THAT.
HE WAS COMMANDED TO ATTACK ME, AND HE DIDN'T.
WHICH MEANS MY DAD IS STILL IN THERE.
MORE LIKELY IT MEANS SOME HAYWIRE CIRCUITRY. A TEMPORARY HICCUP IN HIS PROGRAMMING.
WHICH THE GREENIE SCIENTISTS WILL HAVE FIXED THE NEXT TIME YOU FACE HIM.
LISTEN TO ME: WHAT YOU SHOULD BE CONCENTRATING ON IS AN EXIT STRATEGY.
YOU'VE DEFIED SUPREME SECTOR OVERSEER ZAR TWICE NOW.
HE COULDN'T EXECUTE YOU IN PUBLIC, NOT AFTER YOU'D JUST WON THE ARENA-
--BUT TRUST ME WHEN I SAY HE'S GOING TO FIND SOME OTHER WAY, AND NOTHING IS GOING TO STOP HIM.
NOW, I HAVE SOME FRIENDS WHO--
FORGET IT, GRADY. I'M NOT RUNNING.
MY FATHER IS STILL IN THERE, AND TOMORROW AT THE GLADIATORIAL COMBATANT TRAINING GROUNDS I'M GOING TO PROVE IT.
TOMORROW:
LINE UP IN AN ORDERLY FASHION, HUMANS--
--AND WE WILL TRANSPORT YOU TO THE GLADIATORIAL COMBATANT TRAINING GROUNDS.
GLADIATOR TRAINING TRANSPORT

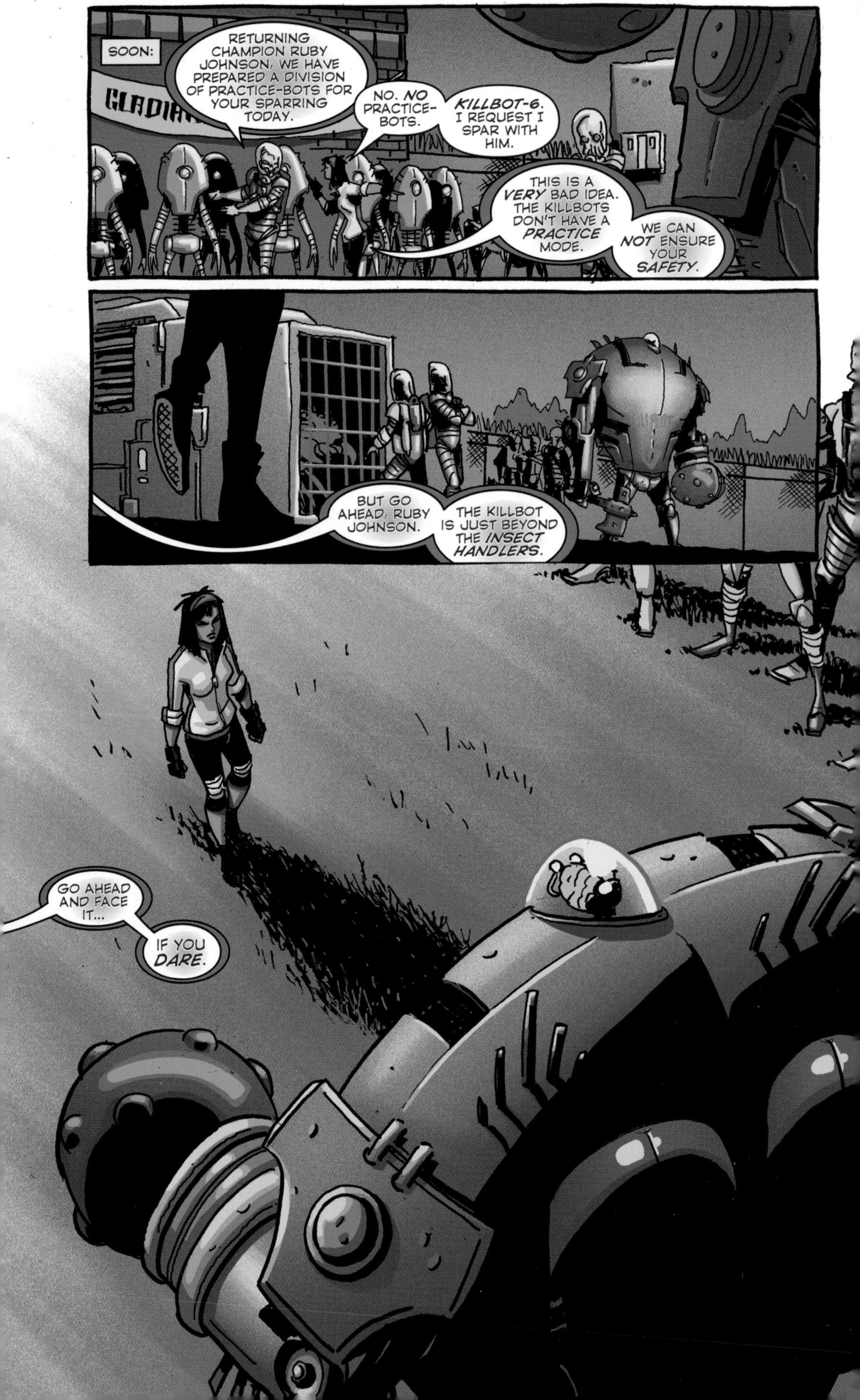
SOON:
RETURNING CHAMPION RUBY JOHNSON, WE HAVE PREPARED A DIVISION OF PRACTICE-BOTS FOR YOUR SPARRING TODAY.
NO. *NO* PRACTICE-BOTS.
KILLBOT-6. I REQUEST I SPAR WITH HIM.
THIS IS A *VERY* BAD IDEA. THE KILLBOTS DON'T HAVE A *PRACTICE* MODE.
WE CAN *NOT* ENSURE YOUR *SAFETY*.
BUT GO AHEAD, RUBY JOHNSON.
THE KILLBOT IS JUST BEYOND THE *INSECT HANDLERS*.
GO AHEAD AND FACE IT...
IF YOU *DARE*.

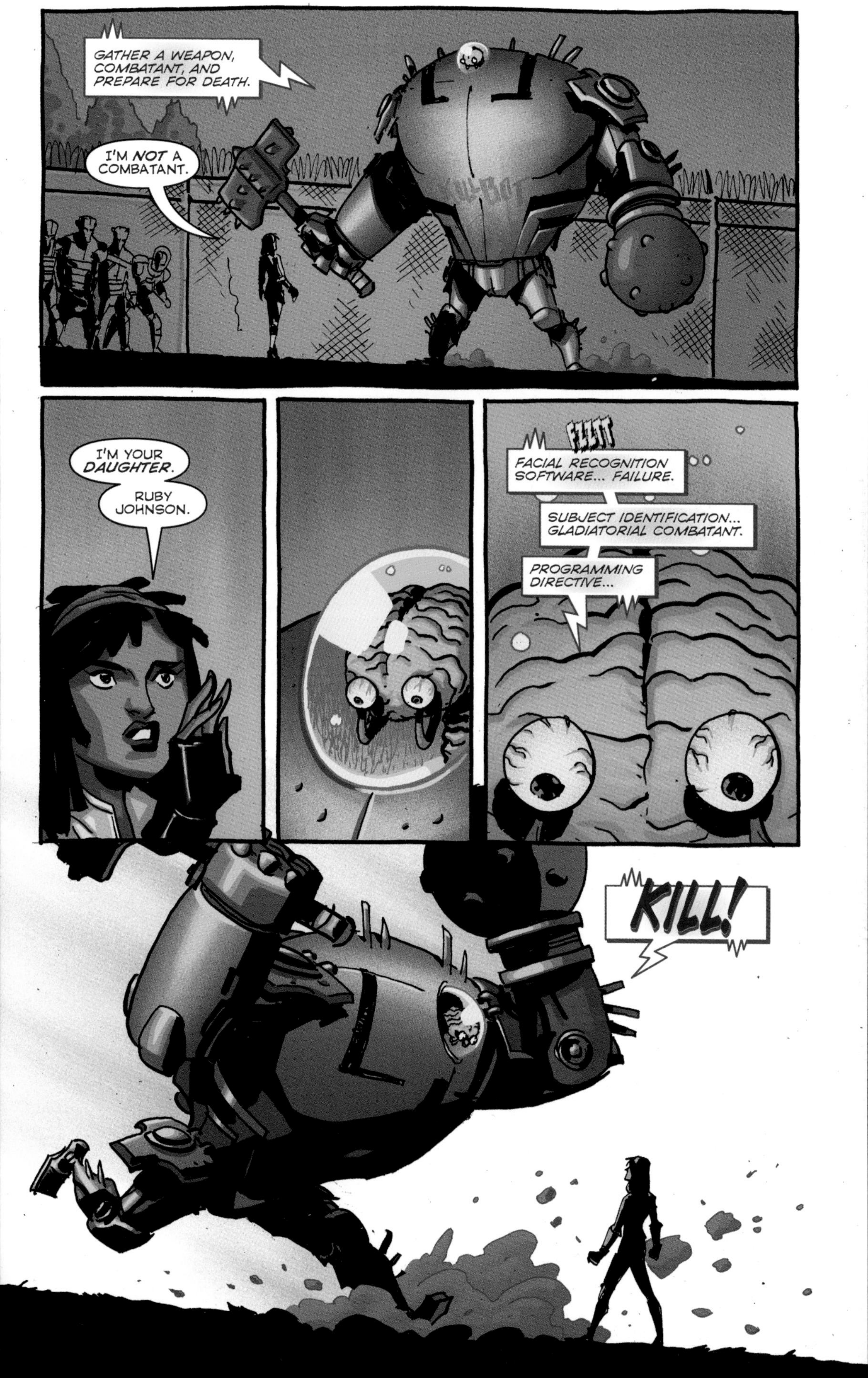
GATHER A WEAPON, COMBATANT, AND PREPARE FOR DEATH.
I'M NOT A COMBATANT.
I'M YOUR DAUGHTER.
RUBY JOHNSON.
FZZTT
FACIAL RECOGNITION SOFTWARE... FAILURE.
SUBJECT IDENTIFICATION... GLADIATORIAL COMBATANT.
PROGRAMMING DIRECTIVE...
KILL!

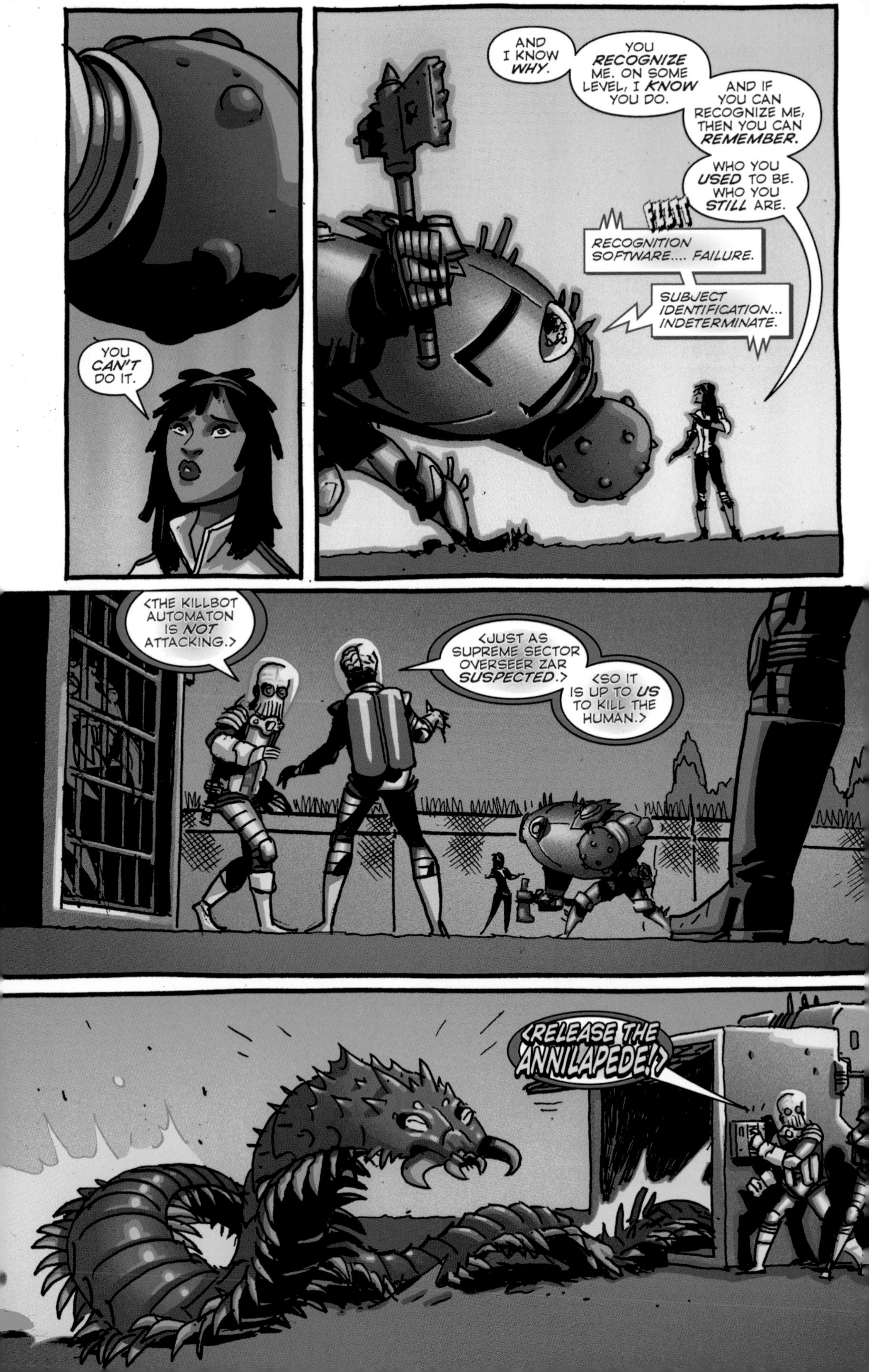
YOU CAN'T DO IT.
AND I KNOW WHY.
YOU RECOGNIZE ME. ON SOME LEVEL, I KNOW YOU DO.
AND IF YOU CAN RECOGNIZE ME, THEN YOU CAN REMEMBER.
WHO YOU USED TO BE. WHO YOU STILL ARE.
FZZTT
RECOGNITION SOFTWARE.... FAILURE.
SUBJECT IDENTIFICATION... INDETERMINATE.
<THE KILLBOT AUTOMATON IS NOT ATTACKING.>
<JUST AS SUPREME SECTOR OVERSEER ZAR SUSPECTED.>
<SO IT IS UP TO US TO KILL THE HUMAN.>
<RELEASE THE ANNILAPEDE!>

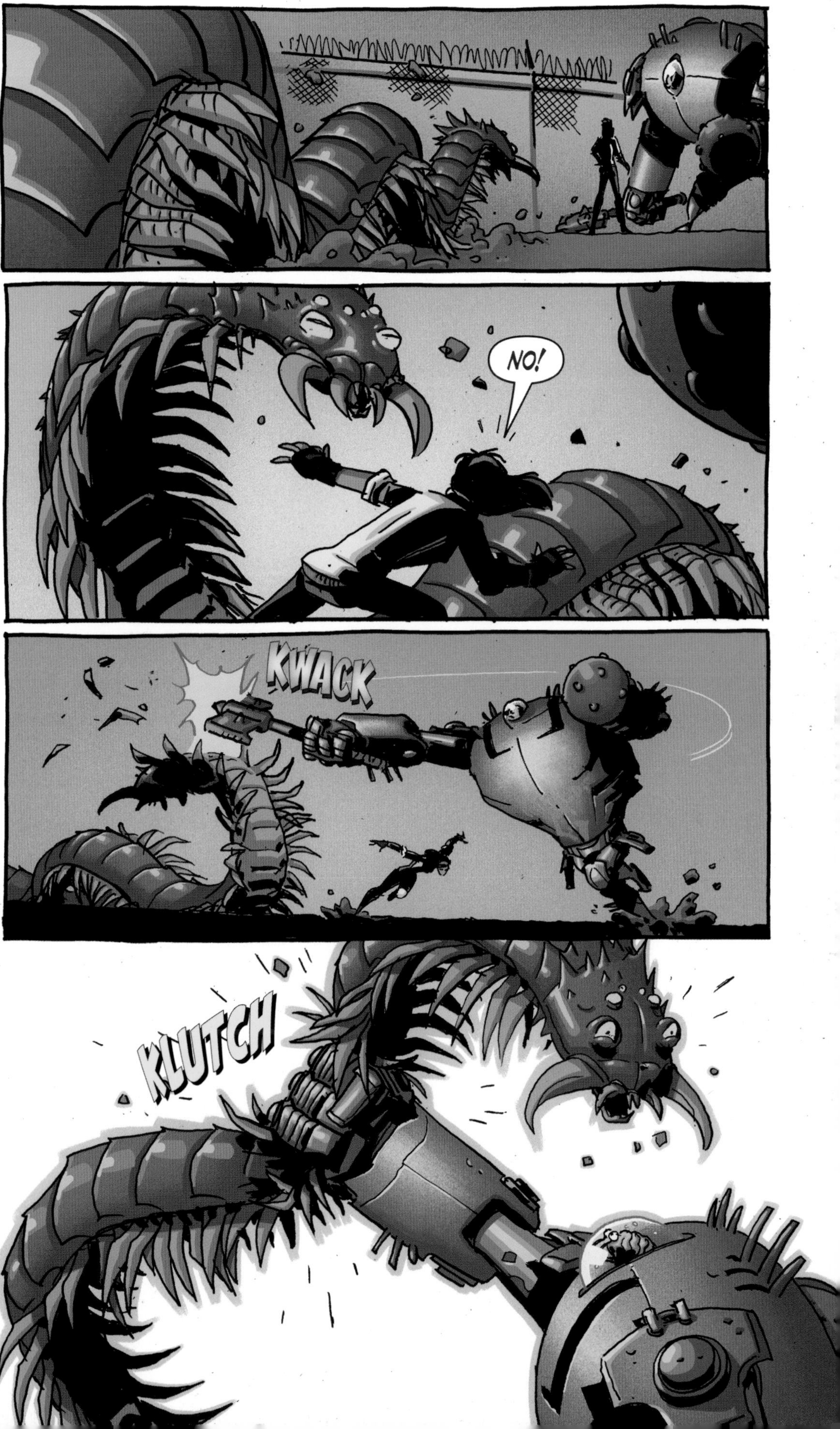
NO!
KWACK
KLUTCH

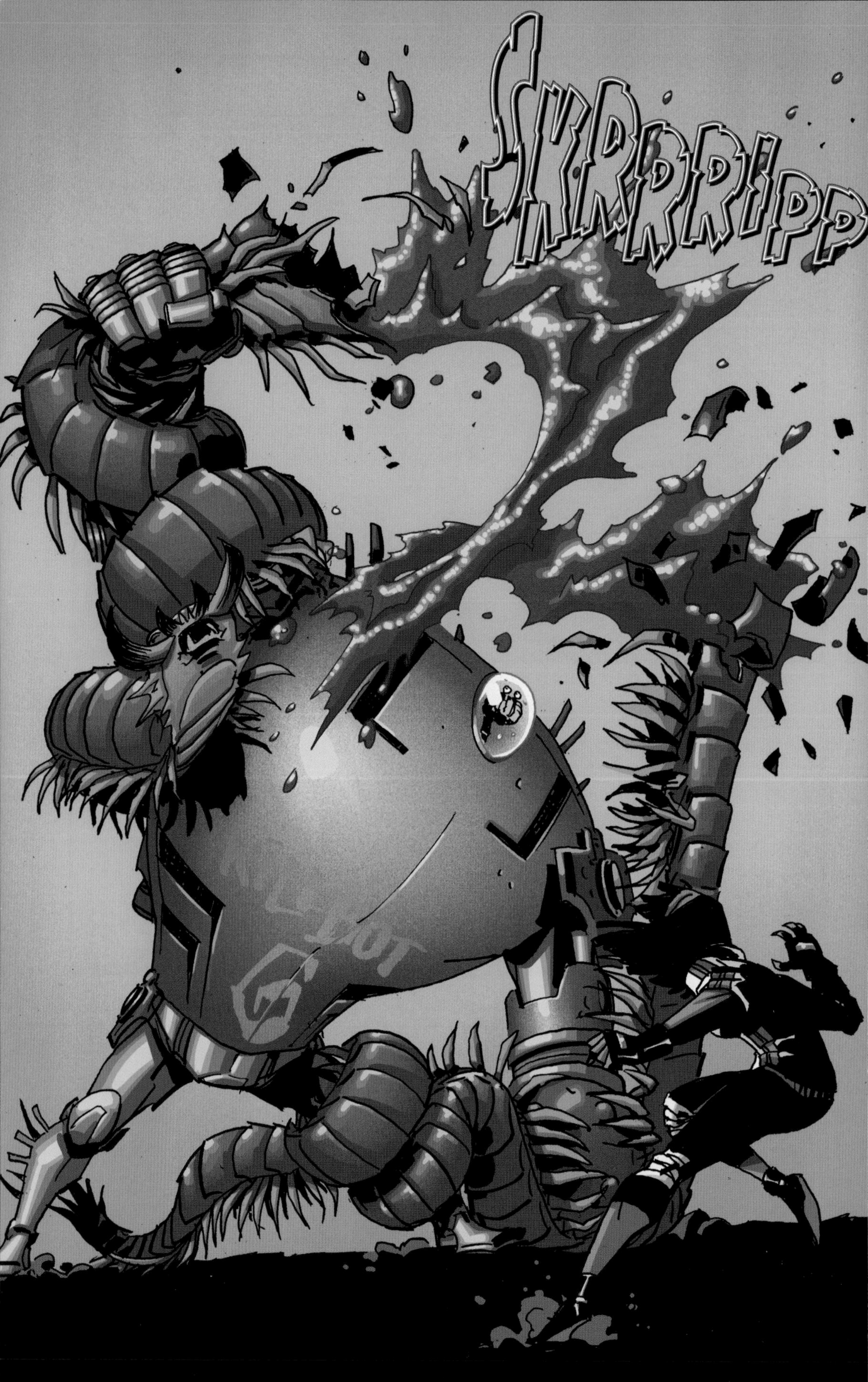
SKRRRIPP

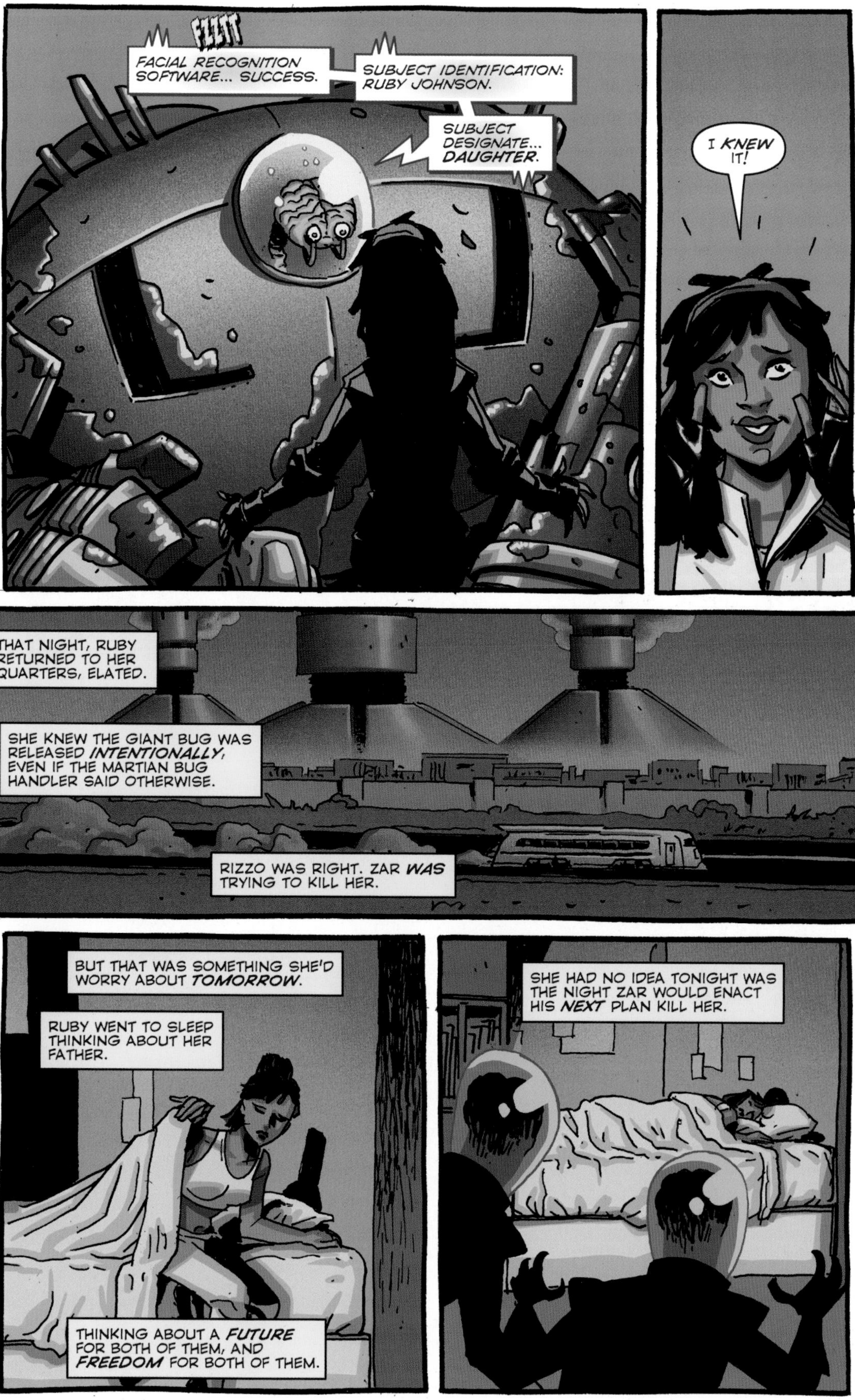
FZZZT
FACIAL RECOGNITION SOFTWARE... SUCCESS.
SUBJECT IDENTIFICATION: RUBY JOHNSON.
SUBJECT DESIGNATE... DAUGHTER.
I KNEW IT!
THAT NIGHT, RUBY RETURNED TO HER QUARTERS, ELATED.
SHE KNEW THE GIANT BUG WAS RELEASED INTENTIONALLY, EVEN IF THE MARTIAN BUG HANDLER SAID OTHERWISE.
RIZZO WAS RIGHT. ZAR WAS TRYING TO KILL HER.
BUT THAT WAS SOMETHING SHE'D WORRY ABOUT TOMORROW.
RUBY WENT TO SLEEP THINKING ABOUT HER FATHER.
THINKING ABOUT A FUTURE FOR BOTH OF THEM, AND FREEDOM FOR BOTH OF THEM.
SHE HAD NO IDEA TONIGHT WAS THE NIGHT ZAR WOULD ENACT HIS NEXT PLAN KILL HER.

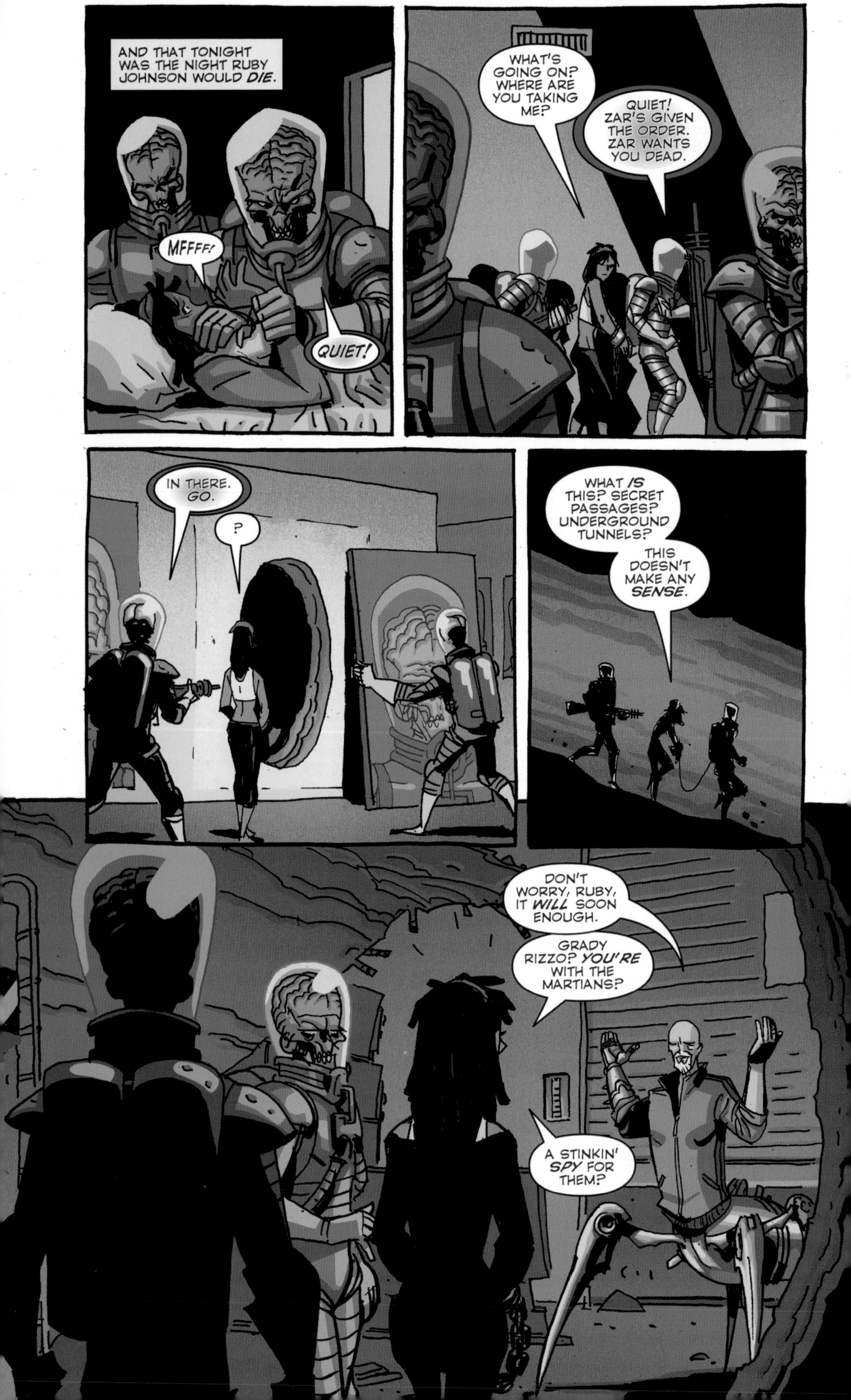

AND THAT TONIGHT WAS THE NIGHT RUBY JOHNSON WOULD *DIE*.
MFFFF!
QUIET!
WHAT'S GOING ON? WHERE ARE YOU TAKING ME?
QUIET! ZAR'S GIVEN THE ORDER. ZAR WANTS YOU DEAD.
IN THERE. *GO*.
?
WHAT *IS* THIS? SECRET PASSAGES? UNDERGROUND TUNNELS?
THIS DOESN'T MAKE ANY *SENSE*.
DON'T WORRY, RUBY, IT *WILL* SOON ENOUGH.
GRADY RIZZO? *YOU'RE* WITH THE MARTIANS?
A STINKIN' *SPY* FOR THEM?

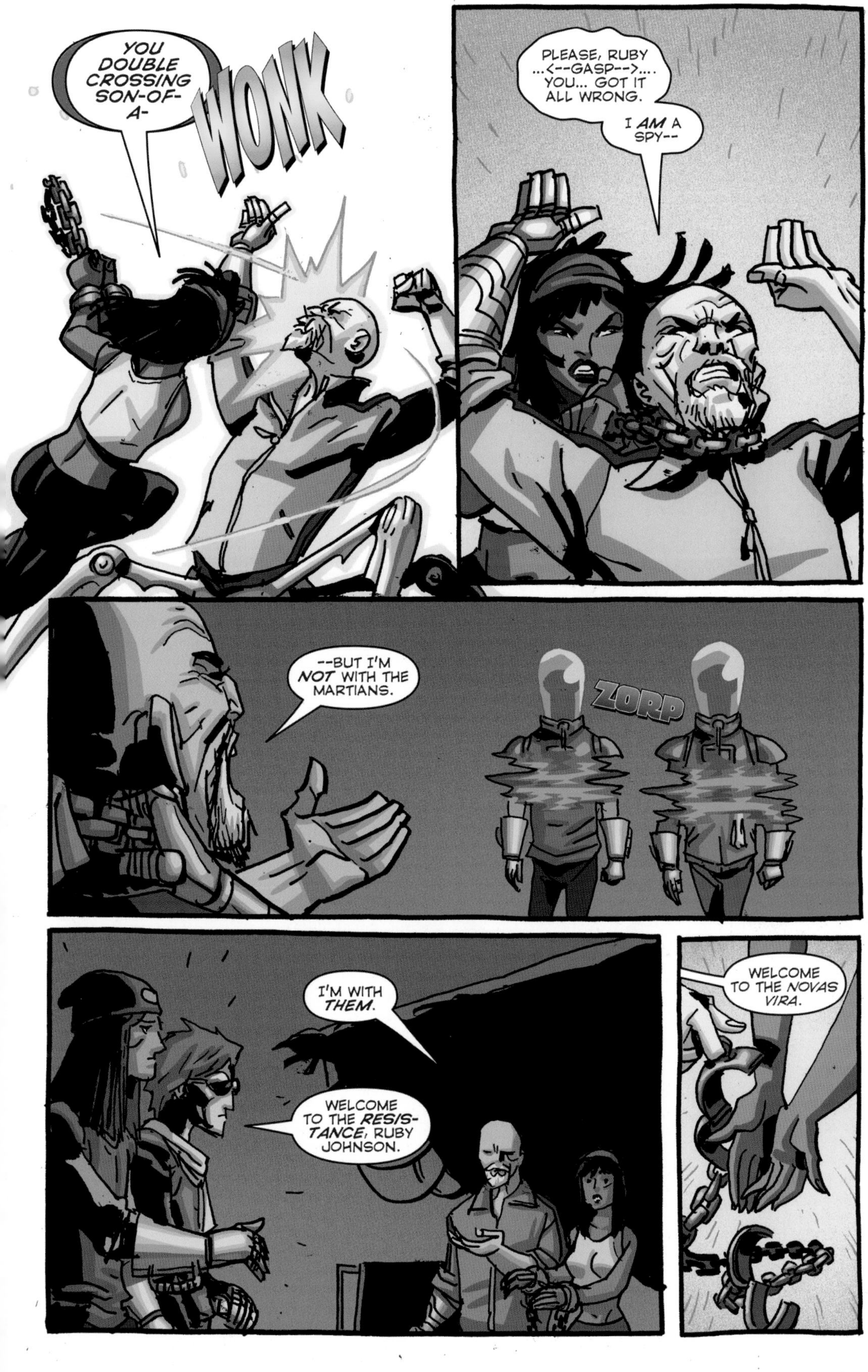

YOU DOUBLE CROSSING SON-OF-A-
WONK
PLEASE, RUBY ...<--GASP-->.... YOU... GOT IT ALL WRONG.
I AM A SPY--
--BUT I'M NOT WITH THE MARTIANS.
ZORP
I'M WITH THEM.
WELCOME TO THE RESISTANCE, RUBY JOHNSON.
WELCOME TO THE NOVAS VIRA.

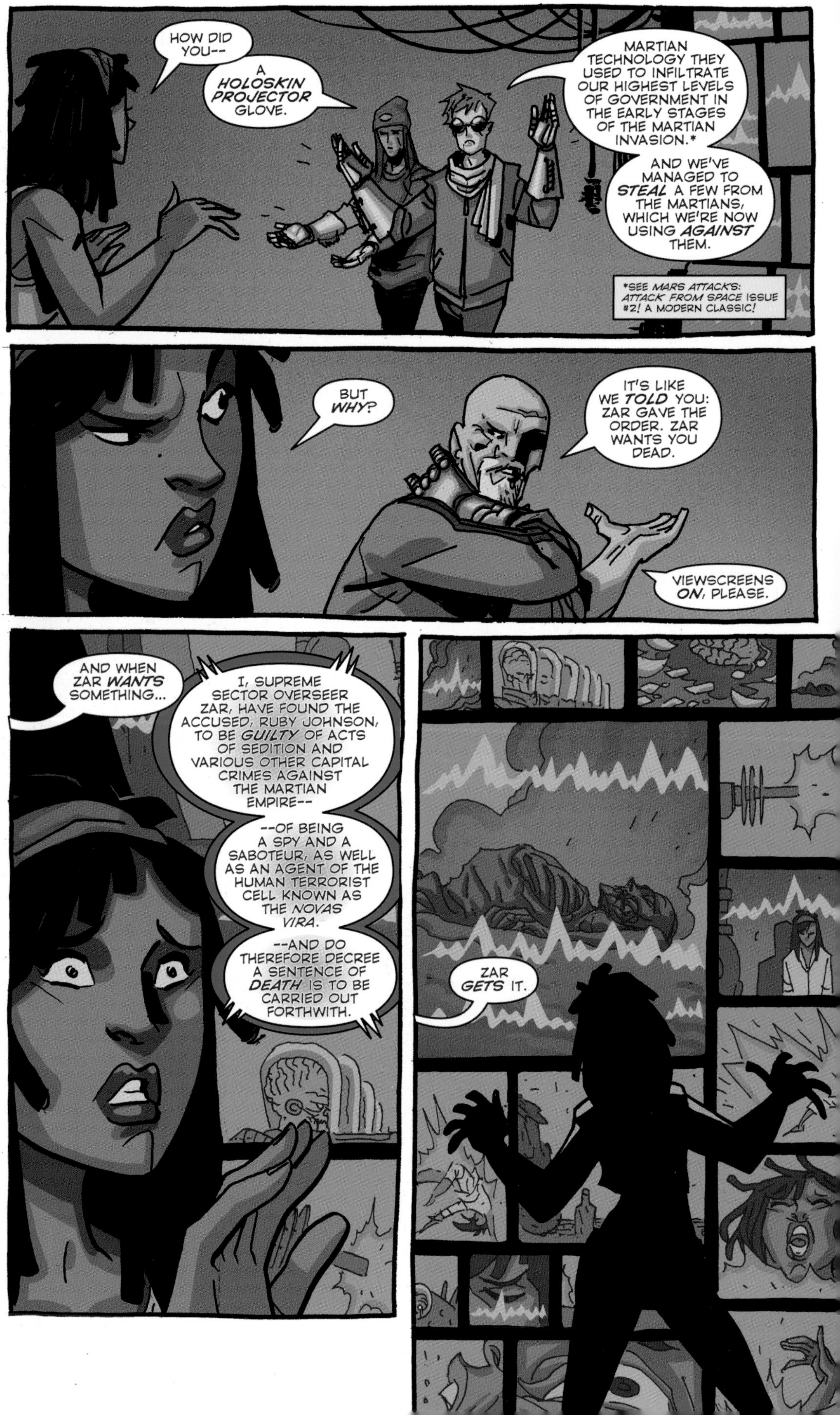
HOW DID YOU--
A HOLOSKIN PROJECTOR GLOVE.
MARTIAN TECHNOLOGY THEY USED TO INFILTRATE OUR HIGHEST LEVELS OF GOVERNMENT IN THE EARLY STAGES OF THE MARTIAN INVASION.*
AND WE'VE MANAGED TO STEAL A FEW FROM THE MARTIANS, WHICH WE'RE NOW USING AGAINST THEM.
*SEE MARS ATTACKS: ATTACK FROM SPACE ISSUE #2! A MODERN CLASSIC!
BUT WHY?
IT'S LIKE WE TOLD YOU: ZAR GAVE THE ORDER. ZAR WANTS YOU DEAD.
VIEWSCREENS ON, PLEASE.
AND WHEN ZAR WANTS SOMETHING...
I, SUPREME SECTOR OVERSEER ZAR, HAVE FOUND THE ACCUSED, RUBY JOHNSON, TO BE GUILTY OF ACTS OF SEDITION AND VARIOUS OTHER CAPITAL CRIMES AGAINST THE MARTIAN EMPIRE--
--OF BEING A SPY AND A SABOTEUR, AS WELL AS AN AGENT OF THE HUMAN TERRORIST CELL KNOWN AS THE NOVAS VIRA.
--AND DO THEREFORE DECREE A SENTENCE OF DEATH IS TO BE CARRIED OUT FORTHWITH.
ZAR GETS IT.

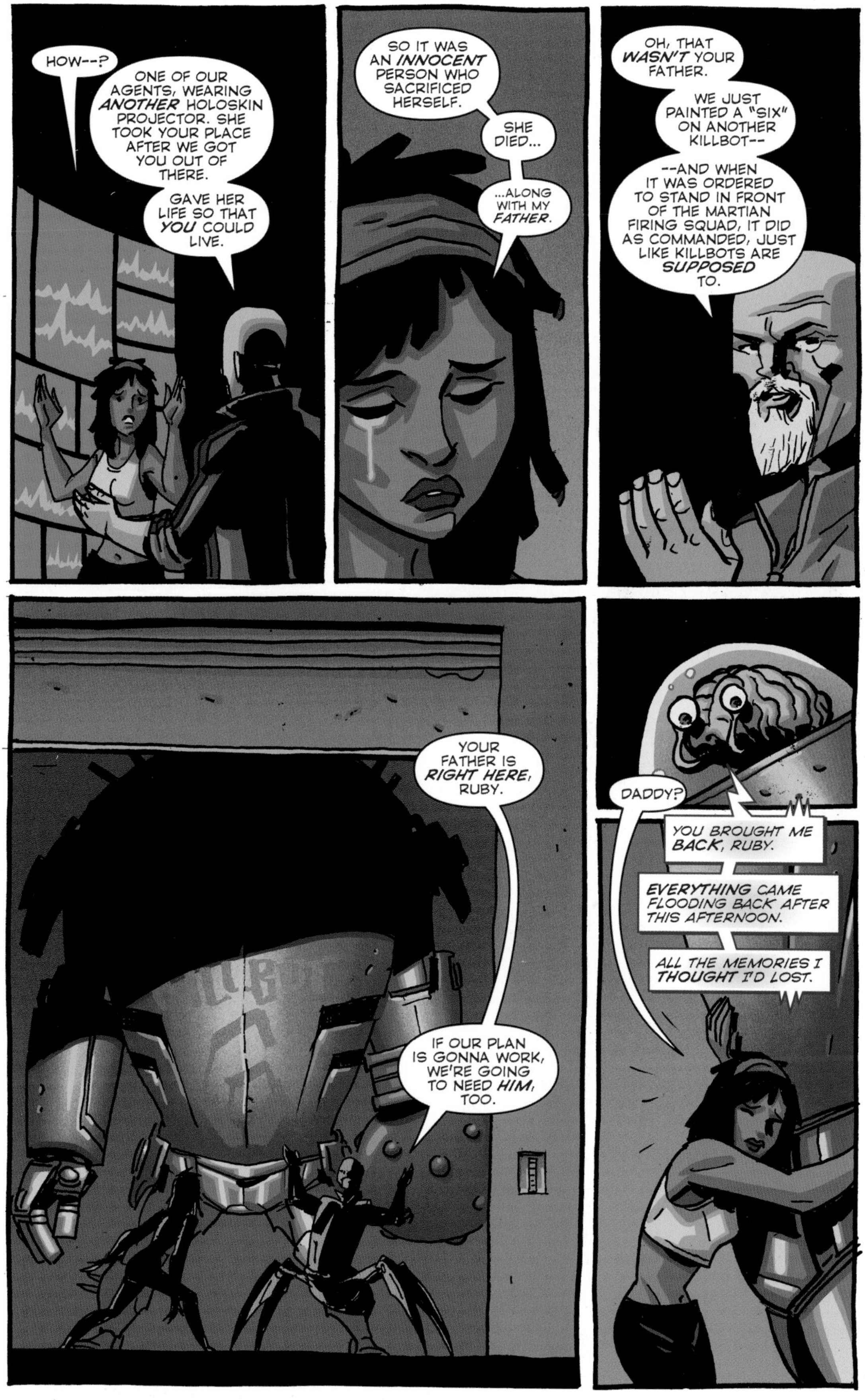

HOW--?
ONE OF OUR AGENTS, WEARING ANOTHER HOLOSKIN PROJECTOR. SHE TOOK YOUR PLACE AFTER WE GOT YOU OUT OF THERE.
GAVE HER LIFE SO THAT YOU COULD LIVE.
SO IT WAS AN INNOCENT PERSON WHO SACRIFICED HERSELF.
SHE DIED...
...ALONG WITH MY FATHER.
OH, THAT WASN'T YOUR FATHER.
WE JUST PAINTED A "SIX" ON ANOTHER KILLBOT--
--AND WHEN IT WAS ORDERED TO STAND IN FRONT OF THE MARTIAN FIRING SQUAD, IT DID AS COMMANDED, JUST LIKE KILLBOTS ARE SUPPOSED TO.
YOUR FATHER IS RIGHT HERE, RUBY.
IF OUR PLAN IS GONNA WORK, WE'RE GOING TO NEED HIM, TOO.
DADDY?
YOU BROUGHT ME BACK, RUBY.
EVERYTHING CAME FLOODING BACK AFTER THIS AFTERNOON.
ALL THE MEMORIES I THOUGHT I'D LOST.

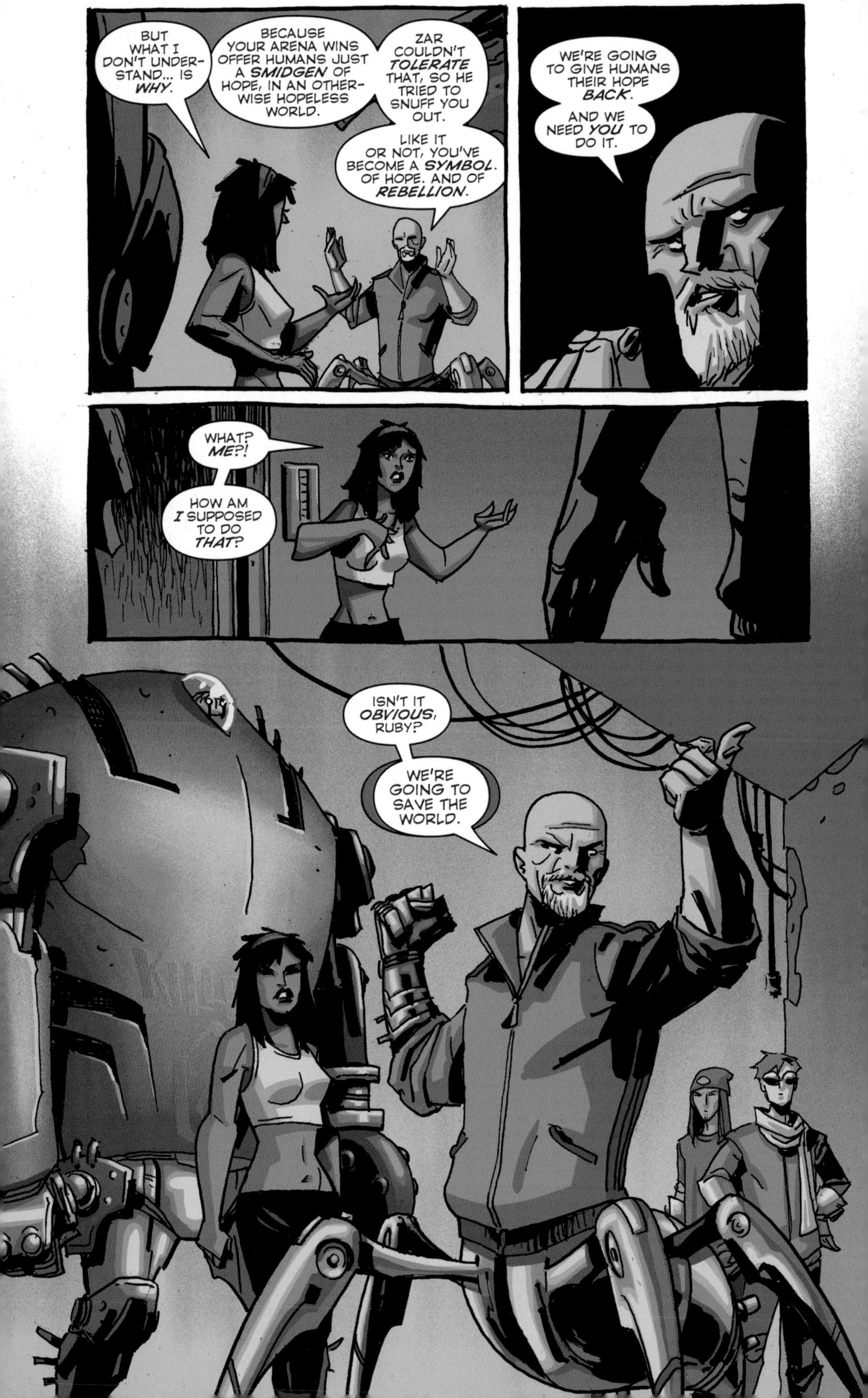

BUT WHAT I DON'T UNDERSTAND... IS WHY.
BECAUSE YOUR ARENA WINS OFFER HUMANS JUST A SMIDGEN OF HOPE, IN AN OTHERWISE HOPELESS WORLD.
ZAR COULDN'T TOLERATE THAT, SO HE TRIED TO SNUFF YOU OUT.
LIKE IT OR NOT, YOU'VE BECOME A SYMBOL. OF HOPE. AND OF REBELLION.
WE'RE GOING TO GIVE HUMANS THEIR HOPE BACK.
AND WE NEED YOU TO DO IT.
WHAT? ME?!
HOW AM I SUPPOSED TO DO THAT?
ISN'T IT OBVIOUS, RUBY?
WE'RE GOING TO SAVE THE WORLD.

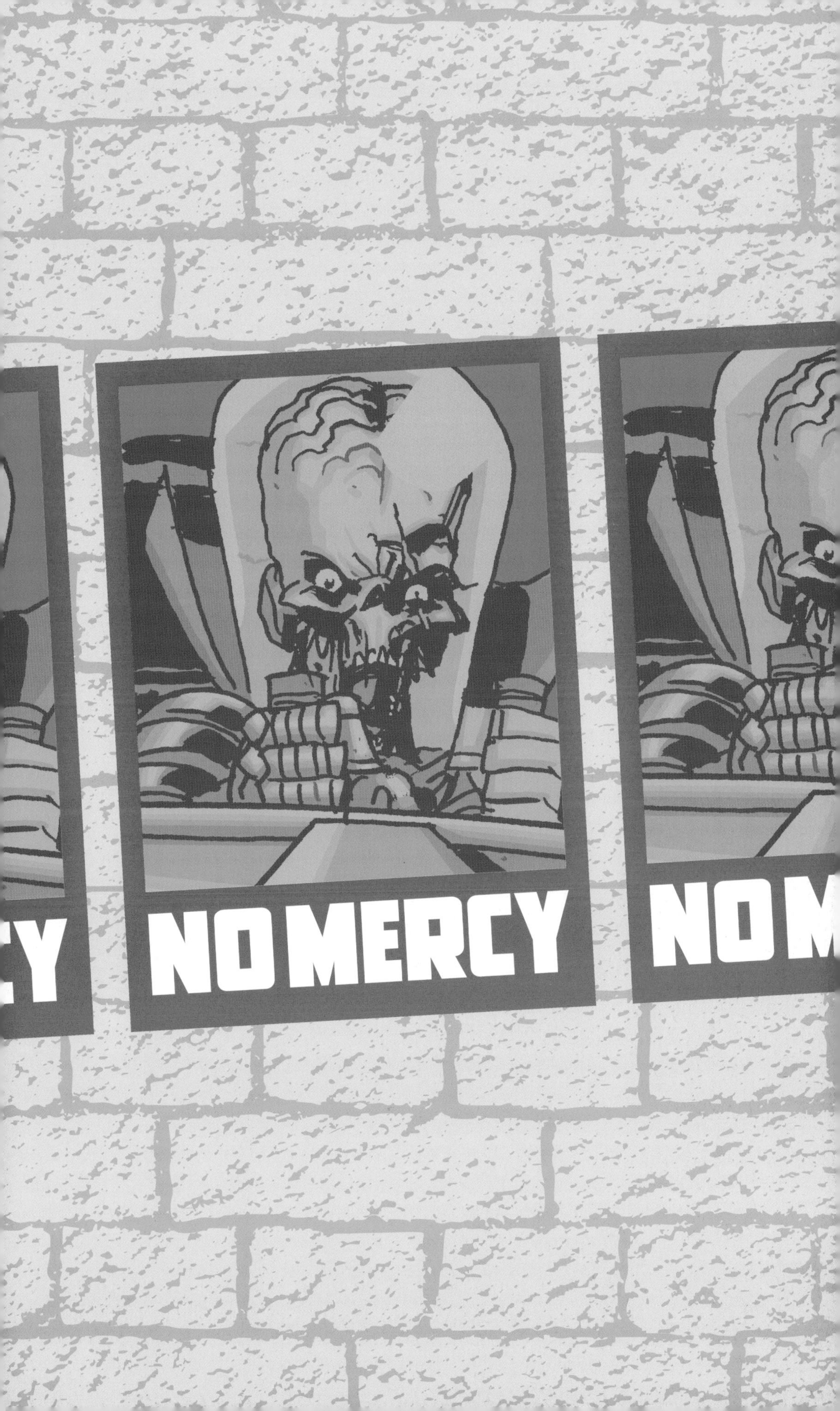
NO MERCY

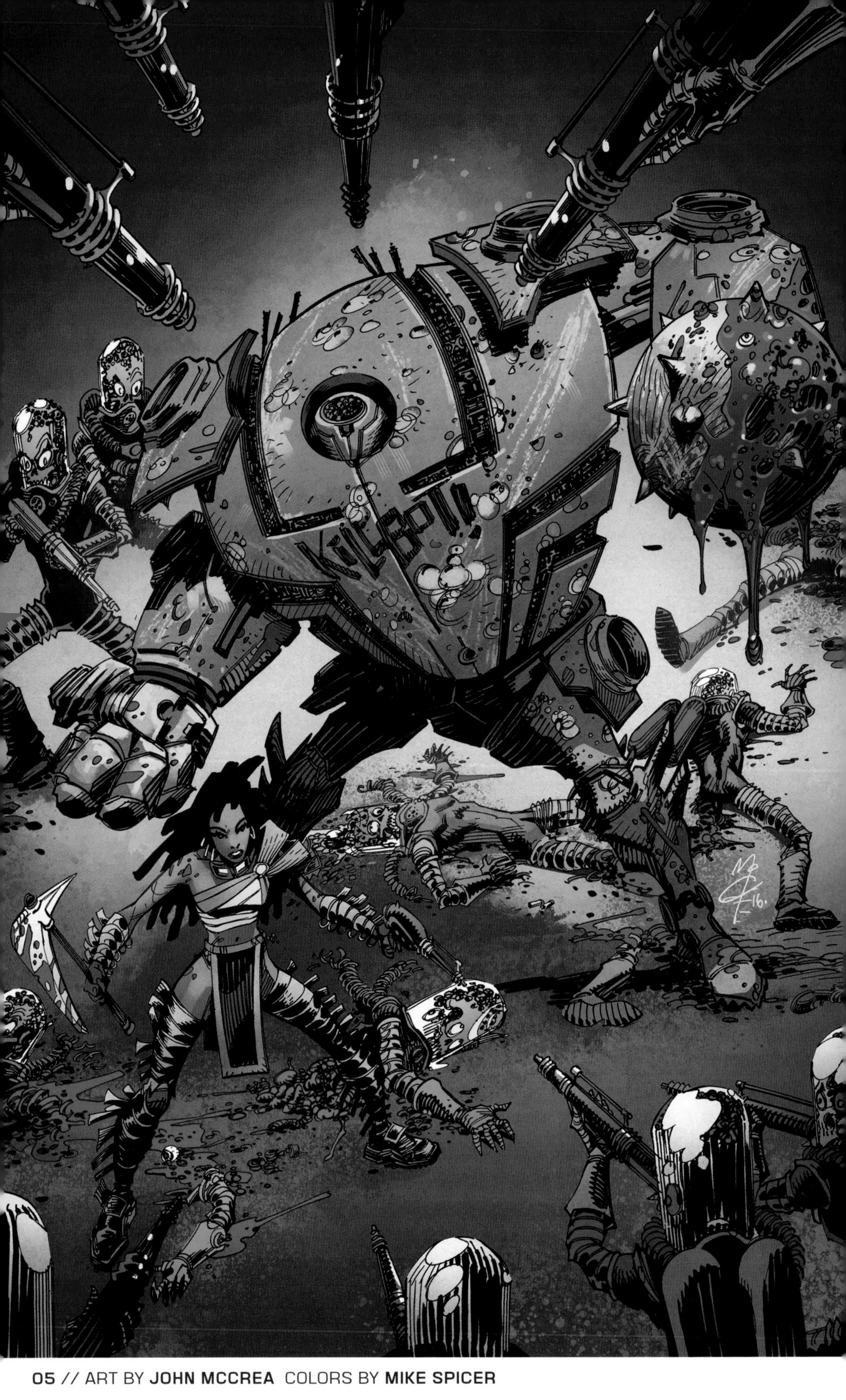
KILLBOT

05 // ART BY **JOHN MCCREA** COLORS BY **MIKE SPICER**

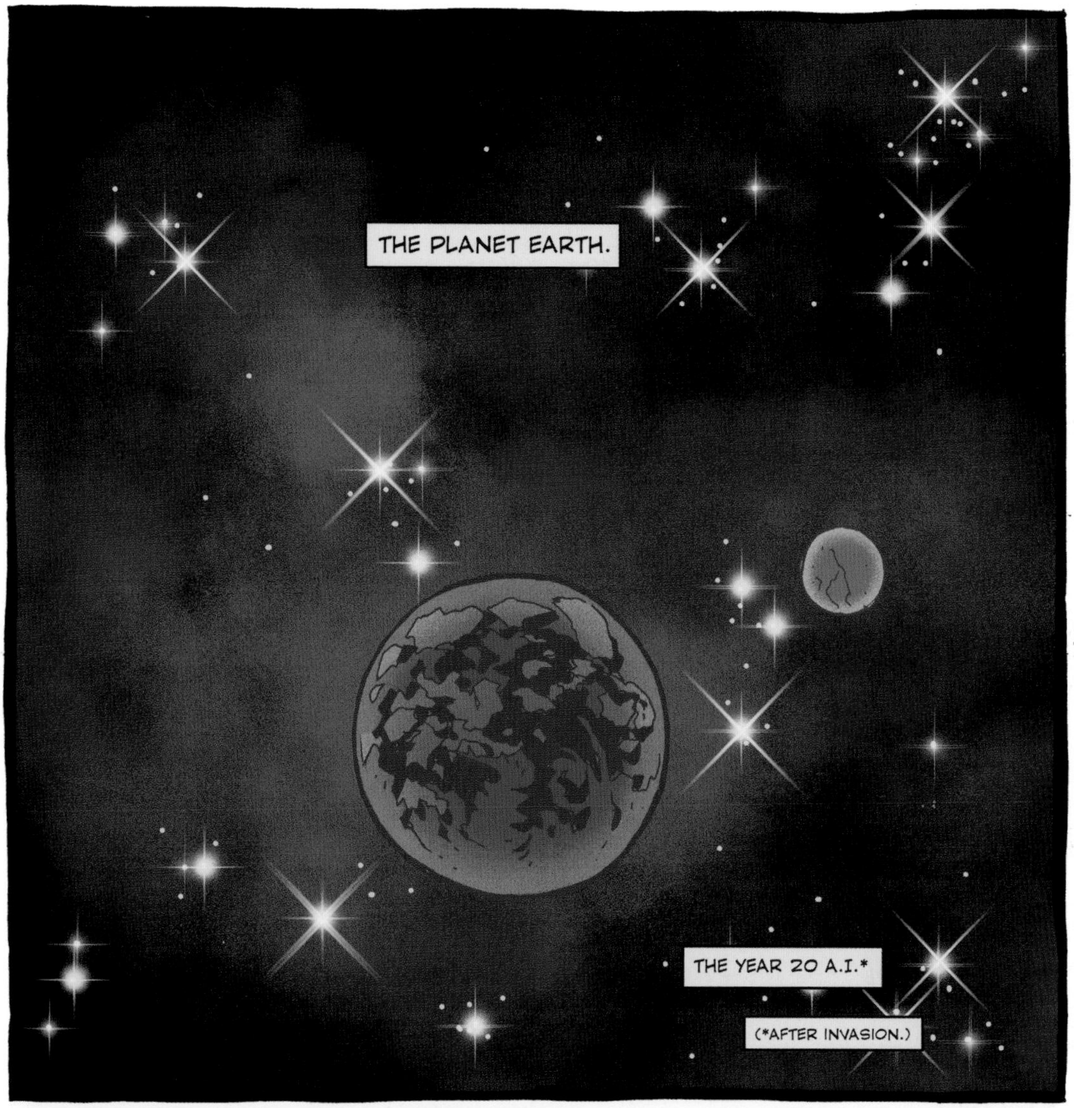
THE PLANET EARTH.
THE YEAR 20 A.I.*
(*AFTER INVASION.)

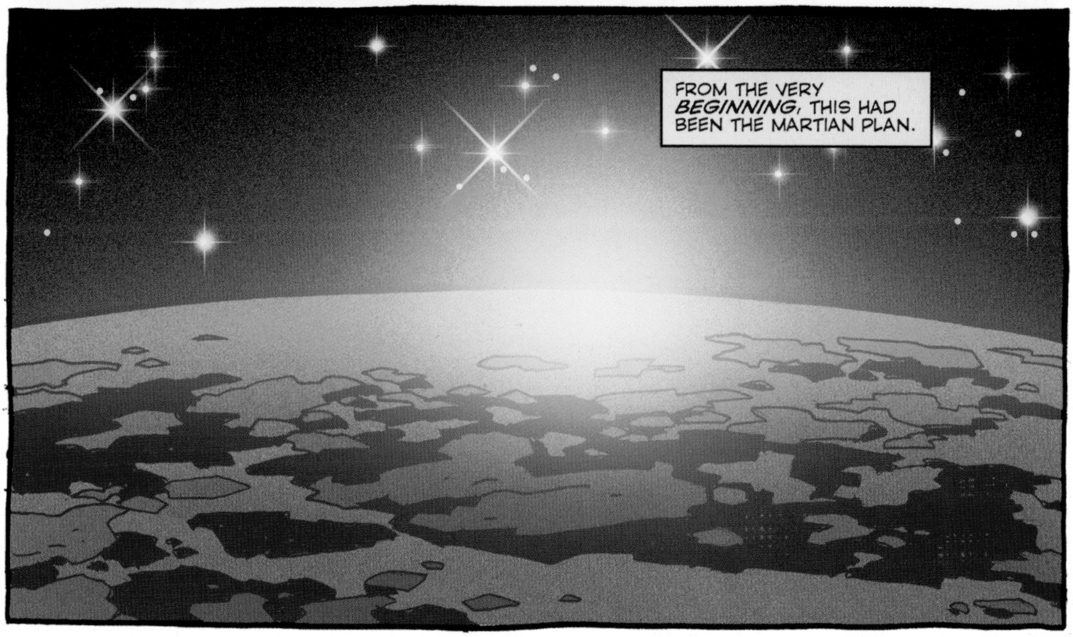
FROM THE VERY *BEGINNING,* THIS HAD BEEN THE MARTIAN PLAN.

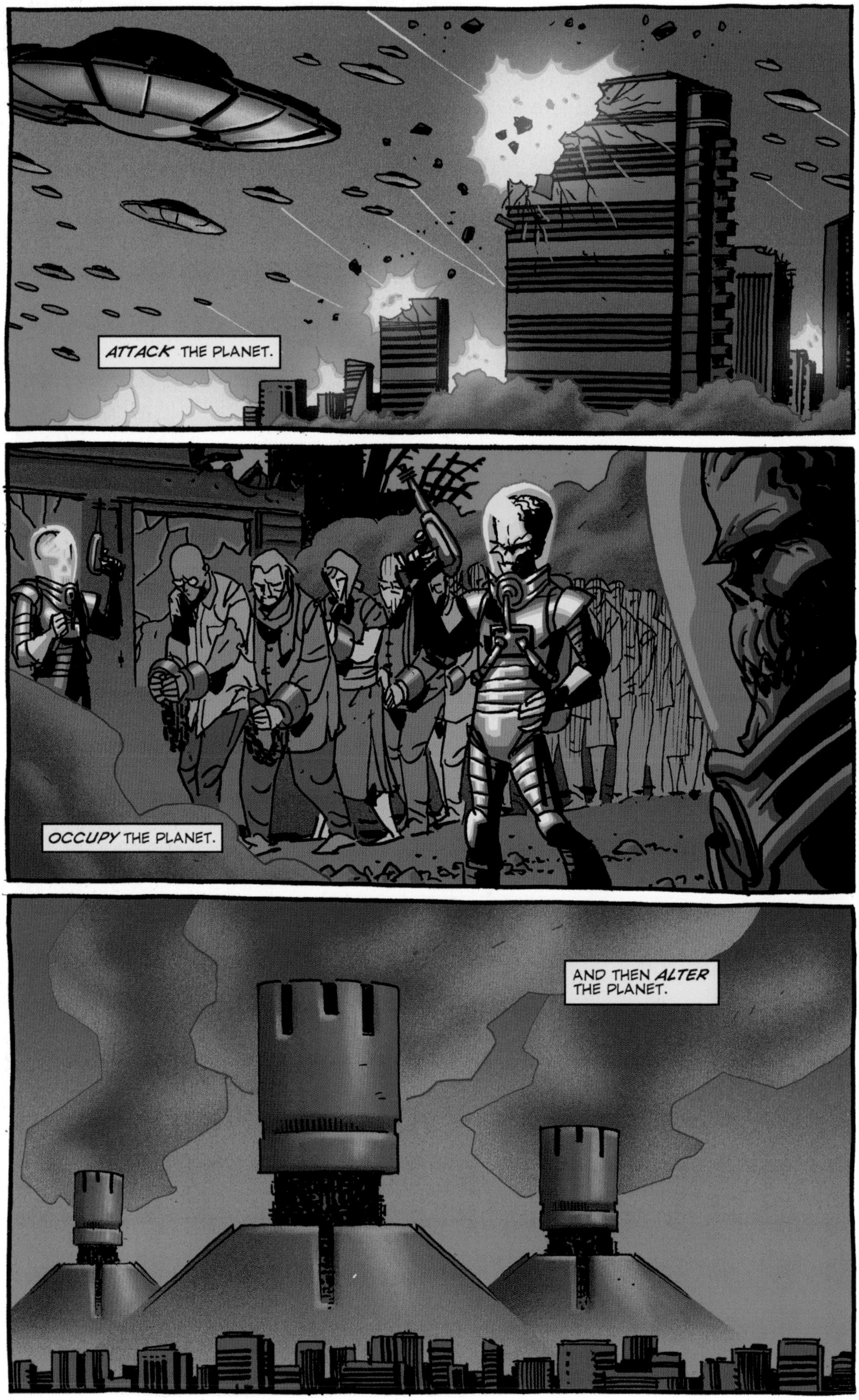
ATTACK THE PLANET.
OCCUPY THE PLANET.
AND THEN ALTER THE PLANET.

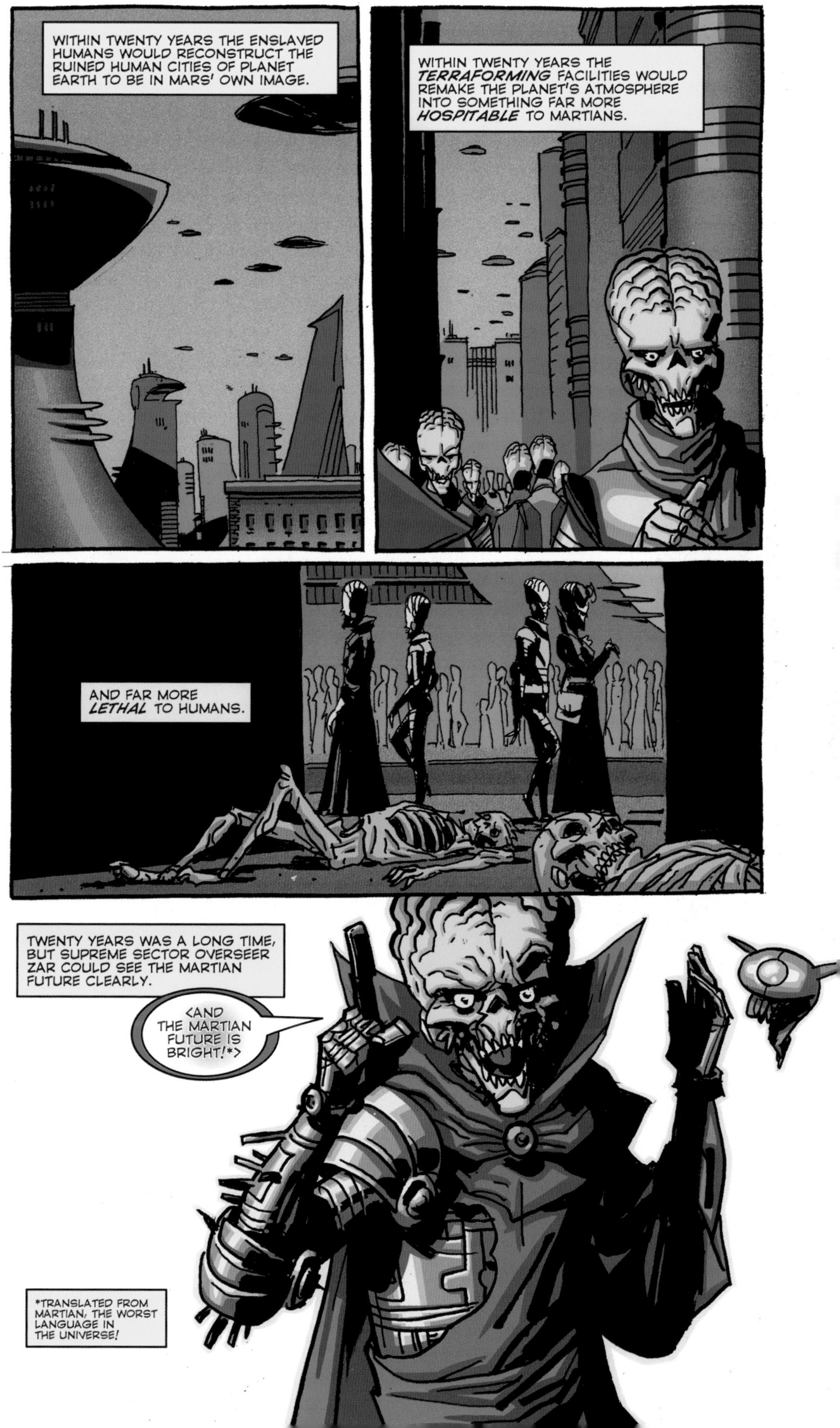
WITHIN TWENTY YEARS THE ENSLAVED HUMANS WOULD RECONSTRUCT THE RUINED HUMAN CITIES OF PLANET EARTH TO BE IN MARS' OWN IMAGE.
WITHIN TWENTY YEARS THE *TERRAFORMING* FACILITIES WOULD REMAKE THE PLANET'S ATMOSPHERE INTO SOMETHING FAR MORE *HOSPITABLE* TO MARTIANS.
AND FAR MORE *LETHAL* TO HUMANS.
TWENTY YEARS WAS A LONG TIME, BUT SUPREME SECTOR OVERSEER ZAR COULD SEE THE MARTIAN FUTURE CLEARLY.
<AND THE MARTIAN FUTURE IS BRIGHT!*>
*TRANSLATED FROM MARTIAN, THE WORST LANGUAGE IN THE UNIVERSE!

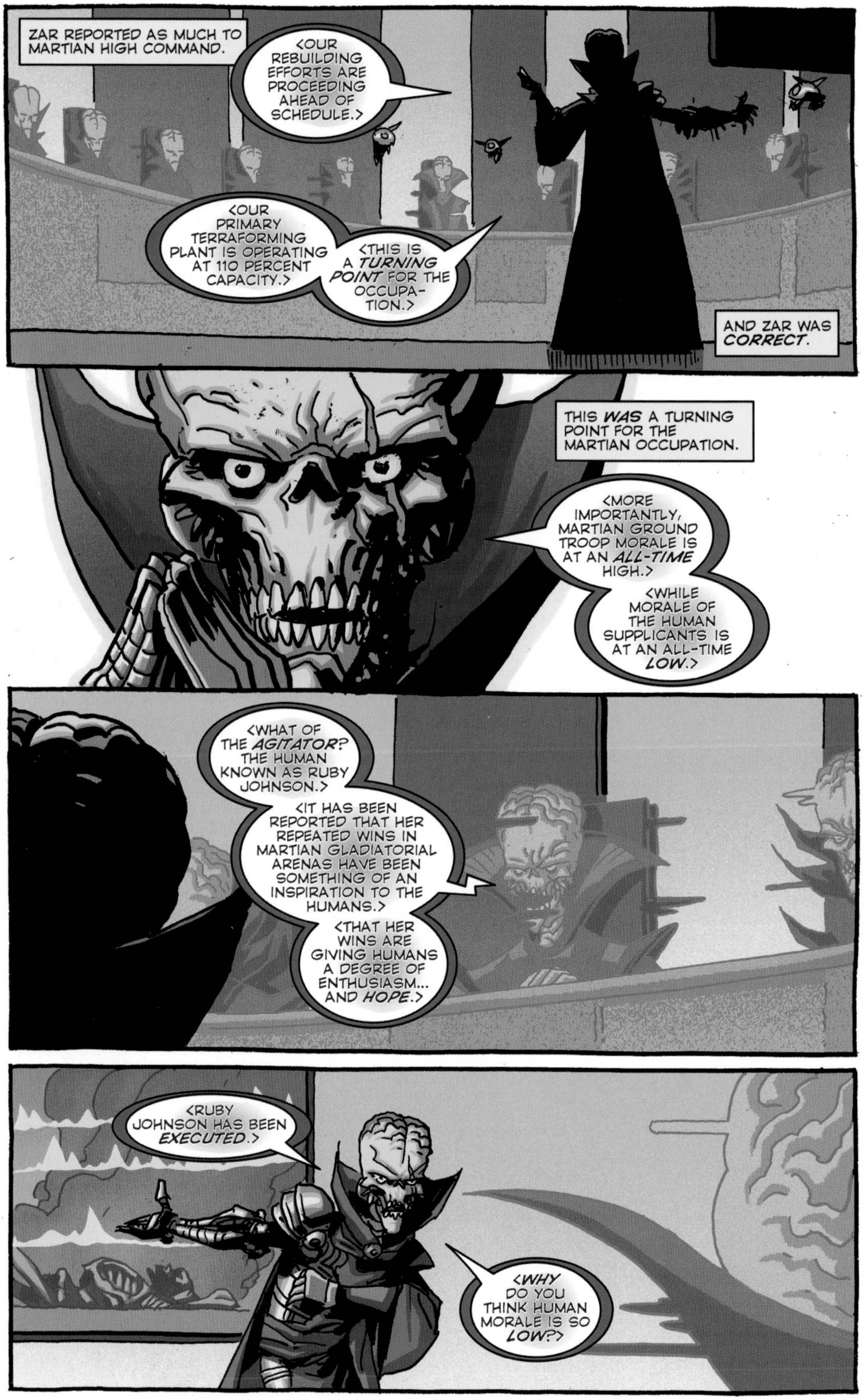
ZAR REPORTED AS MUCH TO MARTIAN HIGH COMMAND.
<OUR REBUILDING EFFORTS ARE PROCEEDING AHEAD OF SCHEDULE.>
<OUR PRIMARY TERRAFORMING PLANT IS OPERATING AT 110 PERCENT CAPACITY.>
<THIS IS A TURNING POINT FOR THE OCCUPATION.>
AND ZAR WAS CORRECT.
THIS WAS A TURNING POINT FOR THE MARTIAN OCCUPATION.
<MORE IMPORTANTLY, MARTIAN GROUND TROOP MORALE IS AT AN ALL-TIME HIGH.>
<WHILE MORALE OF THE HUMAN SUPPLICANTS IS AT AN ALL-TIME LOW.>
<WHAT OF THE AGITATOR? THE HUMAN KNOWN AS RUBY JOHNSON.>
<IT HAS BEEN REPORTED THAT HER REPEATED WINS IN MARTIAN GLADIATORIAL ARENAS HAVE BEEN SOMETHING OF AN INSPIRATION TO THE HUMANS.>
<THAT HER WINS ARE GIVING HUMANS A DEGREE OF ENTHUSIASM... AND HOPE.>
<RUBY JOHNSON HAS BEEN EXECUTED.>
<WHY DO YOU THINK HUMAN MORALE IS SO LOW?>

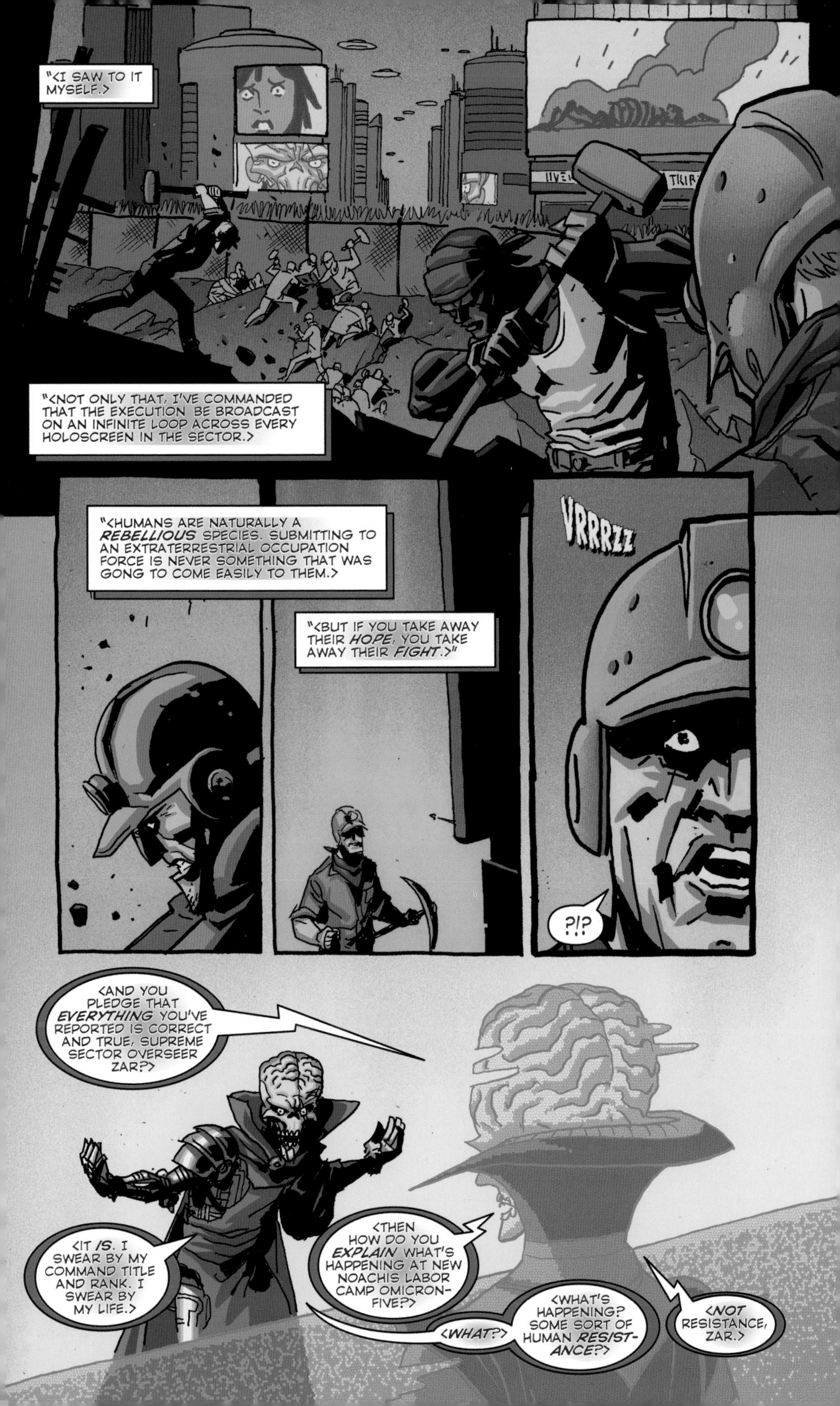
"<I SAW TO IT MYSELF.>
"<NOT ONLY THAT, I'VE COMMANDED THAT THE EXECUTION BE BROADCAST ON AN INFINITE LOOP ACROSS EVERY HOLOSCREEN IN THE SECTOR.>
"<HUMANS ARE NATURALLY A *REBELLIOUS* SPECIES. SUBMITTING TO AN EXTRATERRESTRIAL OCCUPATION FORCE IS NEVER SOMETHING THAT WAS GONG TO COME EASILY TO THEM.>
"<BUT IF YOU TAKE AWAY THEIR *HOPE*, YOU TAKE AWAY THEIR *FIGHT*.>"
VRRRZZ
?!?
<AND YOU PLEDGE THAT *EVERYTHING* YOU'VE REPORTED IS CORRECT AND TRUE, SUPREME SECTOR OVERSEER ZAR?>
<IT *IS*. I SWEAR BY MY COMMAND TITLE AND RANK. I SWEAR BY MY LIFE.>
<THEN HOW DO YOU *EXPLAIN* WHAT'S HAPPENING AT NEW NOACHIS LABOR CAMP OMICRON-FIVE?>
<*WHAT*?>
<WHAT'S HAPPENING? SOME SORT OF HUMAN *RESIST-ANCE*?>
<*NOT* RESISTANCE, ZAR.>

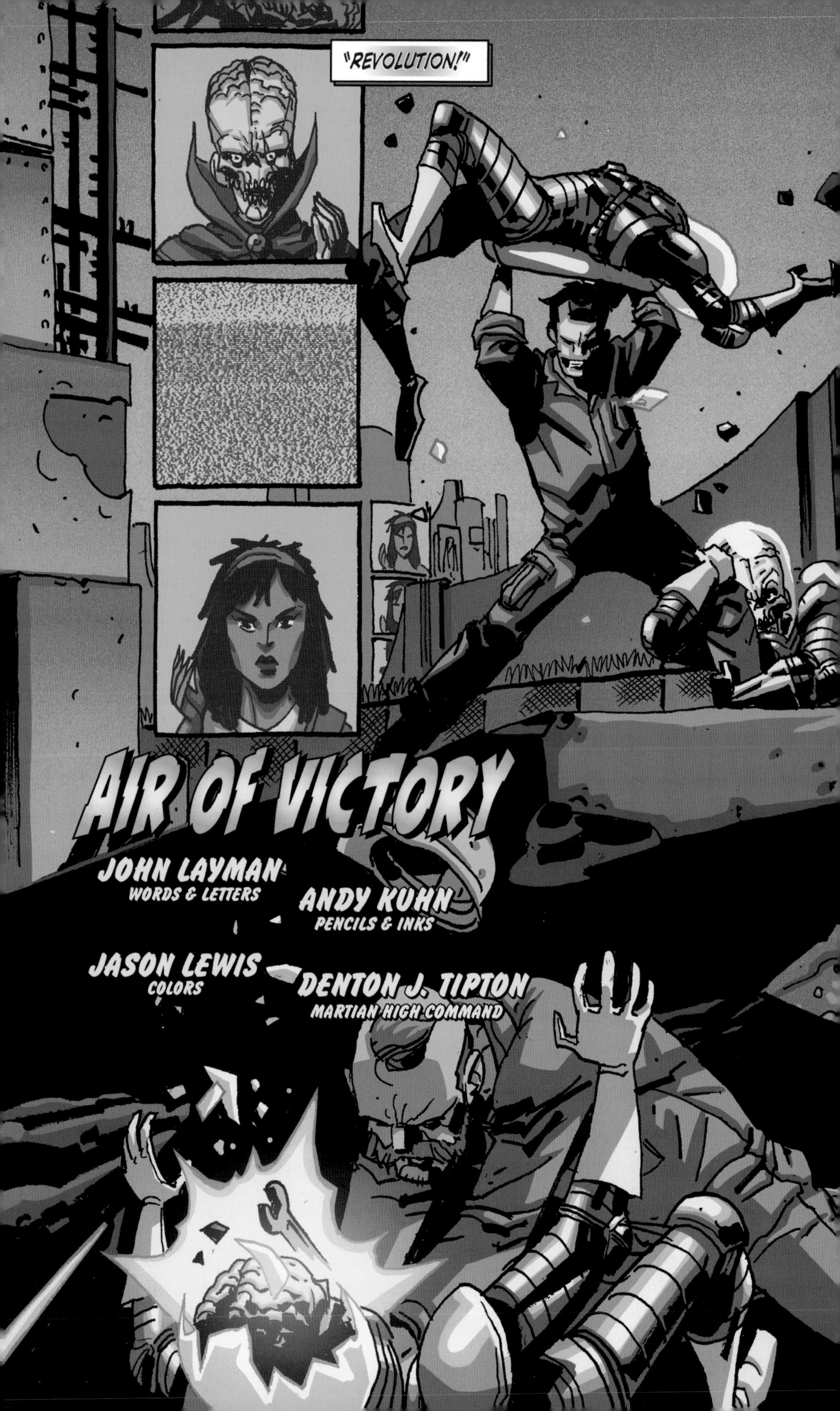
"REVOLUTION!"
AIR OF VICTORY
JOHN LAYMAN
WORDS & LETTERS
ANDY KUHN
PENCILS & INKS
JASON LEWIS
COLORS
DENTON J. TIPTON
MARTIAN HIGH COMMAND

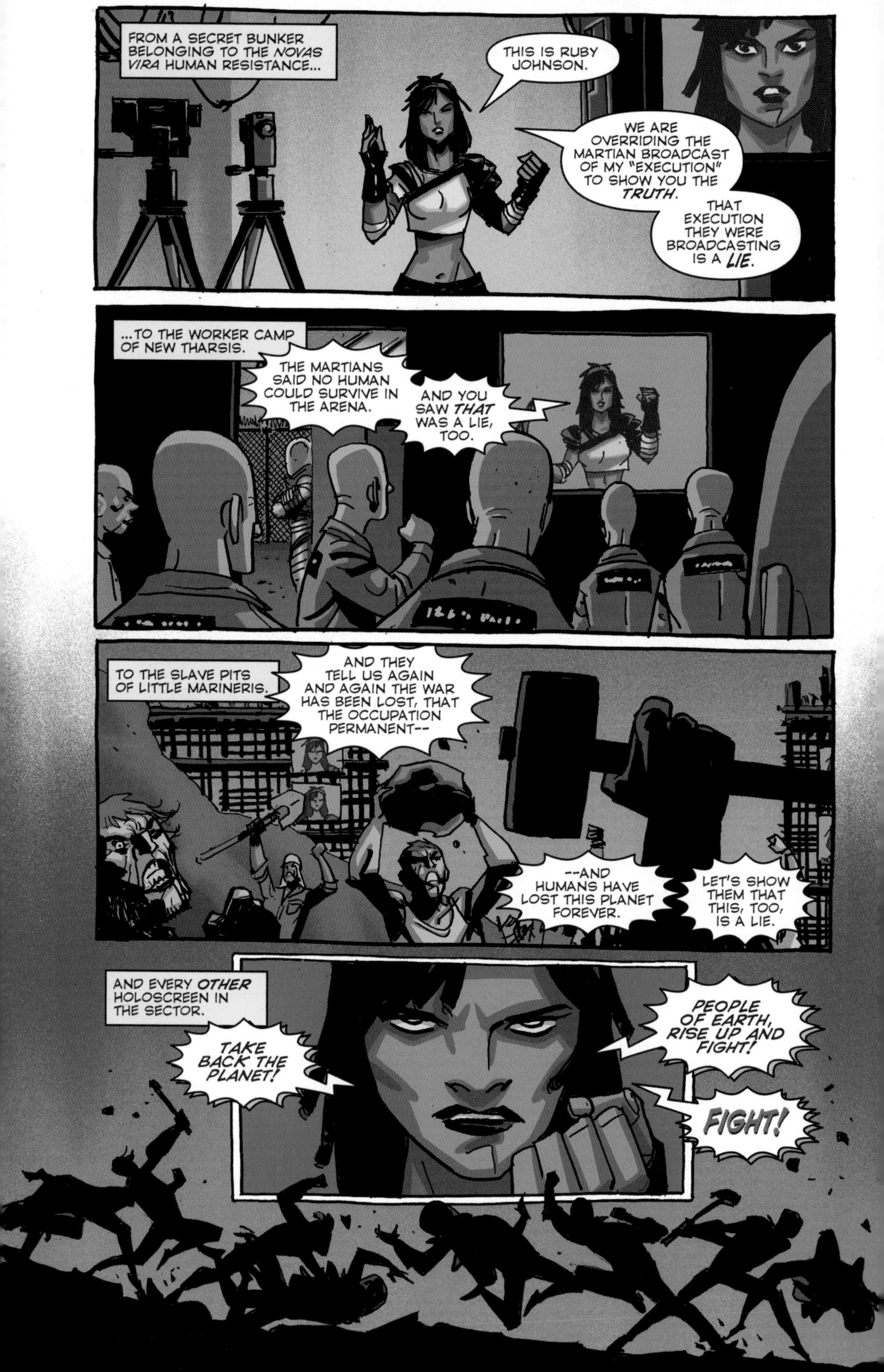
FROM A SECRET BUNKER BELONGING TO THE NOVAS VIRA HUMAN RESISTANCE...
THIS IS RUBY JOHNSON.
WE ARE OVERRIDING THE MARTIAN BROADCAST OF MY "EXECUTION" TO SHOW YOU THE TRUTH.
THAT EXECUTION THEY WERE BROADCASTING IS A LIE.
...TO THE WORKER CAMP OF NEW THARSIS.
THE MARTIANS SAID NO HUMAN COULD SURVIVE IN THE ARENA.
AND YOU SAW THAT WAS A LIE, TOO.
TO THE SLAVE PITS OF LITTLE MARINERIS.
AND THEY TELL US AGAIN AND AGAIN THE WAR HAS BEEN LOST, THAT THE OCCUPATION PERMANENT--
--AND HUMANS HAVE LOST THIS PLANET FOREVER.
LET'S SHOW THEM THAT THIS, TOO, IS A LIE.
AND EVERY OTHER HOLOSCREEN IN THE SECTOR.
TAKE BACK THE PLANET!
PEOPLE OF EARTH, RISE UP AND FIGHT!
FIGHT!

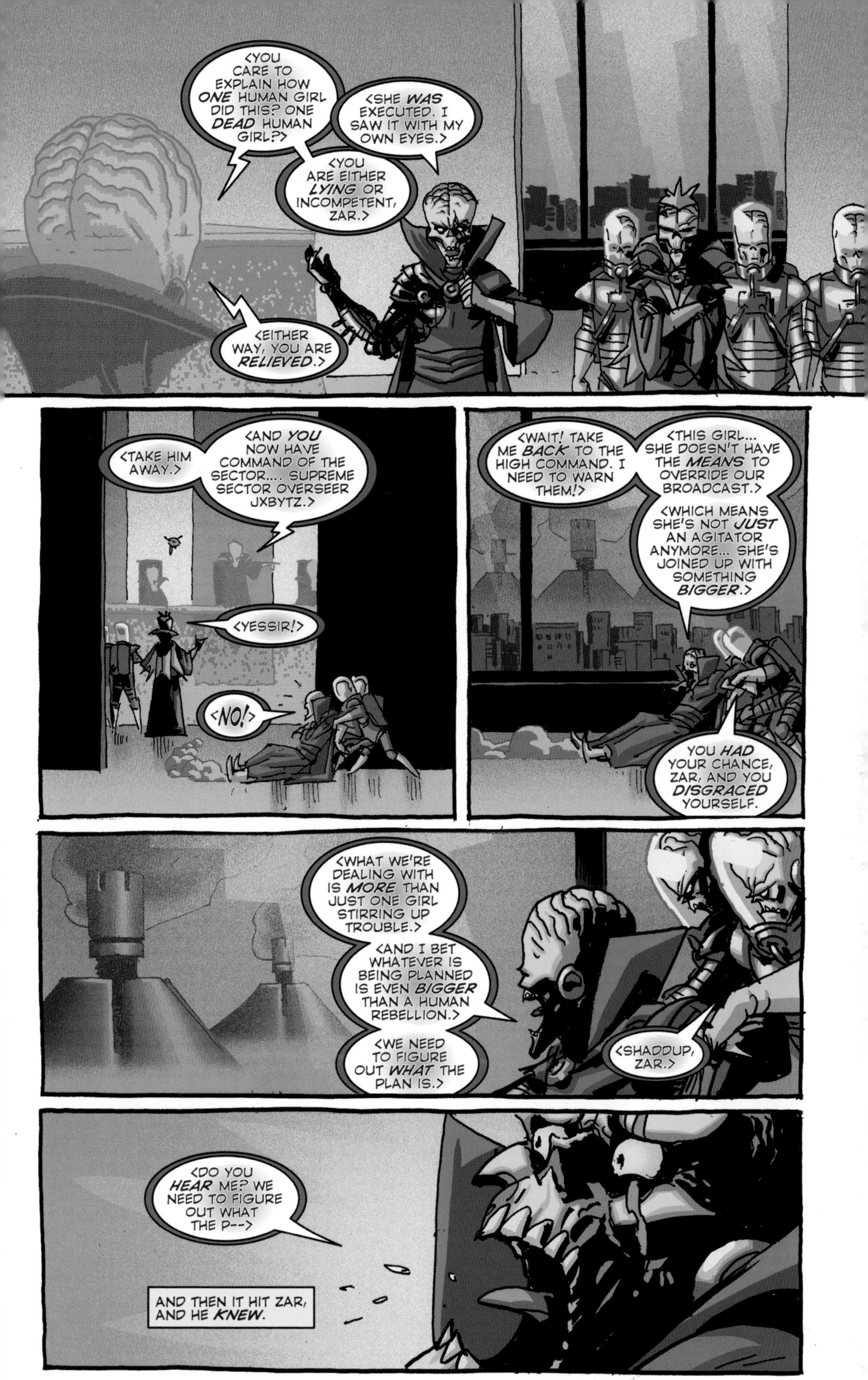
<YOU CARE TO EXPLAIN HOW *ONE* HUMAN GIRL DID THIS? ONE *DEAD* HUMAN GIRL?>
<SHE *WAS* EXECUTED. I SAW IT WITH MY OWN EYES.>
<YOU ARE EITHER *LYING* OR INCOMPETENT, ZAR.>
<EITHER WAY, YOU ARE *RELIEVED*.>
<TAKE HIM AWAY.>
<AND *YOU* NOW HAVE COMMAND OF THE SECTOR.... SUPREME SECTOR OVERSEER JXBYTZ.>
<YESSIR!>
<NO!>
<WAIT! TAKE ME *BACK* TO THE HIGH COMMAND. I NEED TO WARN THEM!>
<THIS GIRL... SHE DOESN'T HAVE THE *MEANS* TO OVERRIDE OUR BROADCAST.>
<WHICH MEANS SHE'S NOT *JUST* AN AGITATOR ANYMORE... SHE'S JOINED UP WITH SOMETHING *BIGGER*.>
YOU *HAD* YOUR CHANCE, ZAR, AND YOU *DISGRACED* YOURSELF.
<WHAT WE'RE DEALING WITH IS *MORE* THAN JUST ONE GIRL STIRRING UP TROUBLE.>
<AND I BET WHATEVER IS BEING PLANNED IS EVEN *BIGGER* THAN A HUMAN REBELLION.>
<WE NEED TO FIGURE OUT *WHAT* THE PLAN IS.>
<SHADDUP, ZAR.>
<DO YOU *HEAR* ME? WE NEED TO FIGURE OUT WHAT THE P-->
AND THEN IT HIT ZAR, AND HE *KNEW*.

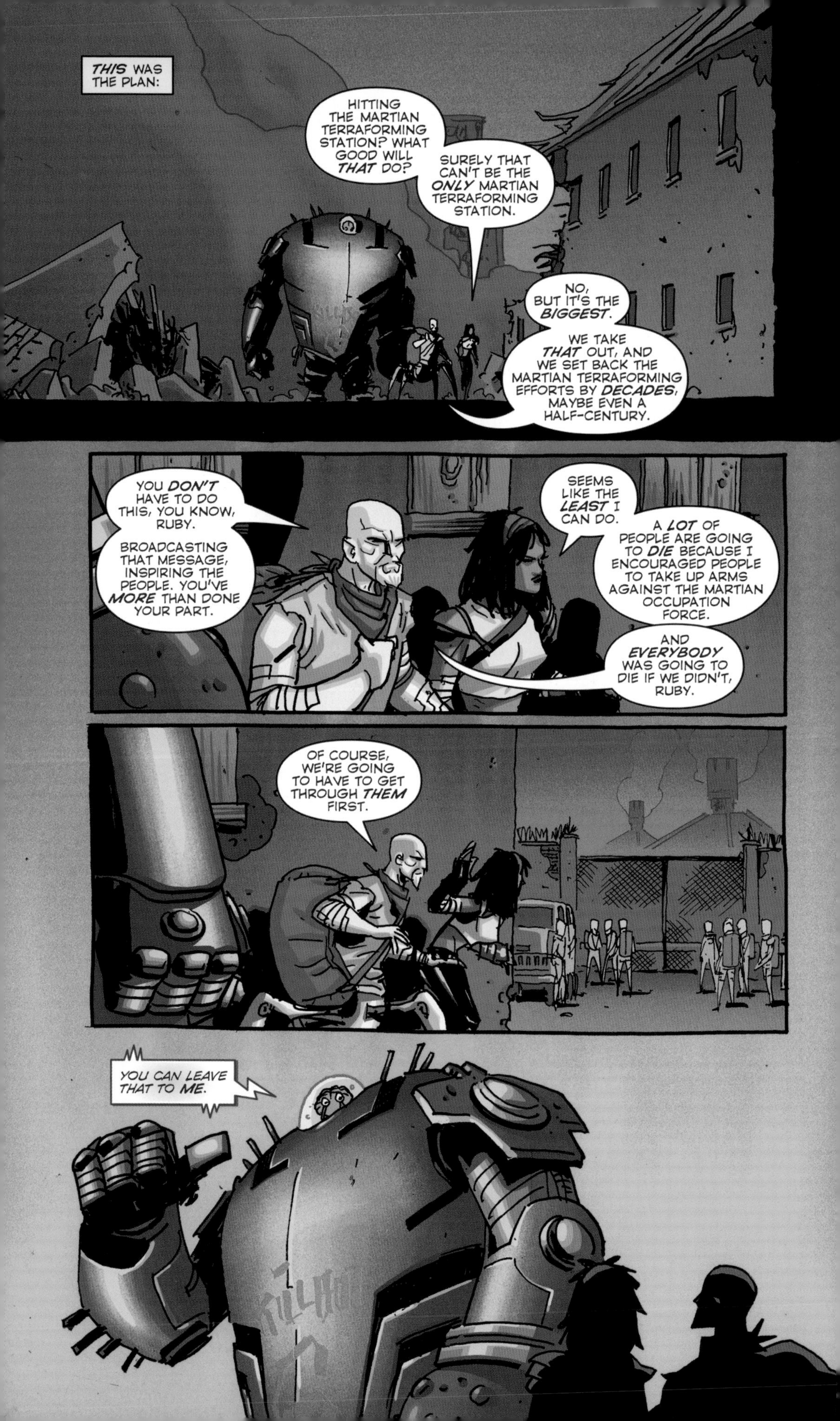
THIS WAS THE PLAN:
HITTING THE MARTIAN TERRAFORMING STATION? WHAT GOOD WILL THAT DO?
SURELY THAT CAN'T BE THE ONLY MARTIAN TERRAFORMING STATION.
NO, BUT IT'S THE BIGGEST.
WE TAKE THAT OUT, AND WE SET BACK THE MARTIAN TERRAFORMING EFFORTS BY DECADES, MAYBE EVEN A HALF-CENTURY.
YOU DON'T HAVE TO DO THIS, YOU KNOW, RUBY.
BROADCASTING THAT MESSAGE, INSPIRING THE PEOPLE. YOU'VE MORE THAN DONE YOUR PART.
SEEMS LIKE THE LEAST I CAN DO.
A LOT OF PEOPLE ARE GOING TO DIE BECAUSE I ENCOURAGED PEOPLE TO TAKE UP ARMS AGAINST THE MARTIAN OCCUPATION FORCE.
AND EVERYBODY WAS GOING TO DIE IF WE DIDN'T, RUBY.
OF COURSE, WE'RE GOING TO HAVE TO GET THROUGH THEM FIRST.
YOU CAN LEAVE THAT TO ME.

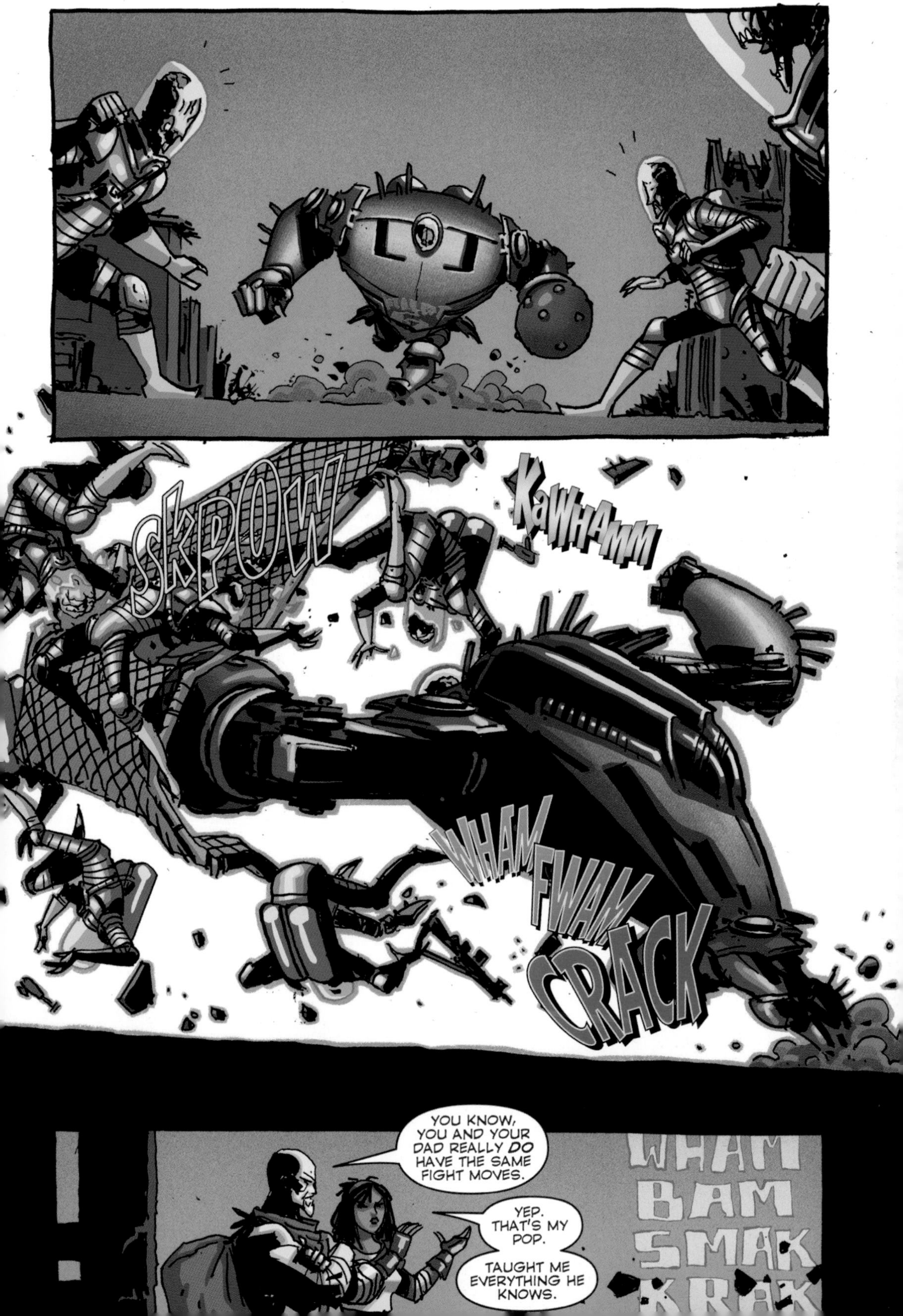
SKPOW
KaWHAMM
WHAM
FWAM
CRACK
YOU KNOW, YOU AND YOUR DAD REALLY DO HAVE THE SAME FIGHT MOVES.
YEP. THAT'S MY POP.
TAUGHT ME EVERYTHING HE KNOWS.
WHAM
BAM
SMAK

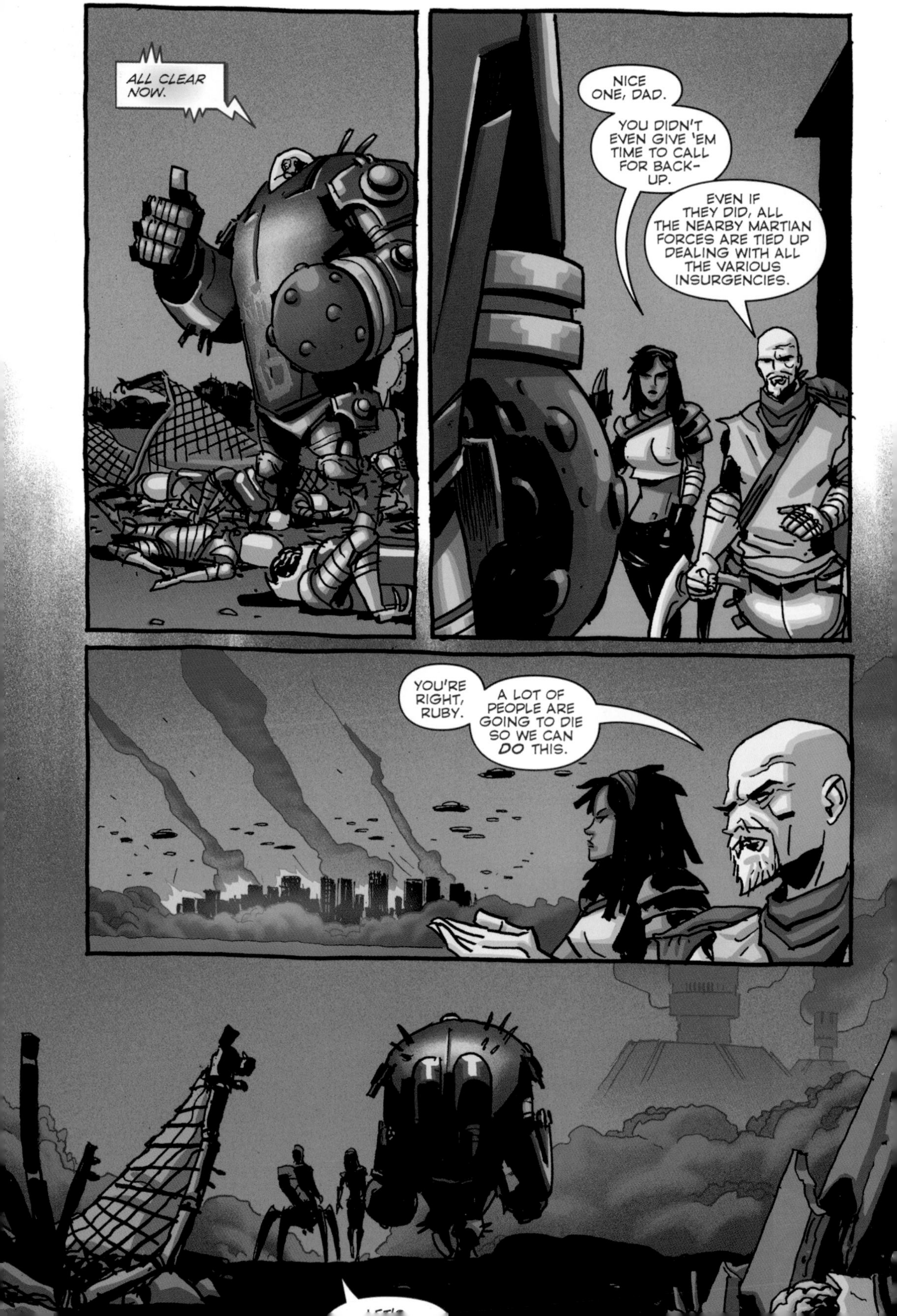
ALL CLEAR NOW.
NICE ONE, DAD.
YOU DIDN'T EVEN GIVE 'EM TIME TO CALL FOR BACK-UP.
EVEN IF THEY DID, ALL THE NEARBY MARTIAN FORCES ARE TIED UP DEALING WITH ALL THE VARIOUS INSURGENCIES.
YOU'RE RIGHT, RUBY.
A LOT OF PEOPLE ARE GOING TO DIE SO WE CAN *DO* THIS.

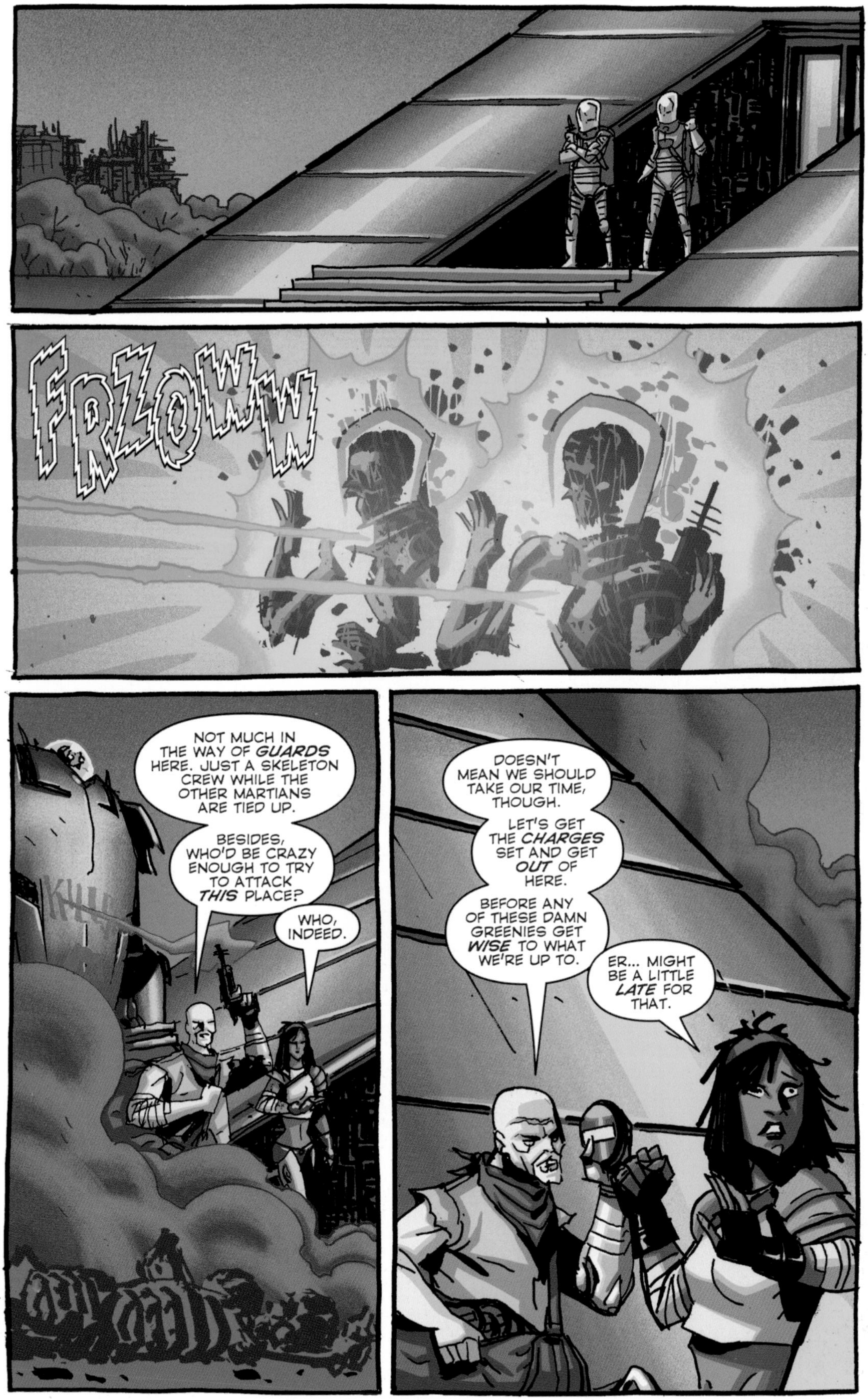
FRZOWW
NOT MUCH IN THE WAY OF GUARDS HERE. JUST A SKELETON CREW WHILE THE OTHER MARTIANS ARE TIED UP.
BESIDES, WHO'D BE CRAZY ENOUGH TO TRY TO ATTACK THIS PLACE?
WHO, INDEED.
DOESN'T MEAN WE SHOULD TAKE OUR TIME, THOUGH.
LET'S GET THE CHARGES SET AND GET OUT OF HERE.
BEFORE ANY OF THESE DAMN GREENIES GET WISE TO WHAT WE'RE UP TO.
ER... MIGHT BE A LITTLE LATE FOR THAT.

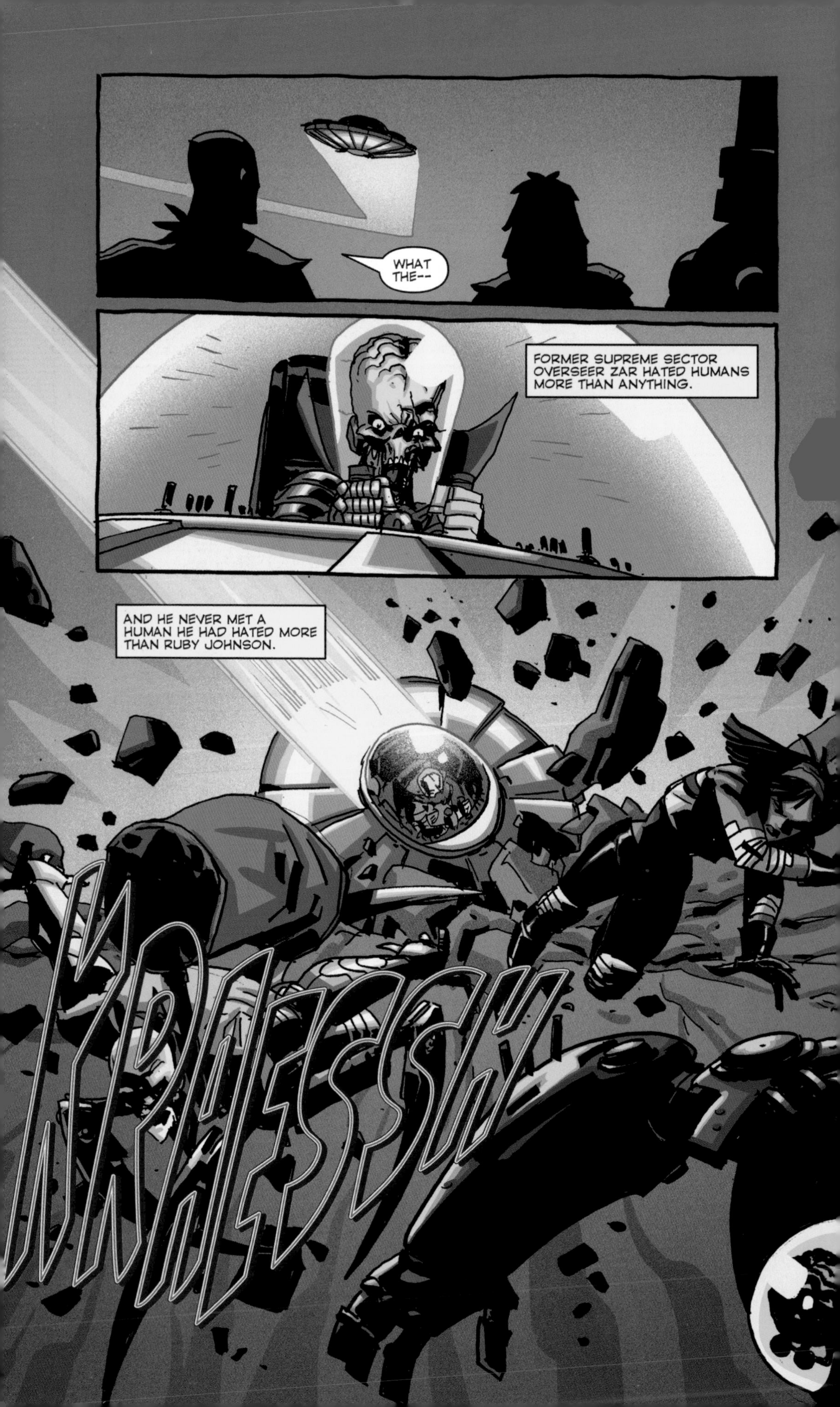
WHAT THE--
FORMER SUPREME SECTOR OVERSEER ZAR HATED HUMANS MORE THAN ANYTHING.
AND HE NEVER MET A HUMAN HE HAD HATED MORE THAN RUBY JOHNSON.

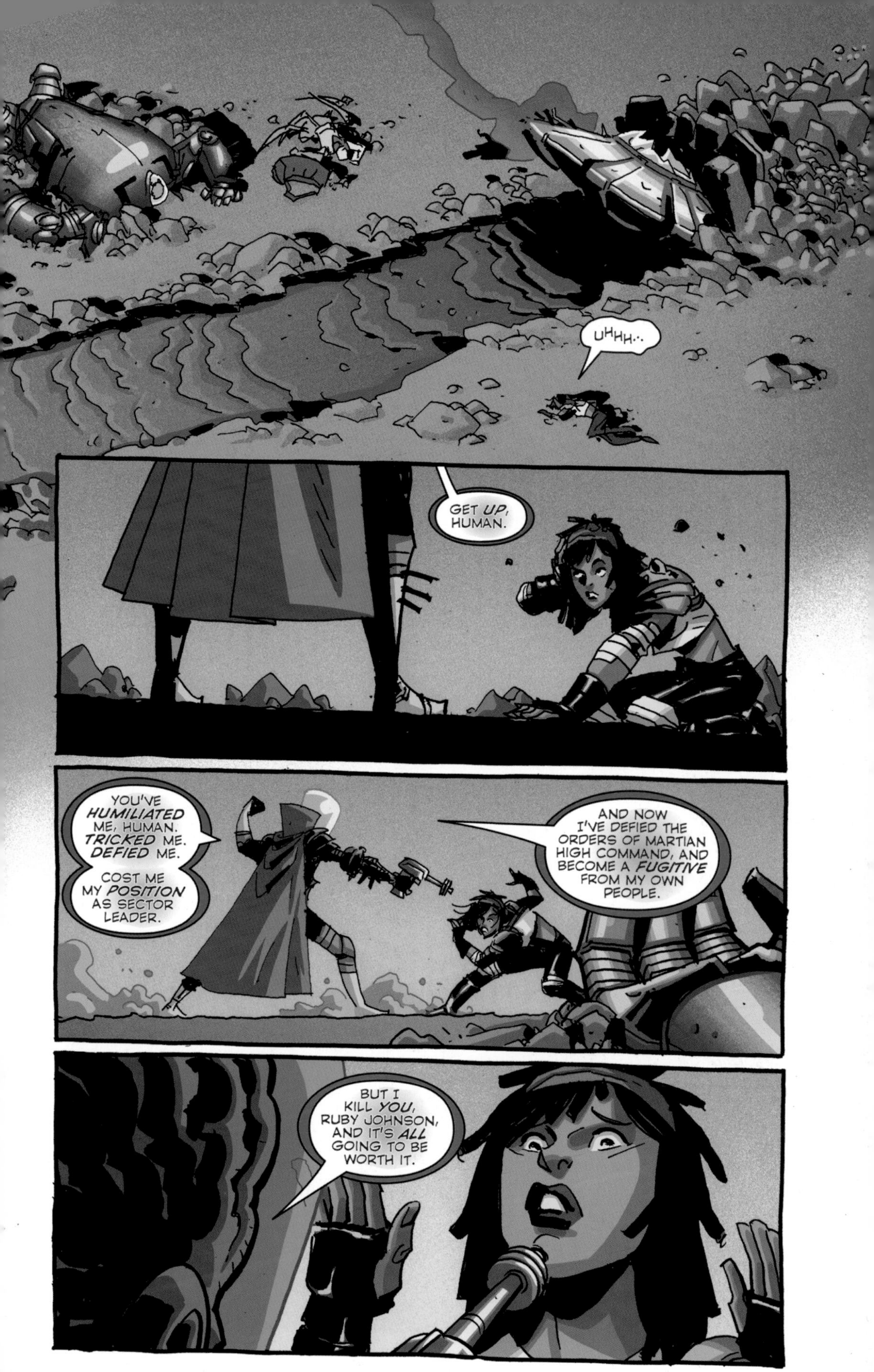

UHHH...
GET UP, HUMAN.
YOU'VE HUMILIATED ME, HUMAN. TRICKED ME. DEFIED ME.
COST ME MY POSITION AS SECTOR LEADER.
AND NOW I'VE DEFIED THE ORDERS OF MARTIAN HIGH COMMAND, AND BECOME A FUGITIVE FROM MY OWN PEOPLE.
BUT I KILL YOU, RUBY JOHNSON, AND IT'S ALL GOING TO BE WORTH IT.

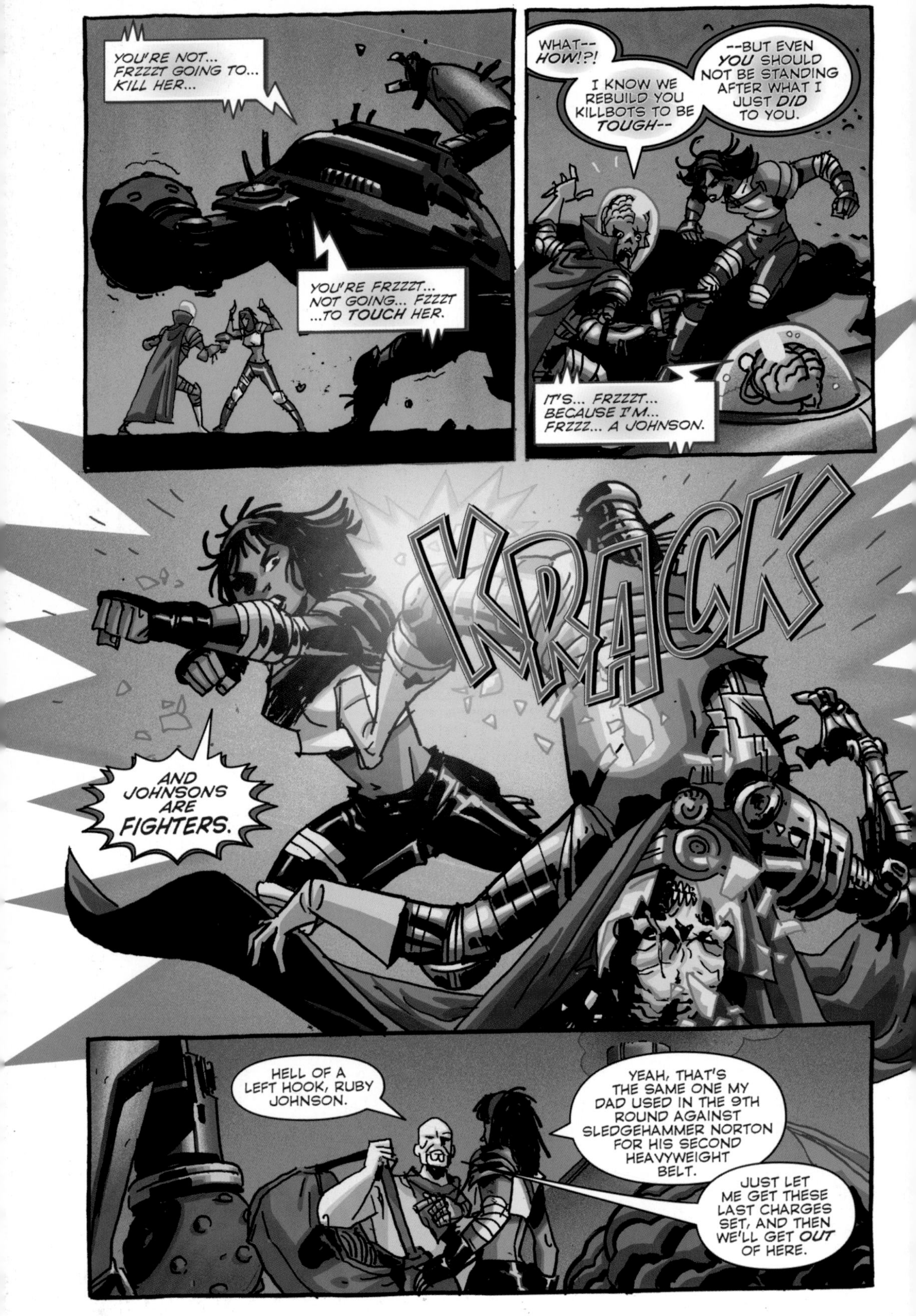
YOU'RE NOT... FRZZZT GOING TO... KILL HER...
YOU'RE FRZZZT... NOT GOING... FZZZT ...TO TOUCH HER.
WHAT-- HOW!?!
I KNOW WE REBUILD YOU KILLBOTS TO BE TOUGH--
--BUT EVEN YOU SHOULD NOT BE STANDING AFTER WHAT I JUST DID TO YOU.
IT'S... FRZZZT... BECAUSE I'M... FRZZZ... A JOHNSON.
KRACK
AND JOHNSONS ARE FIGHTERS.
HELL OF A LEFT HOOK, RUBY JOHNSON.
YEAH, THAT'S THE SAME ONE MY DAD USED IN THE 9TH ROUND AGAINST SLEDGEHAMMER NORTON FOR HIS SECOND HEAVYWEIGHT BELT.
JUST LET ME GET THESE LAST CHARGES SET, AND THEN WE'LL GET OUT OF HERE.

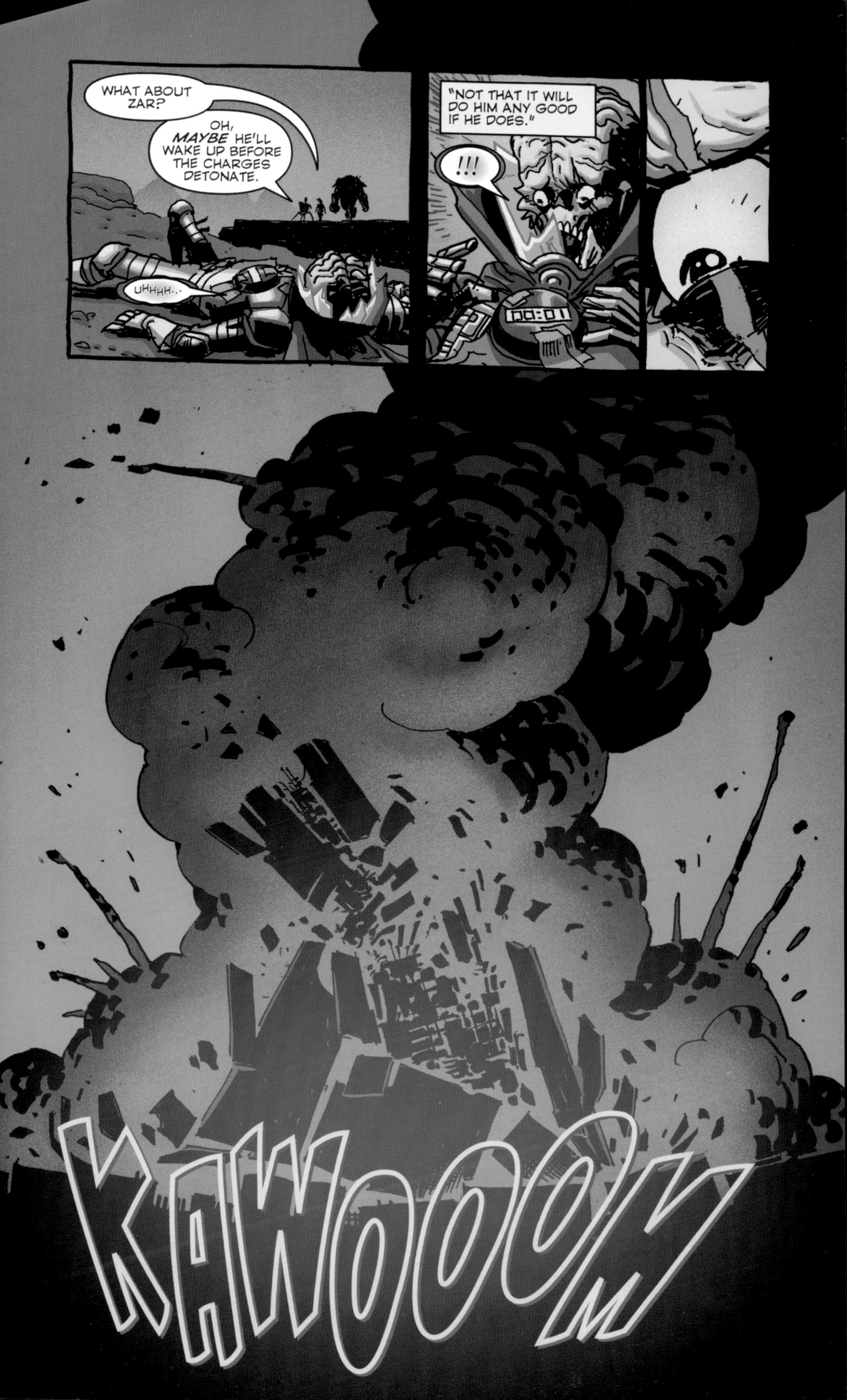
WHAT ABOUT ZAR?
OH, *MAYBE* HE'LL WAKE UP BEFORE THE CHARGES DETONATE.
UHHHH...
"NOT THAT IT WILL DO HIM ANY GOOD IF HE DOES."
!!!
00:01
KAWOOOM

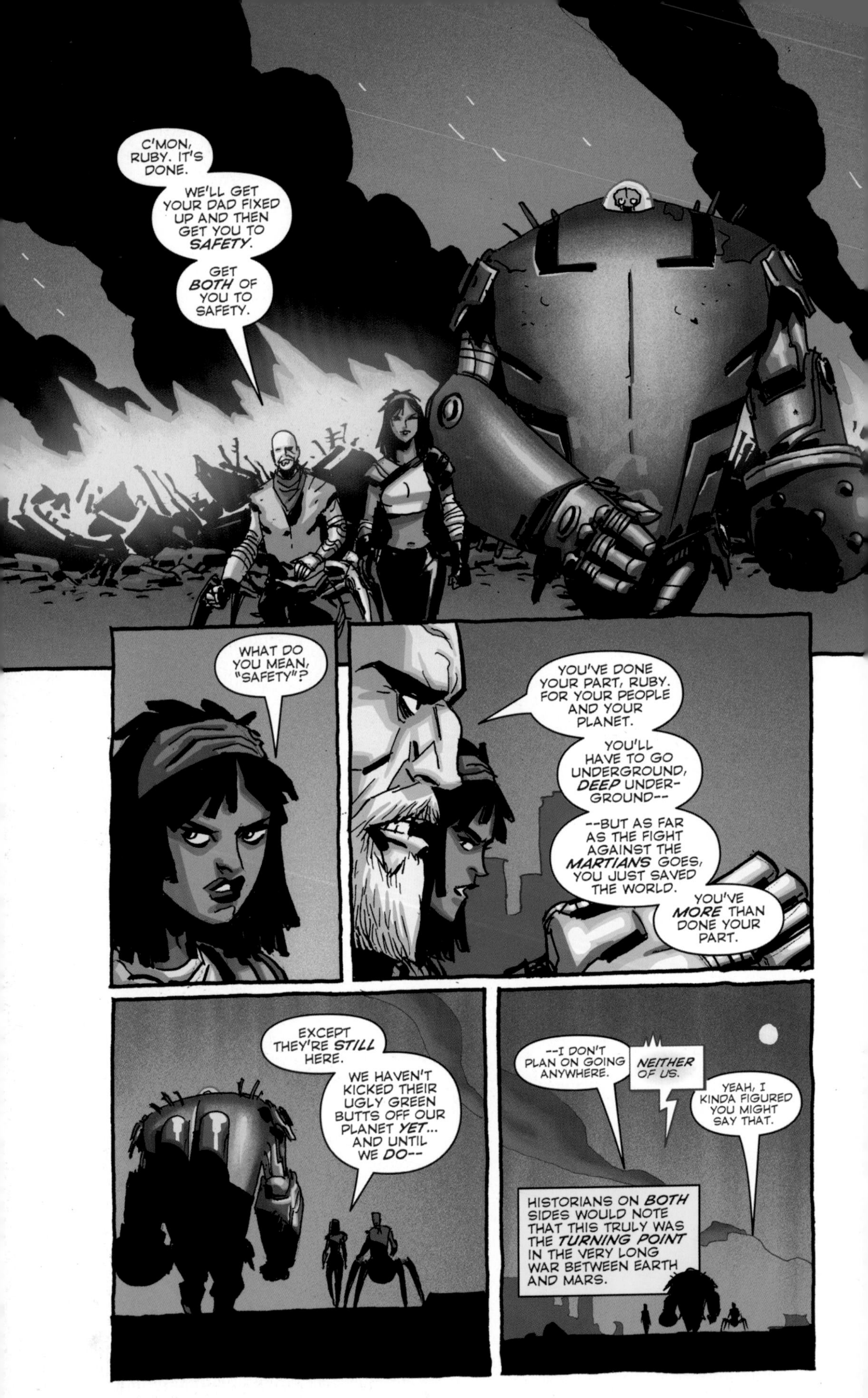
C'MON, RUBY. IT'S DONE.
WE'LL GET YOUR DAD FIXED UP AND THEN GET YOU TO *SAFETY*.
GET *BOTH* OF YOU TO SAFETY.
WHAT DO YOU MEAN, "SAFETY"?
YOU'VE DONE YOUR PART, RUBY. FOR YOUR PEOPLE AND YOUR PLANET.
YOU'LL HAVE TO GO UNDERGROUND, *DEEP* UNDERGROUND--
--BUT AS FAR AS THE FIGHT AGAINST THE *MARTIANS* GOES, YOU JUST SAVED THE WORLD.
YOU'VE *MORE* THAN DONE YOUR PART.
EXCEPT THEY'RE *STILL* HERE.
WE HAVEN'T KICKED THEIR UGLY GREEN BUTTS OFF OUR PLANET *YET*... AND UNTIL WE *DO*--
--I DON'T PLAN ON GOING ANYWHERE.
NEITHER OF US.
YEAH, I KINDA FIGURED YOU MIGHT SAY THAT.
HISTORIANS ON *BOTH* SIDES WOULD NOTE THAT THIS TRULY WAS THE *TURNING POINT* IN THE VERY LONG WAR BETWEEN EARTH AND MARS.

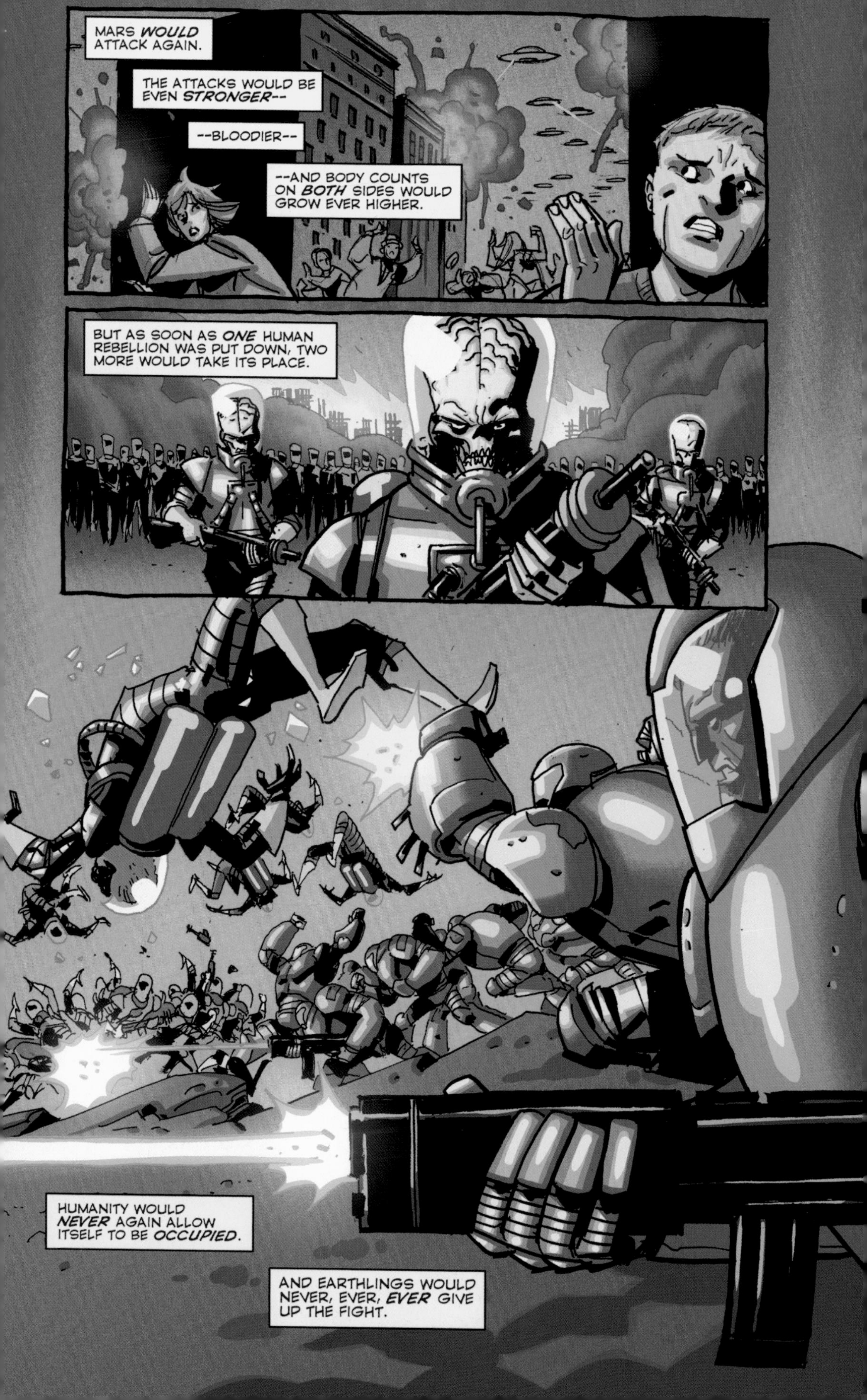
MARS WOULD ATTACK AGAIN.
THE ATTACKS WOULD BE EVEN STRONGER--
--BLOODIER--
--AND BODY COUNTS ON BOTH SIDES WOULD GROW EVER HIGHER.
BUT AS SOON AS ONE HUMAN REBELLION WAS PUT DOWN, TWO MORE WOULD TAKE ITS PLACE.
HUMANITY WOULD NEVER AGAIN ALLOW ITSELF TO BE OCCUPIED.
AND EARTHLINGS WOULD NEVER, EVER, EVER GIVE UP THE FIGHT.

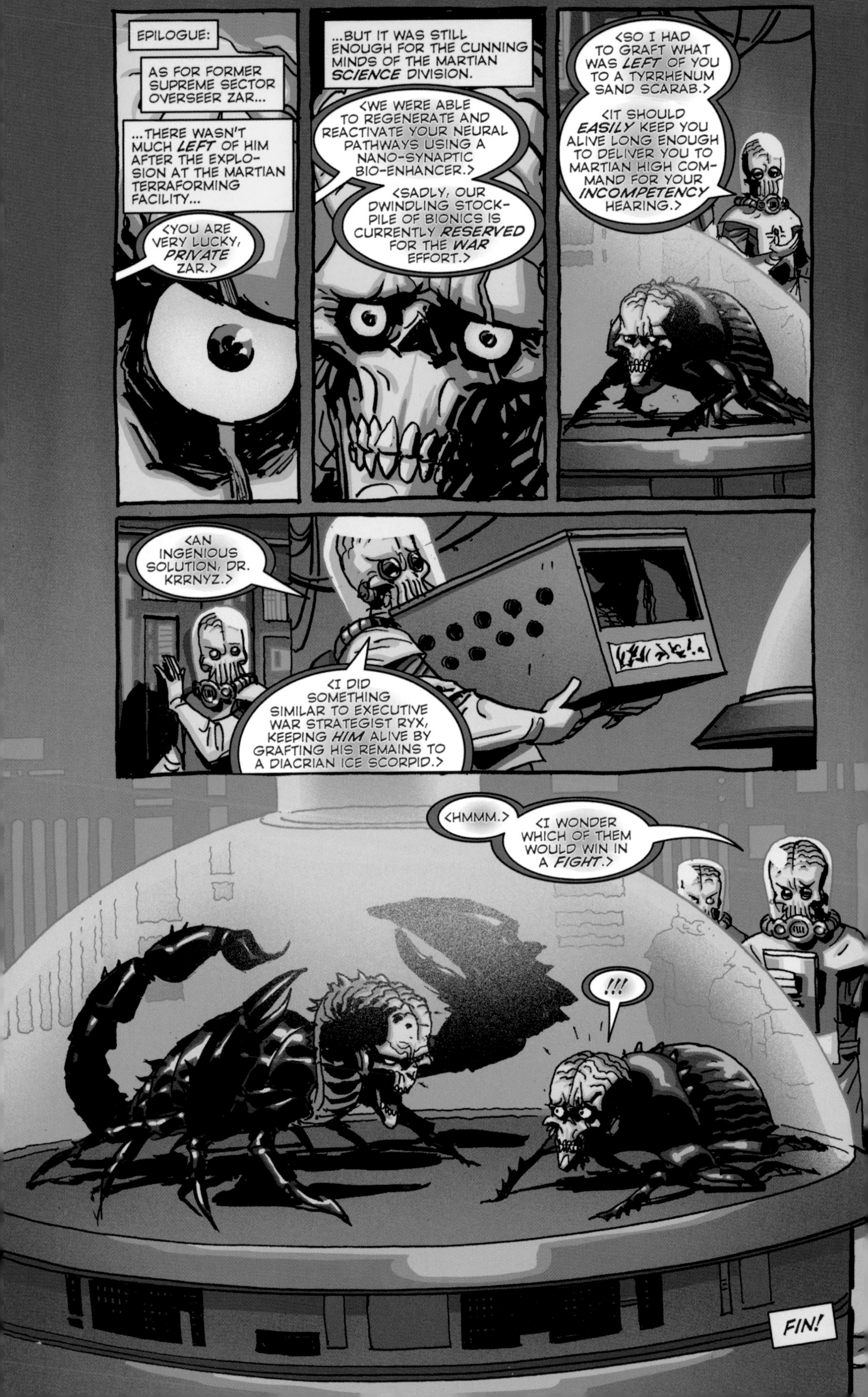
EPILOGUE:
AS FOR FORMER SUPREME SECTOR OVERSEER ZAR...
...THERE WASN'T MUCH LEFT OF HIM AFTER THE EXPLOSION AT THE MARTIAN TERRAFORMING FACILITY...
<YOU ARE VERY LUCKY, PRIVATE ZAR.>
...BUT IT WAS STILL ENOUGH FOR THE CUNNING MINDS OF THE MARTIAN SCIENCE DIVISION.
<WE WERE ABLE TO REGENERATE AND REACTIVATE YOUR NEURAL PATHWAYS USING A NANO-SYNAPTIC BIO-ENHANCER.>
<SADLY, OUR DWINDLING STOCKPILE OF BIONICS IS CURRENTLY RESERVED FOR THE WAR EFFORT.>
<SO I HAD TO GRAFT WHAT WAS LEFT OF YOU TO A TYRRHENUM SAND SCARAB.>
<IT SHOULD EASILY KEEP YOU ALIVE LONG ENOUGH TO DELIVER YOU TO MARTIAN HIGH COMMAND FOR YOUR INCOMPETENCY HEARING.>
<AN INGENIOUS SOLUTION, DR. KRRNYZ.>
<I DID SOMETHING SIMILAR TO EXECUTIVE WAR STRATEGIST RYX, KEEPING HIM ALIVE BY GRAFTING HIS REMAINS TO A DIACRIAN ICE SCORPID.>
<HMMM.>
<I WONDER WHICH OF THEM WOULD WIN IN A FIGHT.>
!!!
FIN!

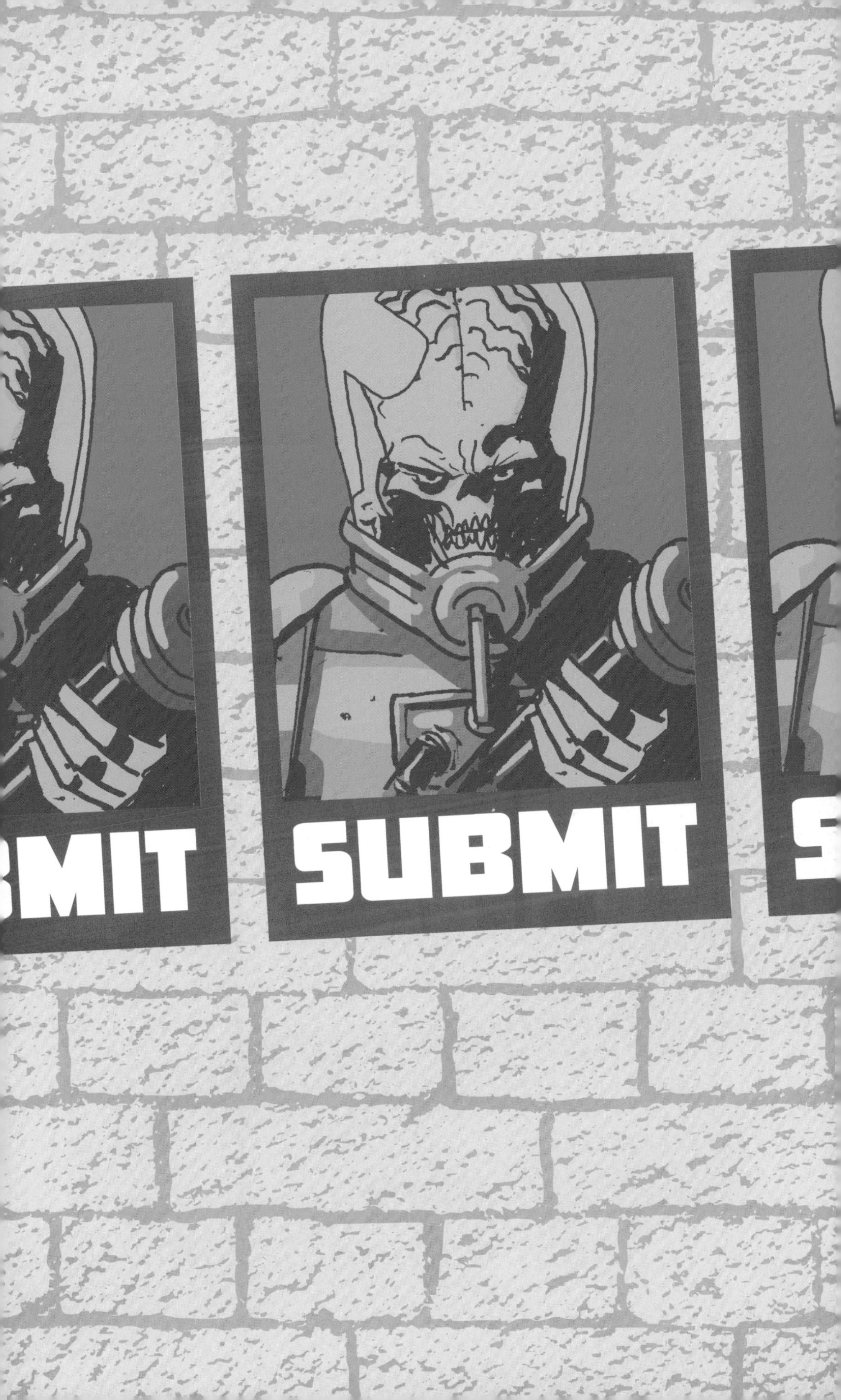
BMIT
SUBMIT
S

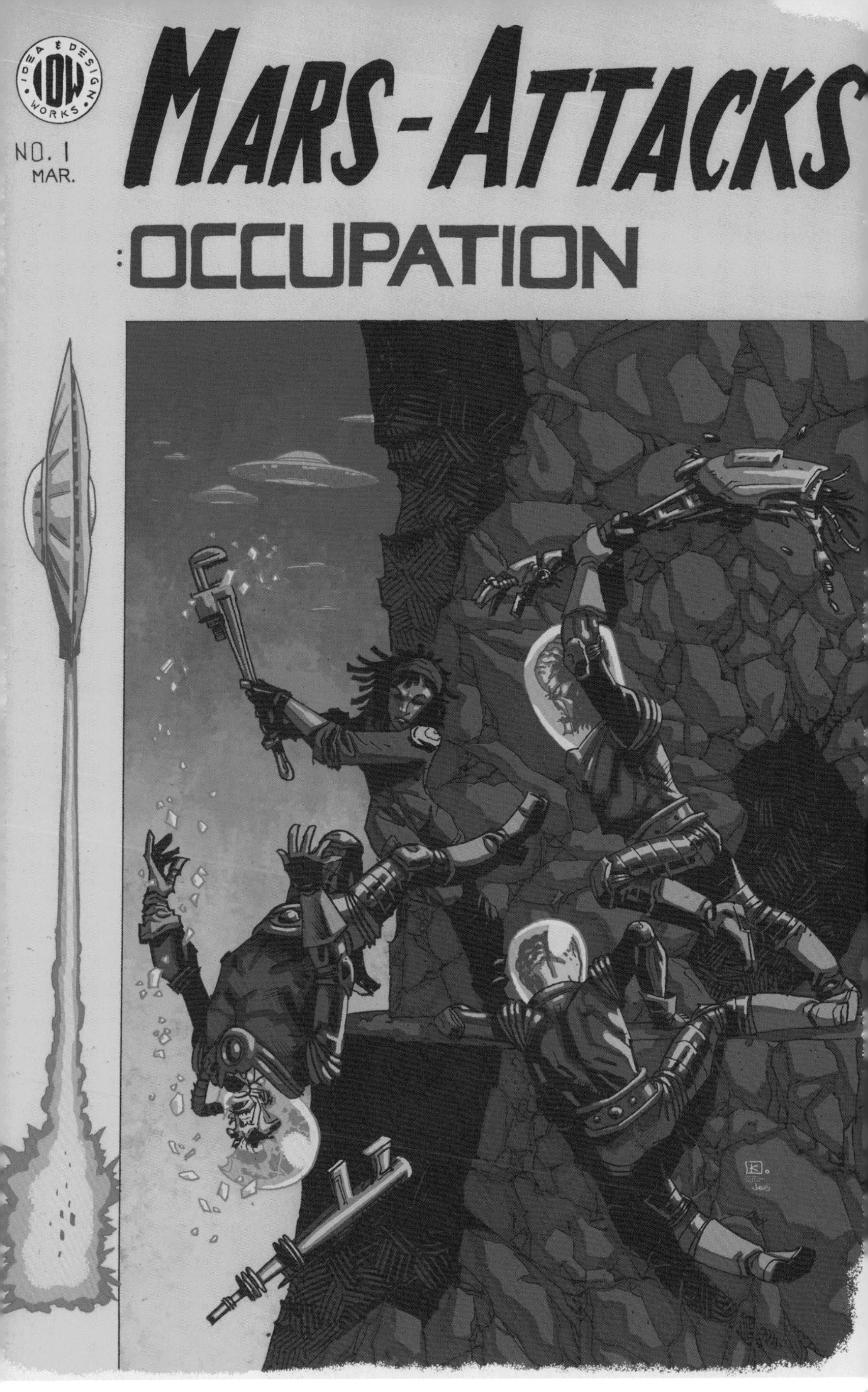
IDEA & DESIGN WORKS
IDW
NO. 1
MAR.
MARS-ATTACKS
:OCCUPATION

ART BY **ANDY KUHN** COLORS BY **JASON LEWI**

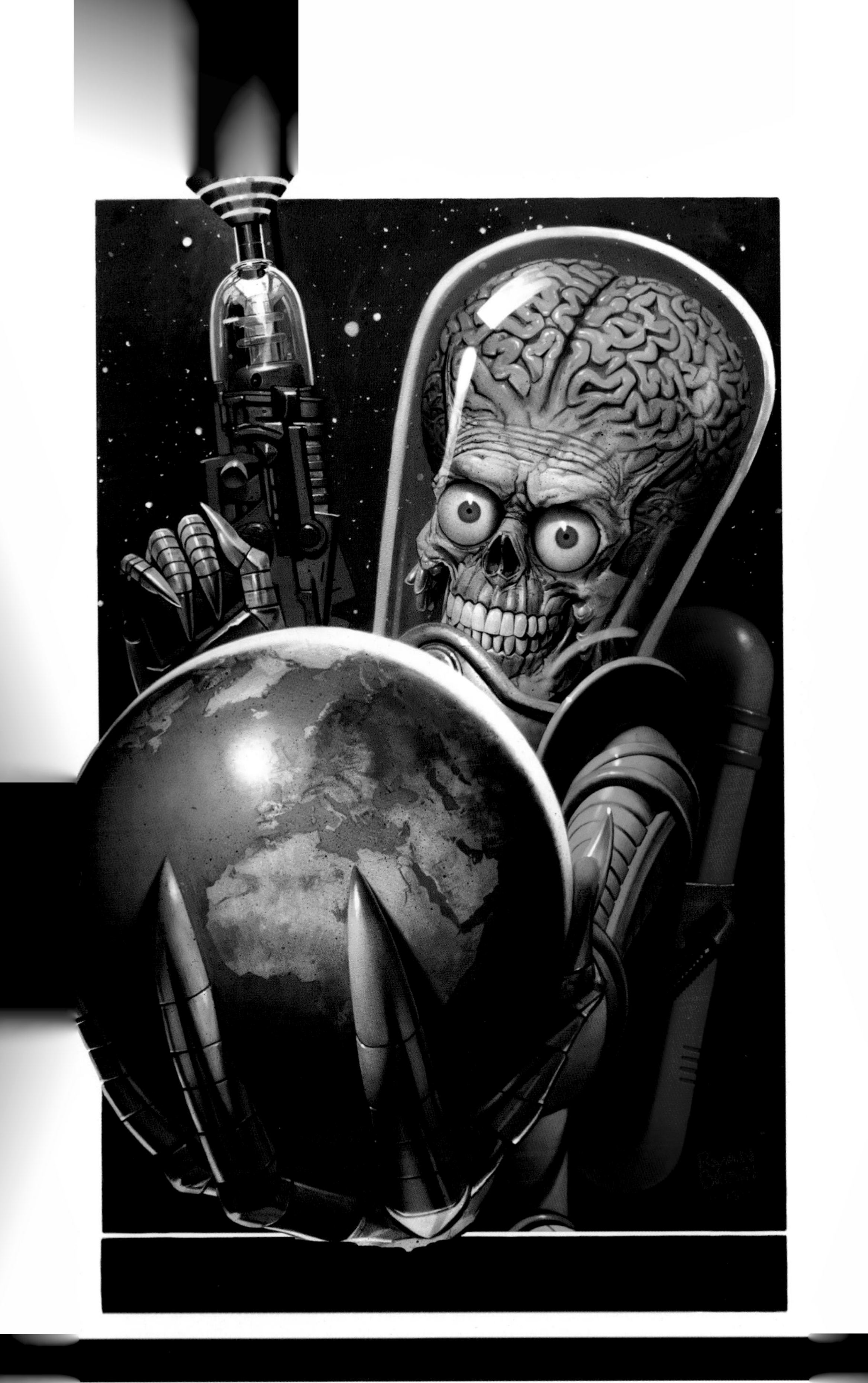

ART BY **RYAN BRO**

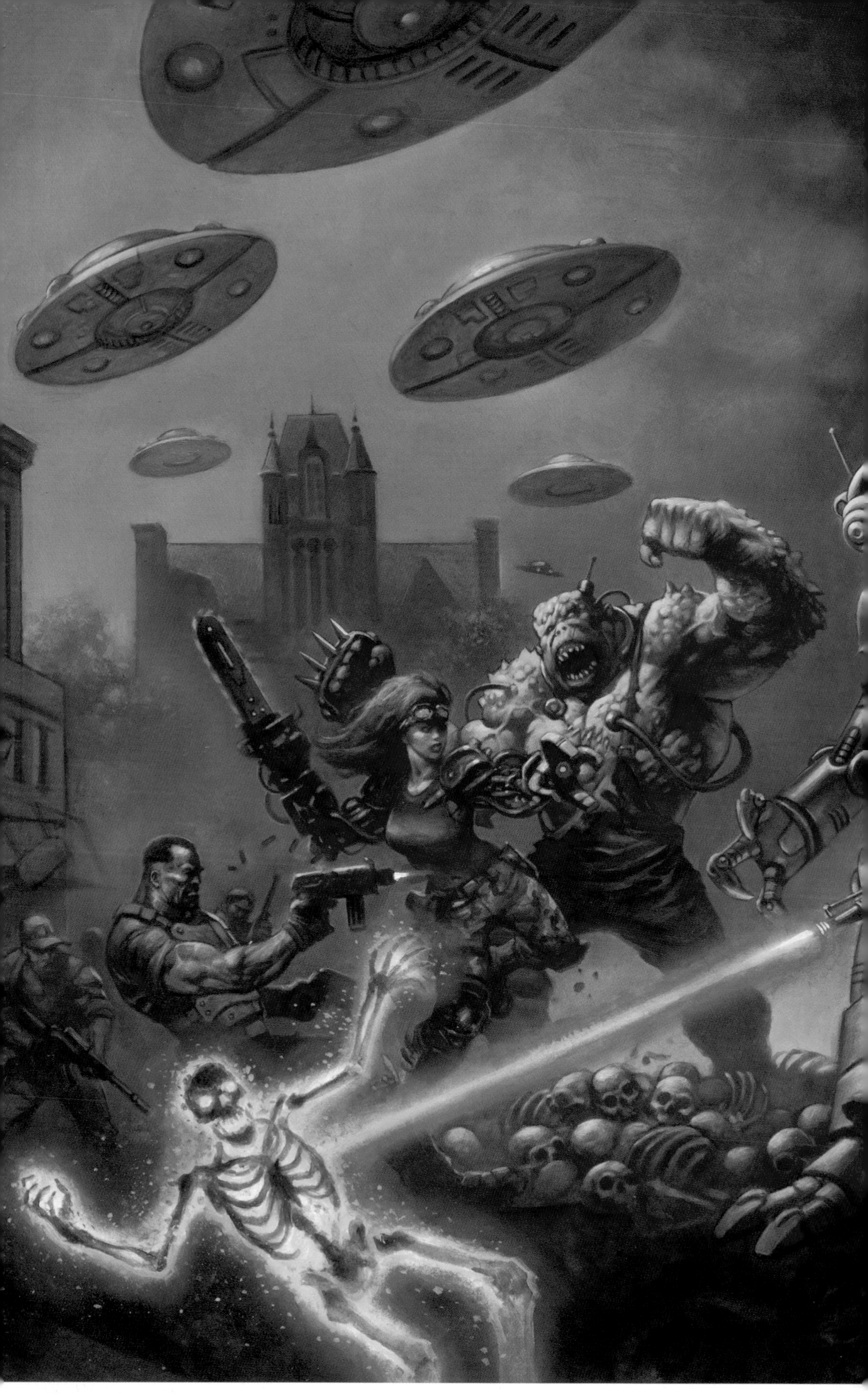

ART BY **ALEX HORLEY**

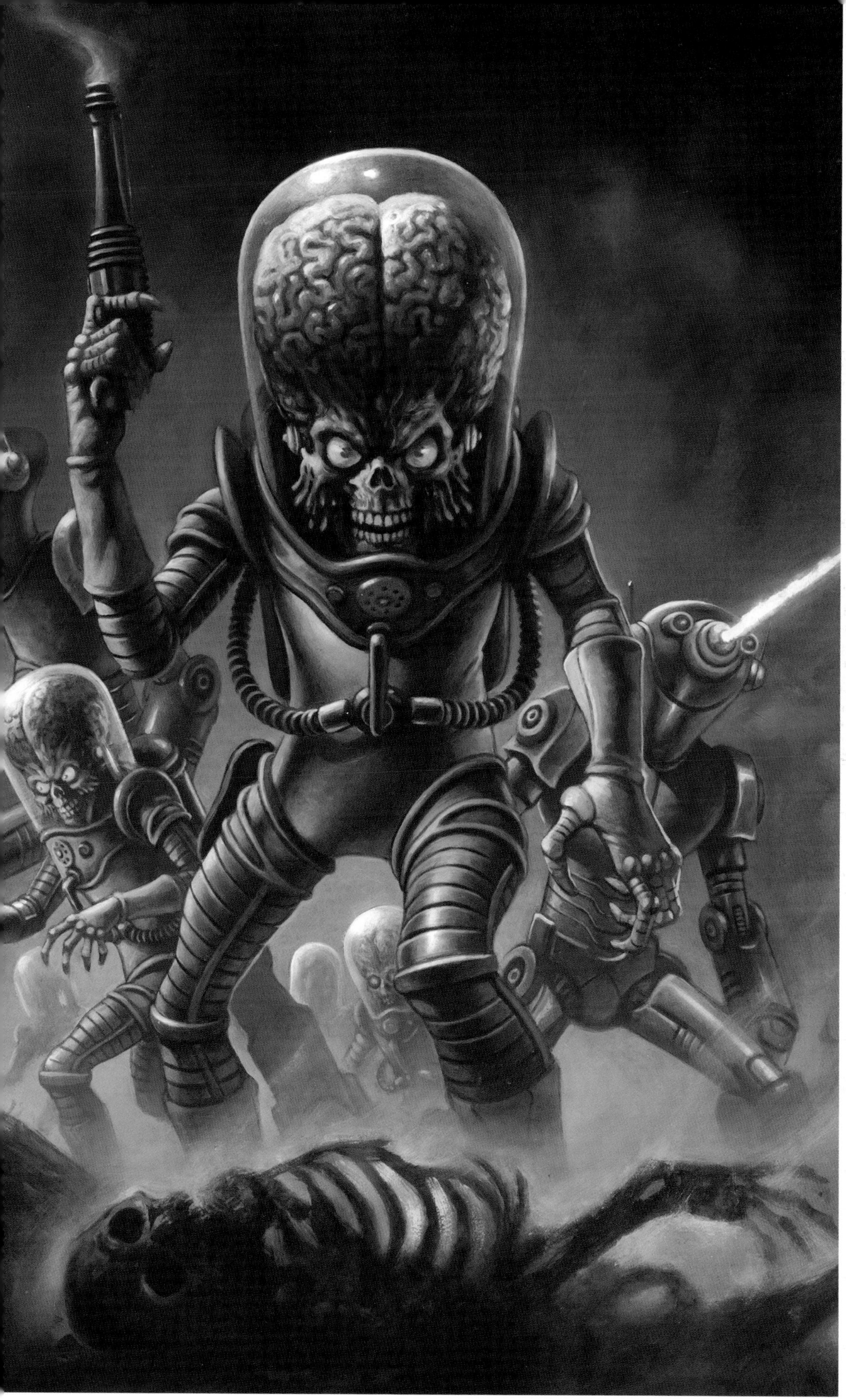

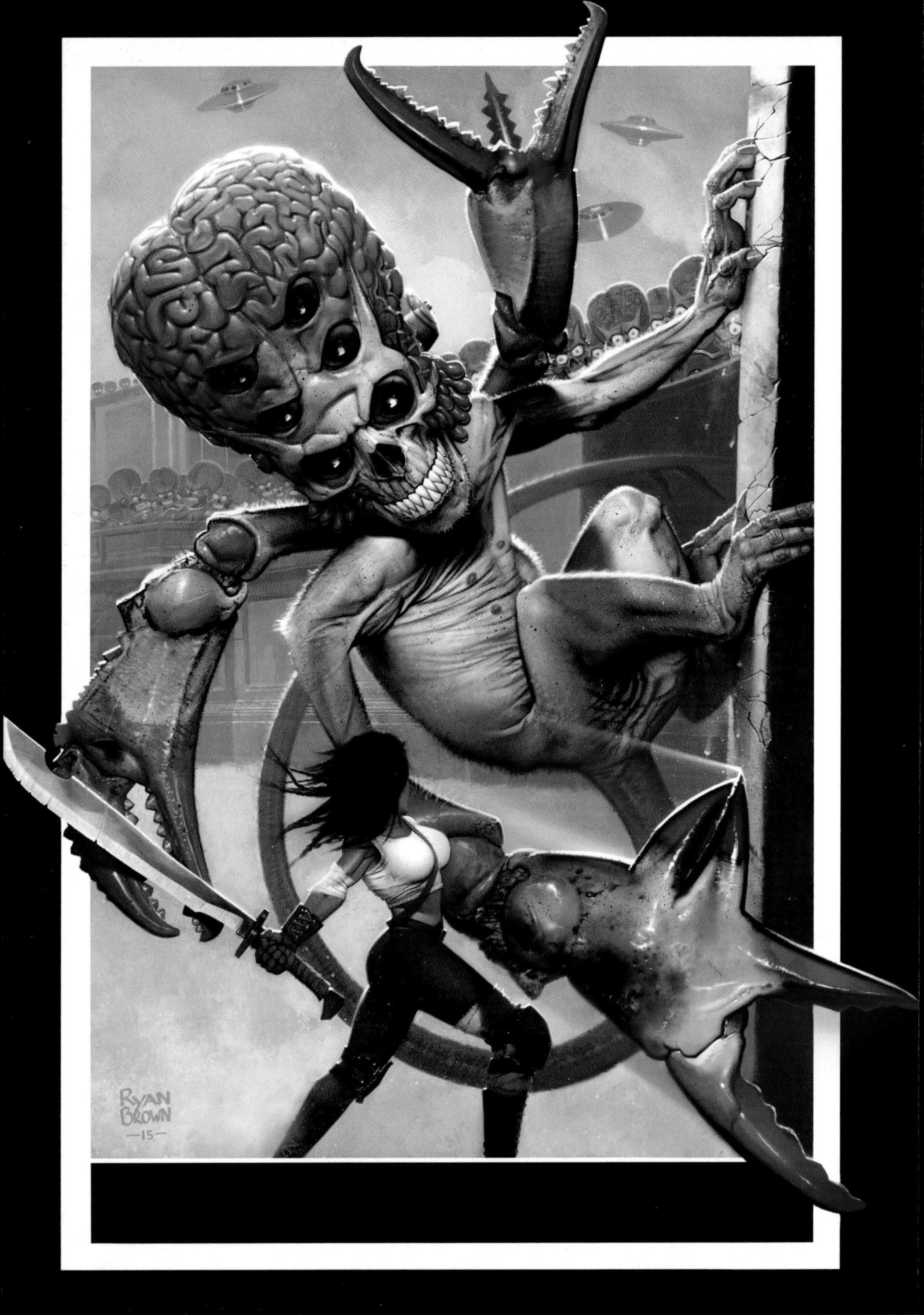
RYAN
BROWN
-15-

ART BY **RYAN BROWN**

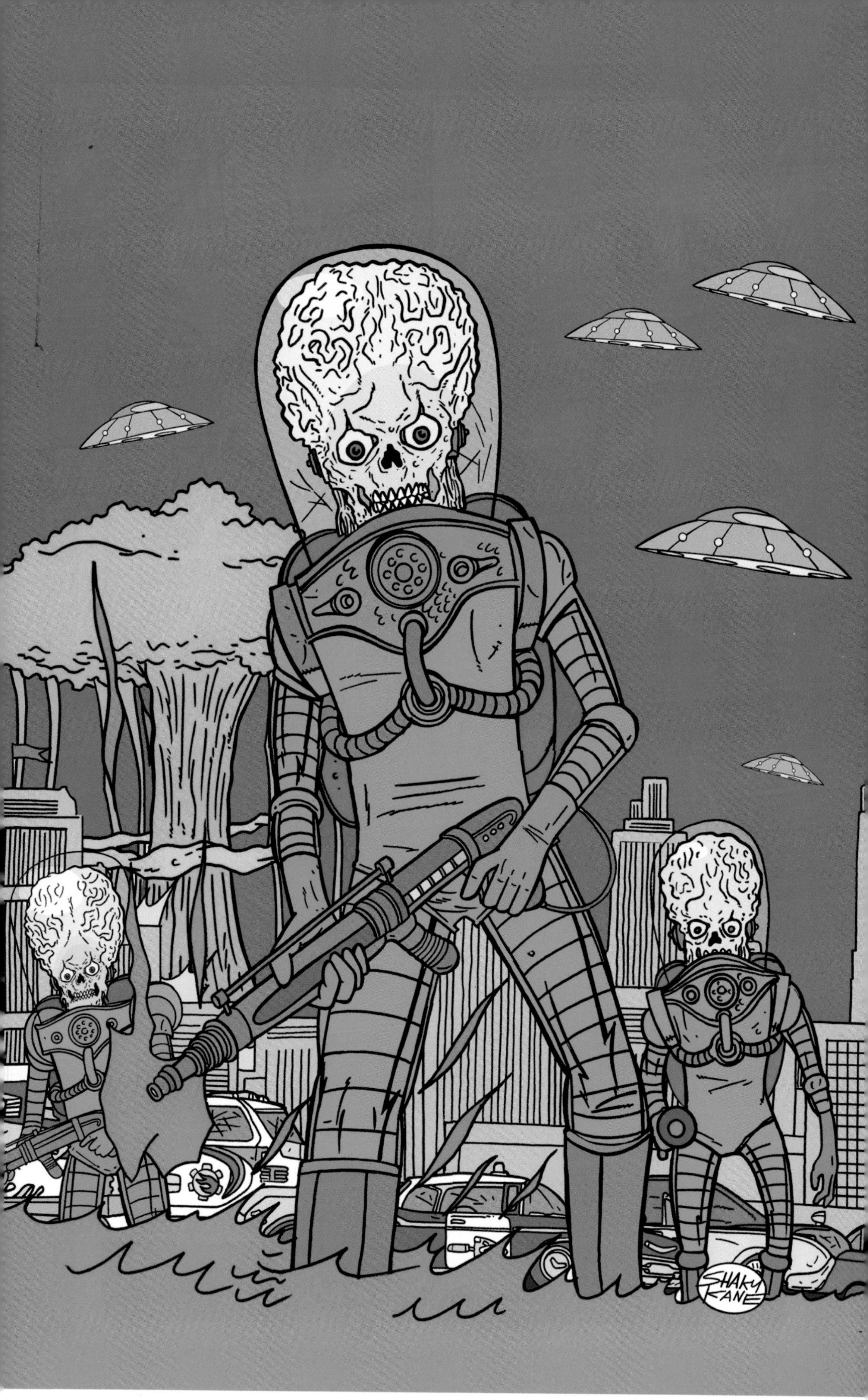
SHAKY KANE

ART BY **SHAKY KANE**

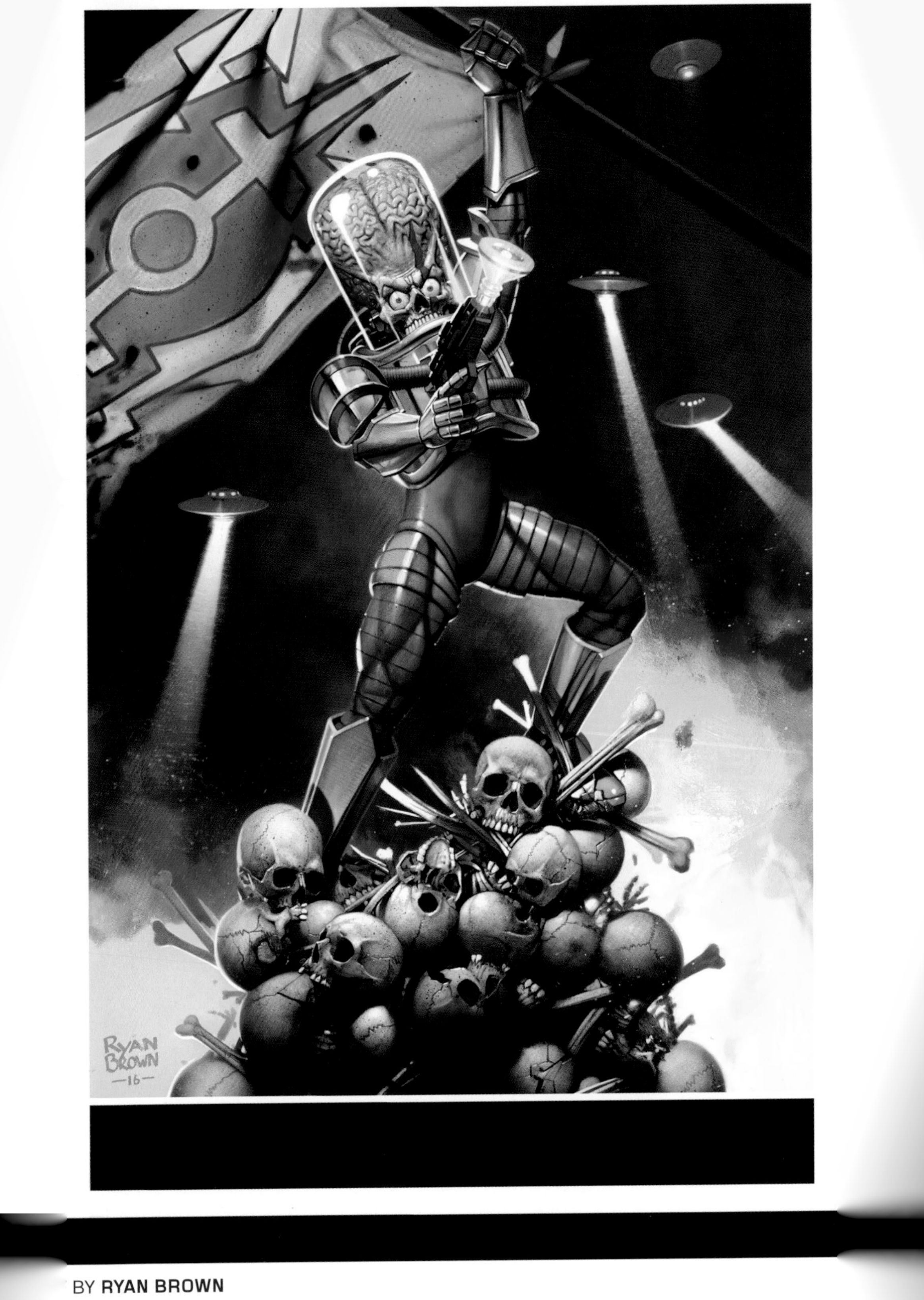
RYAN
BROWN
-16-

BY **RYAN BROWN**

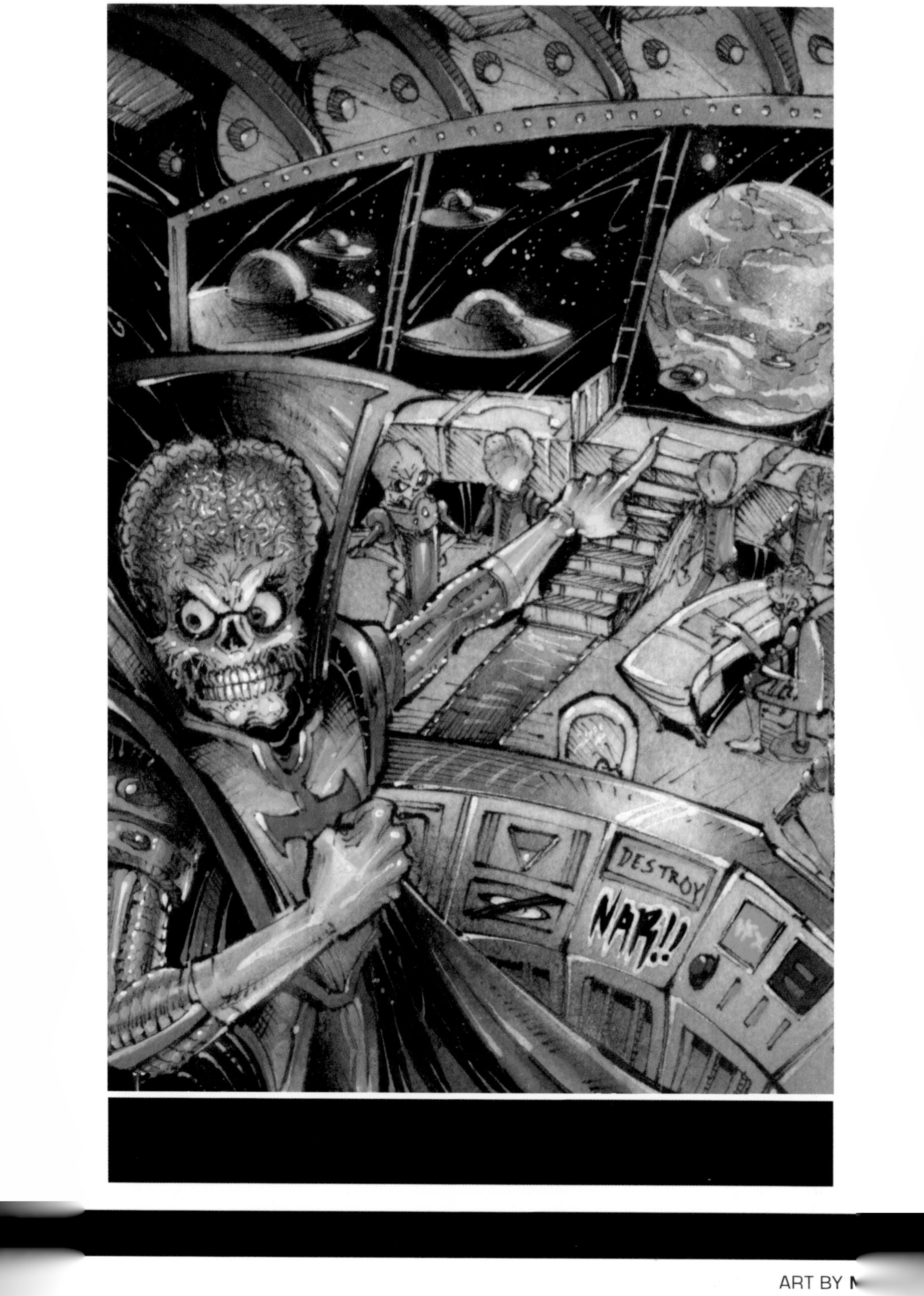
DESTROY
NAR!!

ART BY M

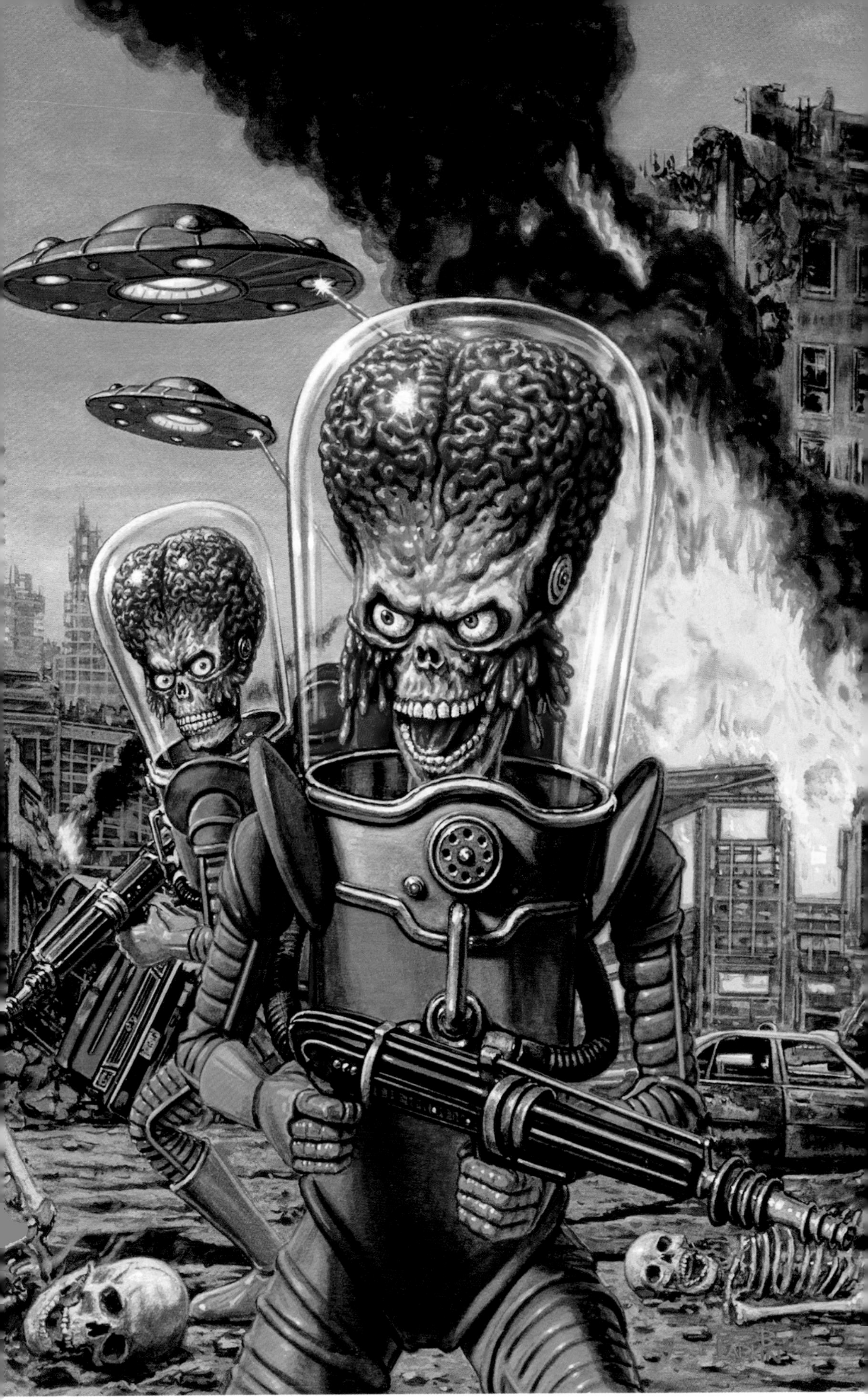

ART BY **BOB LARKIN**

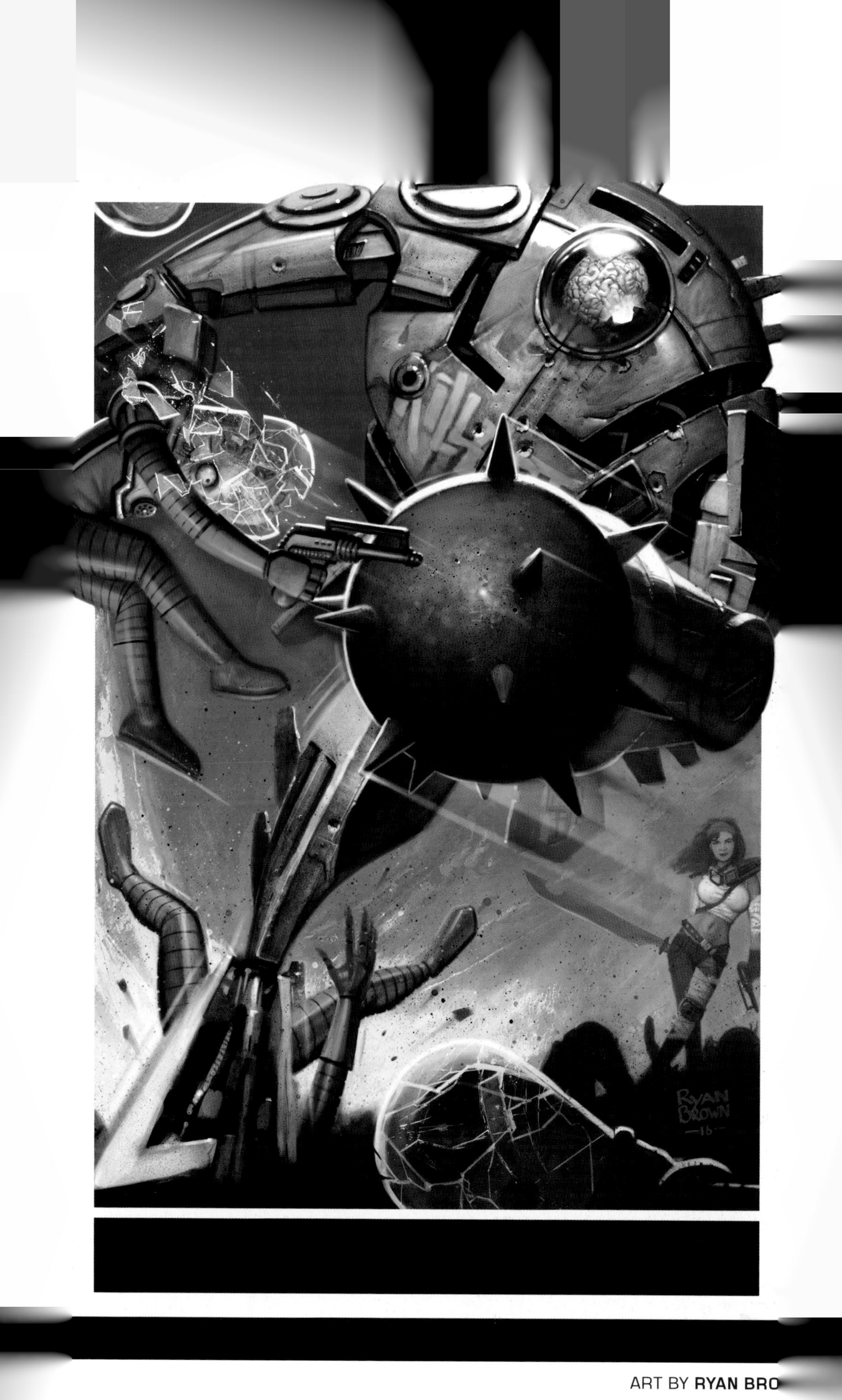
RYAN
BROWN
-16-

ART BY **RYAN BRO**

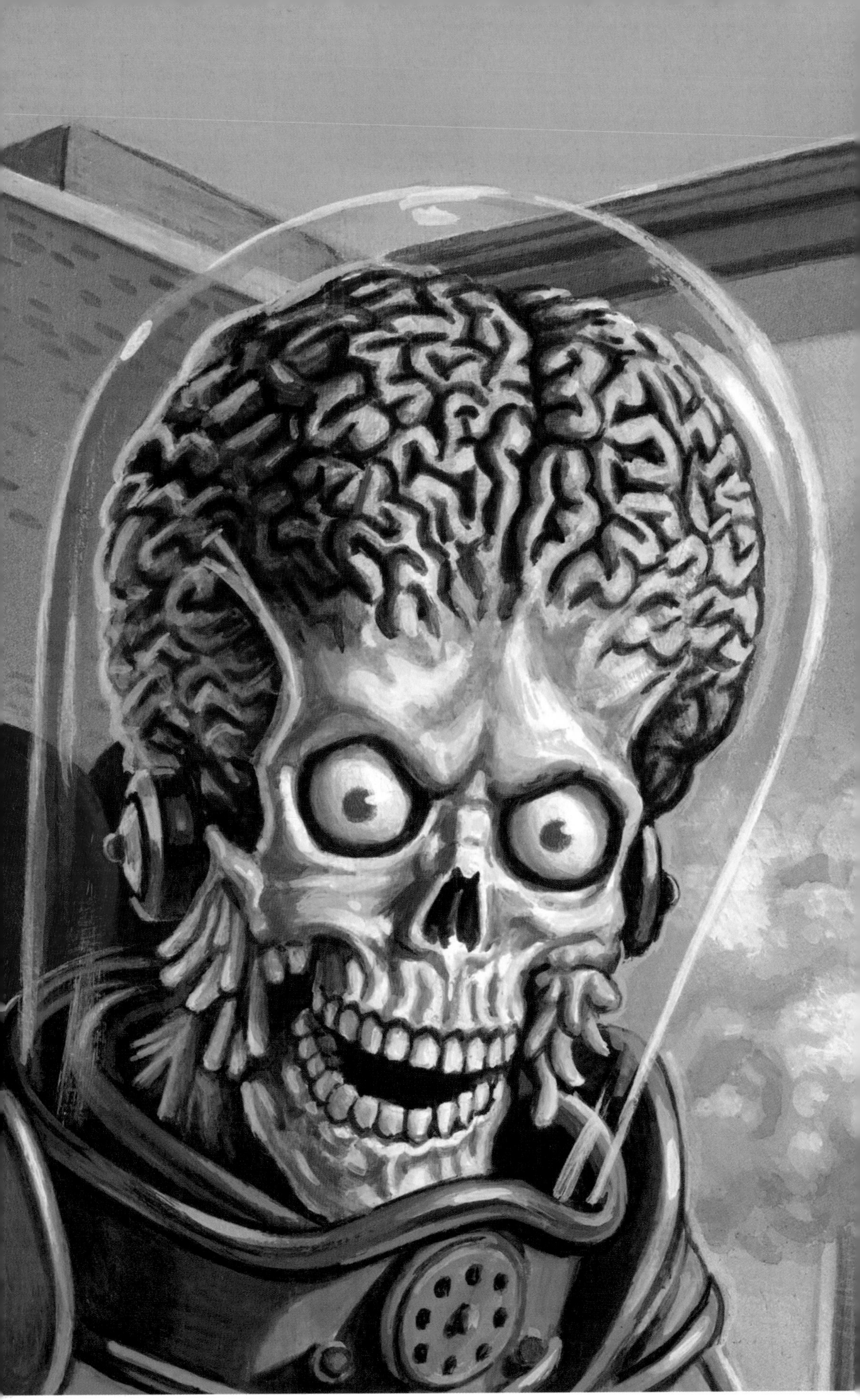
ART BY **ED REPKA**

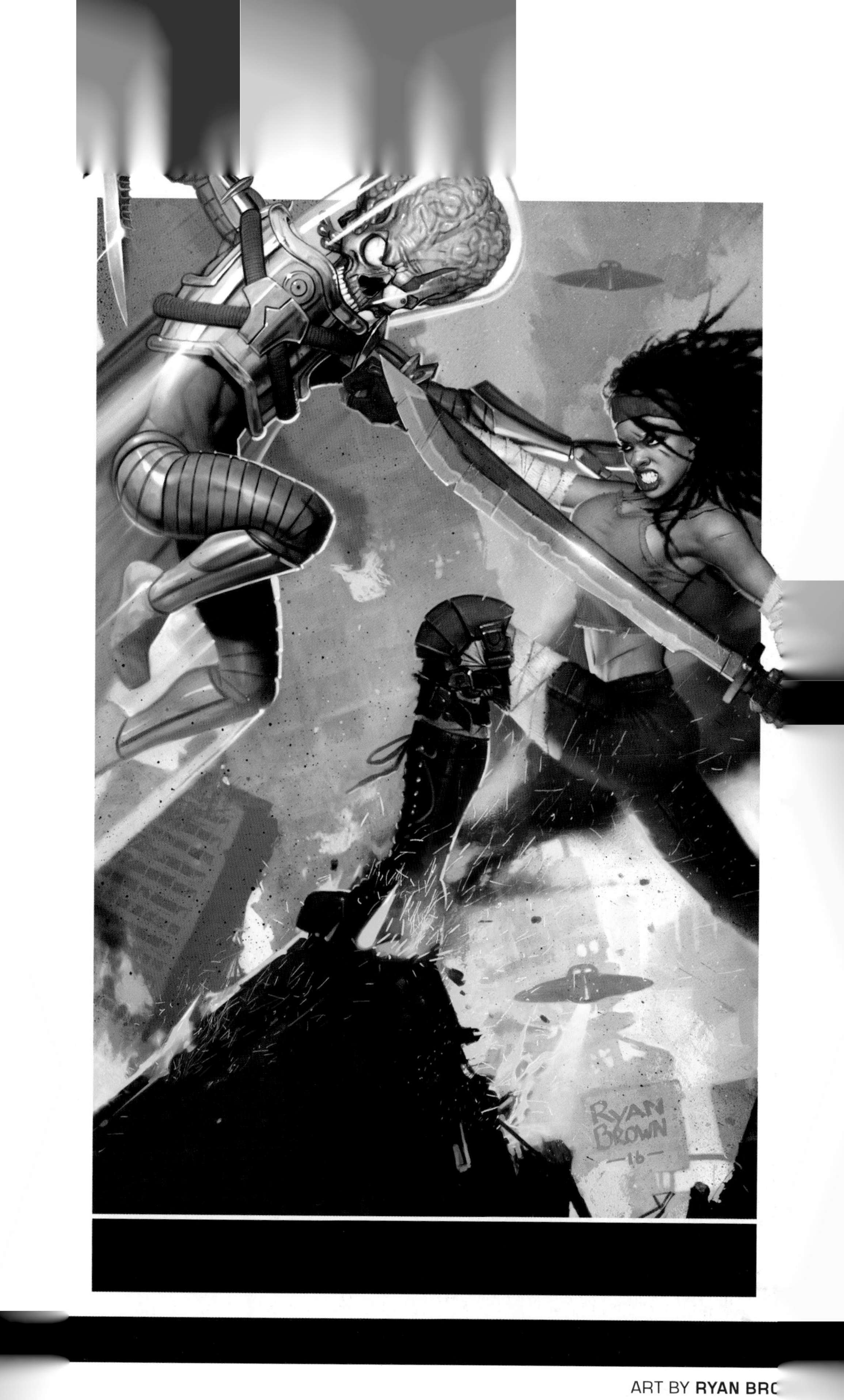
RYAN BROWN
-16-

ART BY **RYAN BRO**

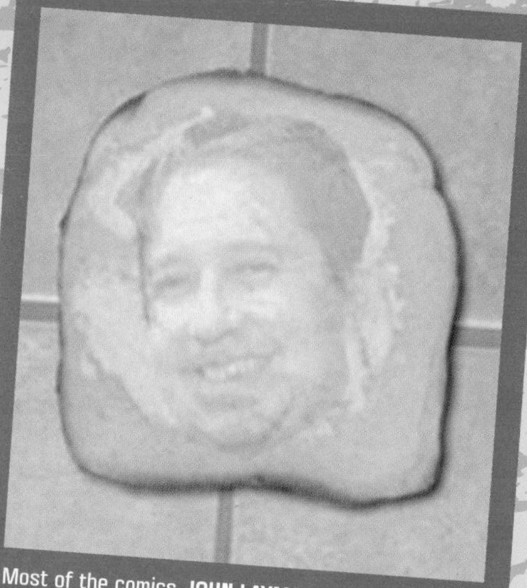

Most of the comics **JOHN LAYMAN** writes and letters suck, except for the stuff he's written for IDW, which are all masterpieces. This includes a previous 10-issue run of *Mars Attacks* with John McCrea, *Scarface: Scarred for Life*, and *Godzilla: Gangsters & Goliaths*. He also writes and letters *CHEW* for Image comics, which does not completely suck.

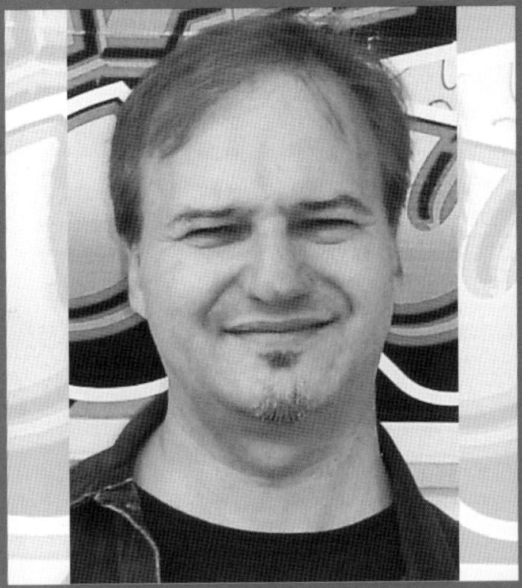

Artist **ANDY KUHN** is co-creator of the comic series *Firebreather*, with writer Phil Hester. In 2010 *Firebreather* was adapted into an Emmy Award-winning animated film for Cartoon Network. Recently, he has drawn *Teenage Mutant Ninja Turtles*, *Doctor Who*, *Samurai Jack*, *Mutanimals*, and *Zombies vs. Robots* for IDW. Also, *Justice League 3000* and *Sinestro* for DC, and *Conan the Barbarian* for Dark Horse. He lives and works in New Mexico.

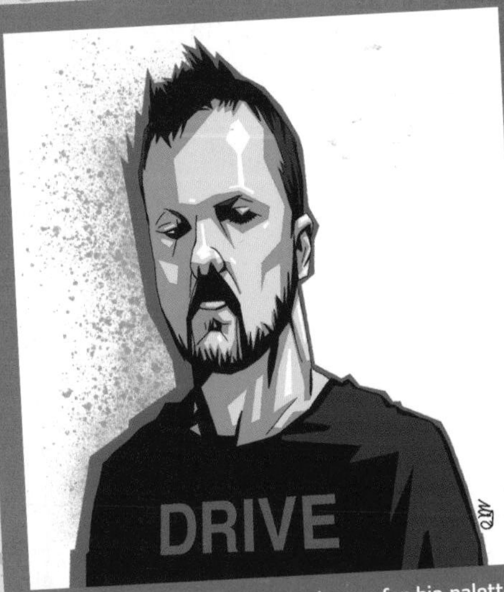
DRIVE

Colorist **JASON LEWIS** is best known for his palettes on IDW's groundbreaking miniseries *Drive*. He's probably not an alien life form in disguise. Ask him how many black band t-shirts a man his age should responsibly own.

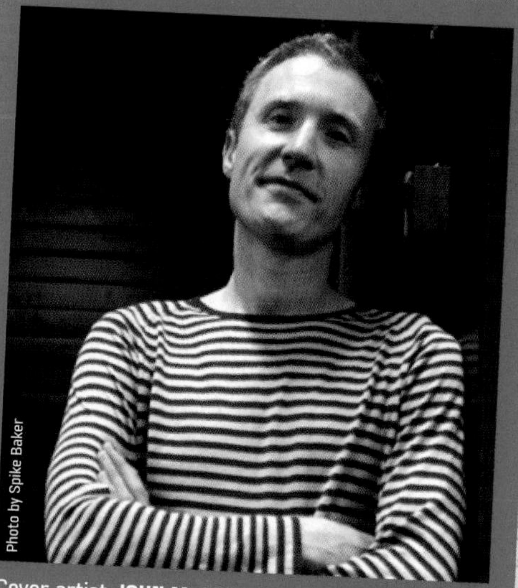
Photo by Spike Baker

Cover artist **JOHN McCREA** has been drawing comics for 27 years and has recently worked on *Deadpool* for Marvel, *Batman*, *Catwoman*, and *Plastic Man* for DC Comics, and *Judge Dredd* for 2000 AD. He is drawing a new creator-owned book for Image with Phil Hester called *Mythic*, and *Section 8* with Garth Ennis for DC.

Website: www.johnmccrea.com Twitter: @mccreaman.

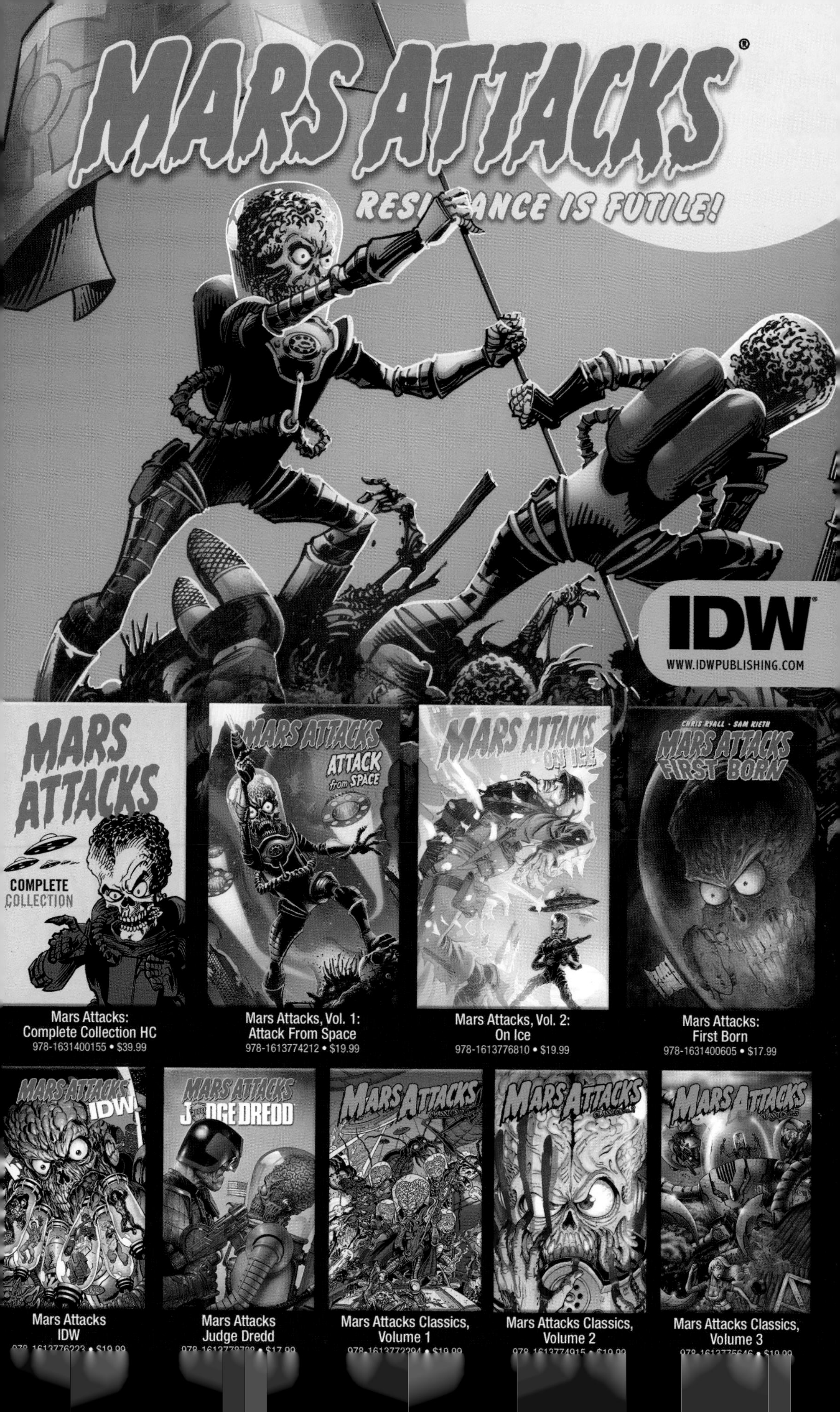

MARS ATTACKS®
RESISTANCE IS FUTILE!
IDW®
WWW.IDWPUBLISHING.COM
MARS ATTACKS
COMPLETE COLLECTION
Mars Attacks:
Complete Collection HC
978-1631400155 • $39.99
MARS ATTACKS
ATTACK from SPACE
Mars Attacks, Vol. 1:
Attack From Space
978-1613774212 • $19.99
MARS ATTACKS
ON ICE
Mars Attacks, Vol. 2:
On Ice
978-1613776810 • $19.99
CHRIS RYALL • SAM KIETH
MARS ATTACKS
FIRST BORN
Mars Attacks:
First Born
978-1631400605 • $17.99
MARS ATTACKS
IDW
Mars Attacks
IDW
978-1613776223 • $19.99
MARS ATTACKS
JUDGE DREDD
Mars Attacks
Judge Dredd
978-1613778708 • $17.99
MARS ATTACKS
Mars Attacks Classics,
Volume 1
978-1613772294 • $19.99
MARS ATTACKS
Mars Attacks Classics,
Volume 2
978-1613774915 • $19.99
MARS ATTACKS
Mars Attacks Classics,
Volume 3
978-1613775646 • $19.99

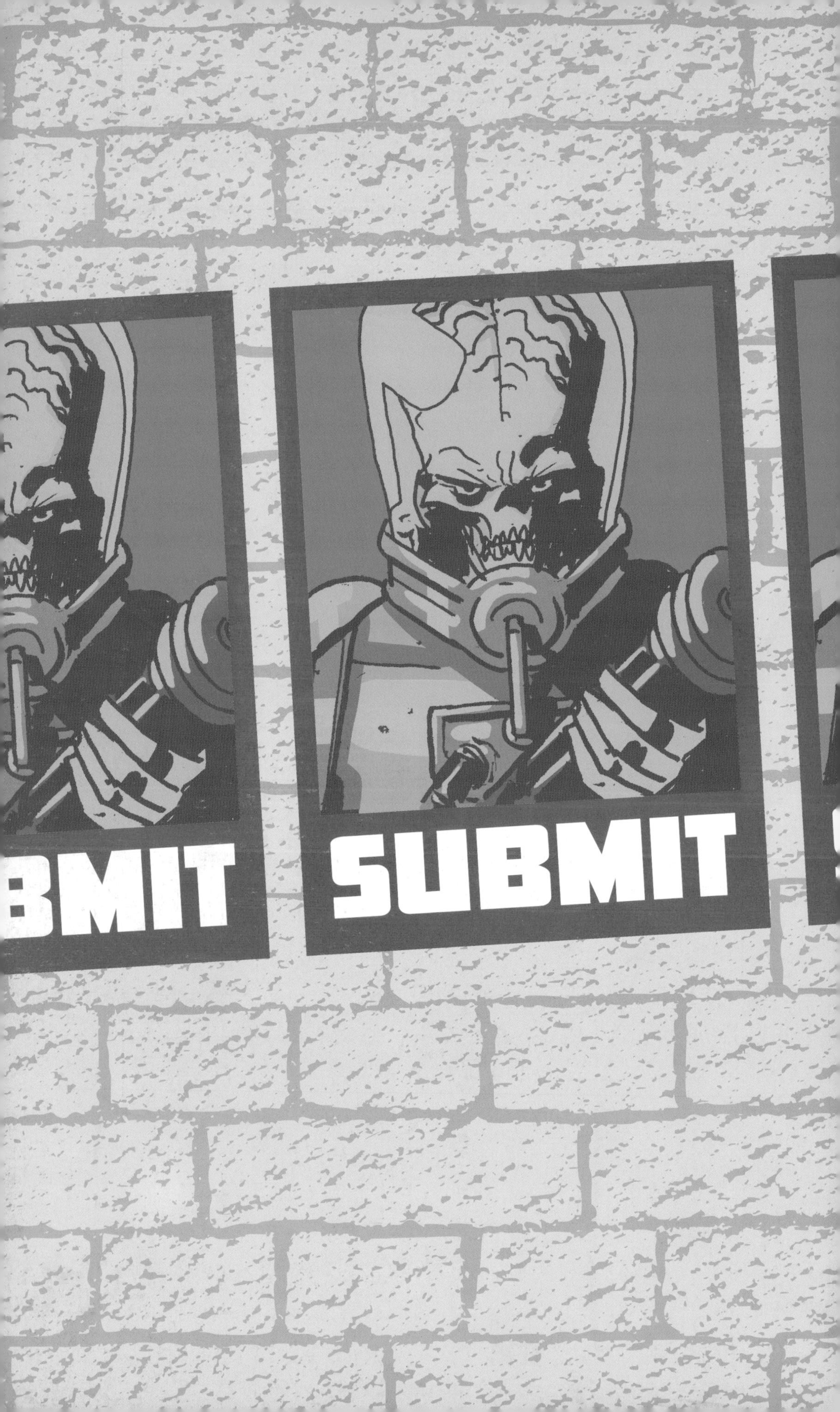
SUBMIT